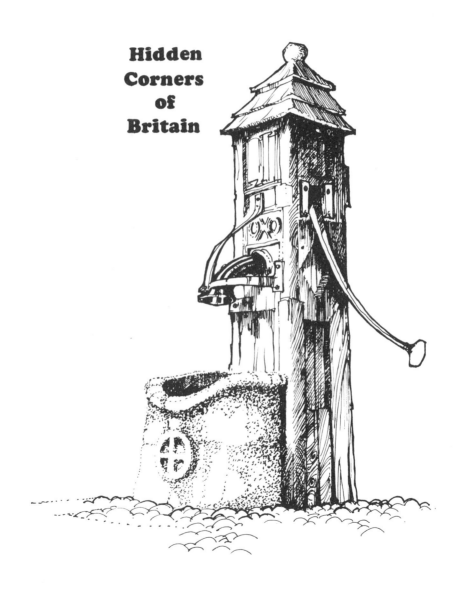

Hidden Corners of Britain

Hidden Corners of Britain

written and illustrated by
David Yeadon

W · W · NORTON & COMPANY
New York · London

Printed in the United States of America.

First American edition 1982

Library of Congress Cataloging in Publication Data

Yeadon, David.
   Hidden corners of Britain.

   Includes index.
   1. Great Britain—Description and travel—
1971-   —Guide-books.   I. Title.
DA650.Y4   1982   914.1′04858   81-22539
                          AACR2

W. W. Norton & Company, Inc. 500 Fifth Avenue, New York, N.Y. 10110
W. W. Norton & Company Ltd. 37 Great Russell Street, London WC1B 3NU
1   2   3   4   5   6   7   8   9   0

ISBN 0-393-01460-6

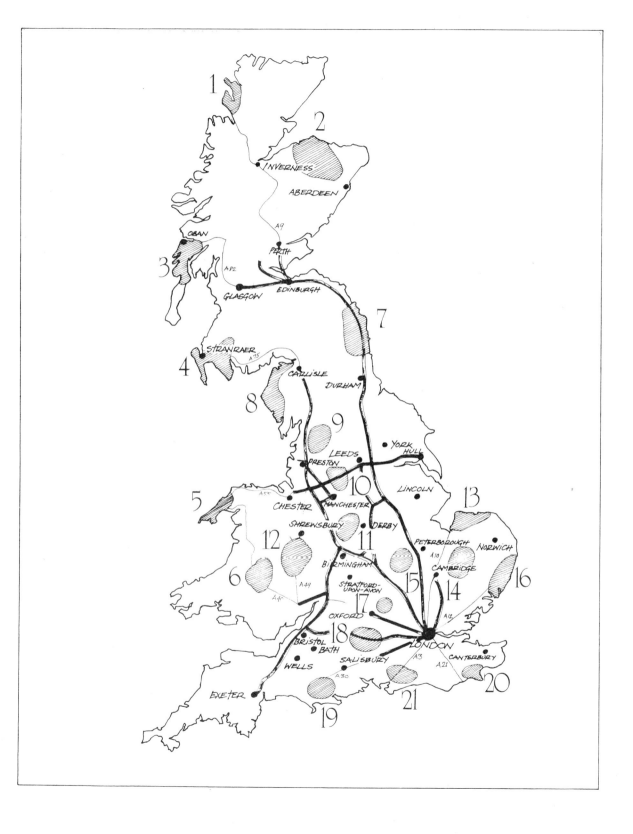

Contents

introduction

It may be hard to believe that Britain, this small, overpopulated country, still contains delightfully undiscovered hidden corners away from the hurly-burly of cities and coach-crowds. Yet for every hundred tourists struggling for their few square feet of beach or standing in sweaty lines around the rococo bedrooms of some popular palace, only a handful of travellers meander the country lanes in search of this other Britain of empty seashores, cosy hamlets hidden valleys, strange traditions, and some of the friendliest people anywhere in the world.

Of course, the credit goes to Fred. It was he who initiated most of the impromptu friendships we made on our ramble together. No sooner had we paused in some doe-eyed village snoozing the afternoon away in a fold of hills, than he'd be out of the camper (our true 'mobile home') and off sniffing, purring and rubbing up against anything capable of responding amicably. His tailless stump had a way of waggling that captivated the most reticent resident. 'It's a Manx cat, then?' was the familiar query which brought the explanation that no, Fred was not a Manx but merely an impetuous puss who had escaped an early end by inches but sacrificed his tail in the process to the wheel of a manic motorist. After the grins and guffaws we invariably found ourselves the guest of some rumbustical countryman, an expert in unlikely legends and brimming with tales of doings in the hills that would make even the most ardent folklorist blush and wriggle.

Through Fred's capacity for making instant friends we ate better than any expense-account super-salesman and learned of places we might easily have overlooked. We were told the mysteries of Kingley Vale and of Otmoor; we met the flint-knappers of Brandon and the kippermen of Craster; we discovered an eerie museum of childhood in wildest Scotland, and a Cotswold-like region a hundred miles from the Cotswolds. We were entertained by a fisherman in Tarbert who cooked up a memorable 'Cullen Skink' for us, we crossed the 'Great East Anglian Desert', followed in the footsteps of Rev. Kilvert and A. E. Housman, and explored the Pendle witch-country. On and on we meandered, never quite knowing where we'd be next, who we'd meet or what tempting little by-ways might lead us off into fresh adventures and new friendships.

If readers – both residents and travellers from abroad – share this spirit of exploration and delight in discovering a countryside unspoilt by crowds, rambling the 'real' Britain, staying in country inns (far less expensive than their tourist-centre equivalents), eating the regional dishes and, best of all, meeting the people of these quiet corners, then they will enjoy these journeys as much as we did.

David Yeadon

York, 1980

Hidden
Corners
of
Britain

HANDA ISLAND

to:
CAPE
WRATH

Point of
Stoer

Eddrachillis
Bay

KYLESTROME

Cluas Deas

UNAPOOL

ACHNACARNIN

DRUMBEG

Loch
Glencoul

CLASHNESSIE

Quinag

Eas Chual Aluinn

STOER

CLACHTOLL

Baddidarach

Skiag Bridge

Ardvreck Castle

ACHMELVICH

LOCHINVER

Loch
Assynt

INCHNADAMPH

Glencansip
Lodge

INVERKIRKAIG

Canisp

Caves

Ben More
Assynt

Suilven

Enard Bay

COIGACH

A837

Rubha
Mor

BRAE of ACHNAHAIRD

Cul Mor

INVERPOLLY Res.

Auld
Dornie

Stac Polly

Knockan
Cliff

SUMMER
ISLES

ACHILTIBUIE

Cul Beag

Loch
Lurgain

Tanera
Beg

Tanera
More

Old Drumrunie Lodge

CULNACRAIG

Beinn
Ghabhlach

ULLAPOOL

Loch Broom

to:
INVERNESS

5 MILES 10

1. The Lochinver Peninsula

It was a rather inauspicious start.

The morning began with one of those sticky west-coast sea mists and Fred, my feline companion, left the camper for a stroll into the heather after breakfast. I went looking for him, tripped in a rabbit hole and twisted my ankle.

'Two days rest – no walking' said the doctor.

'Oh dear, you poor dear' said my mother on the phone.

Fred said nothing, at least, nothing very consoling, and mewed incessantly for his next meal.

My ankle healed quickly and after a convalescence spent gazing over Ullapool harbour and the hazy reaches of Loch Broom I was off, leaving behind the little tourist town with its West Highland Woollen Shop and hourly – on the hour – invasions by Japanese and German tourists. I shared a final pint with the fishermen in the pub across from the boat dock. They'd been restless too, waiting for the weather to change, sipping beer half-heartedly and exchanging gruff intimacies like a huddle of Italian housewives. I'd learned a little about fishing and a lot about the men who work the boats. I was to learn much more on my journeys.

A crisp sun shone over Beinn Ghabhlach on the south wall of the loch, the air was heathery and time was all mine. Leaving the main road behind I vanished down the byways of the Lochinver peninsula, deep into the Inverpolly Nature Reserve. With an area of almost 27,000 acres, the reserve stretches from the towering Knockan Cliff (where an earth shift 400 million years ago tangled the ancient rocks and left a dramatic geological record) to the lochans necklaced over the moors below the sugar-loaf outline of Suilven. This is primitive territory. Golden eagles, pine martens, wildcats, roe deer and the less frequent red, inhabit the bogs, screes and eyries. Ragged remnants of birch forest, branches brittle as bones, occupy the glens, and sharp-beaked seabirds skim the frothy tops of waves in Enard Bay.

I had telegraph poles for company and not much else on the backroad down from the Old Drumrunie Lodge and alongside Loch Lurgain. Ahead of me rose Stac Polly (Pollaidh), at 2,009 ft hardly a mountain and yet possessing immense stature – an almost regal presence topped by a bristling crown of frost-shattered gneiss. Behind and visible after a struggle up a rocky gulley lay the glacier-smoothed bleaks of Coigach.

Almost immediately the mood was broken. An irate sign scribbled on a board below Stac Polly read: 'Any unauthorised dogs found on the

Inverpolly Estate will be shot.' It's always a problem mixing people and wilderness. The southern peninsulas around Loch Torridon and the Isle of Skye face a constant summer conflict between walkers, motorists and campers on the one hand and landowners, farmers and crofters on the other. There's no easy solution. Even the Lochinver peninsula is beginning to suffer during the height of the season. Most travellers bypass it, moving on rapidly up the A835 over the Kylestrome ferry and on into Sutherland, but the few exploring its narrow byways soon fill the passing places and reduce that sense of isolation which attracted them in the first place. I prefer to leave late July and August to the tourists and arrange my journeys here in early summer or after mid September.

Yet fortunately, even in the busier weeks, one need only stroll a few yards from the road to find a deserted world of babbling burns, silky waterfalls and sheep tracks meandering alongside nameless lochans. This is crisp walking country. From the high point of the Loch Assynt road to Unapool hikers can make the return journey to the red peak of Quinag (2,651 ft) in a few hours, or seek out Britain's largest waterfall at the head of Loch Glencoul, Eas Chual Aluinn (the Maiden's Tresses), after a climb over the Bealoch a' Bhurich pass. Here the milky curve of the stream vanishes into rainbow haloes and divides briefly before rejoining to cascade into pools at the base of a 658-ft drop.

Further south I travelled to the ancient crofting village of Achiltibuie, littered with shells of abandoned homes but still supporting a hotel, a shed for fish-smoking and a corrugated-iron post office painted brilliant silver. I took a boat out to the Summer Isles lying like a school of basking porpoises in the bay. Visitors come for the sea fishing (forty-three different species are said to breed here), claimed to be the best in Europe. I spent my time rambling rocky coves and watching seals off Tanera Beg and Tanera More, once centres of a prosperous fishing station. There's little vegetation and the breezes are always cooler than those on the peninsula. Once back on land, walkers can follow a rock-road through Culnacraig and back into Ullapool if they miss home comforts so soon.

In the north-western corner is the rugged Point of Stoer, bleak and windswept with its rock pillar, 'The Old Man of Stoer'. Crofting has always been marginal here, a struggle between subsistence and despair with the latter apparently winning in recent years. Hardscrabble acres of half-moor are devoid of sheep or cultivation. Cottages with corrugated-iron roofs peer out empty-eyed at a steel-grey ocean. Some are the typical butt-and-bens normally associated with the rigorous highland life and designed to house both family and livestock under the same small roof.

Such primitive conditions have been common in the north for centuries.

Crofter's Cottage near Achiltibuie

Parish records for Assynt in 1700 suggest that 300 families lived on less than 280 acres of land, and poor land at that. The lot of the crofter worsened considerably after the defeat of the Jacobite rebellion at Culloden in 1745 and the subsequent eradication of the clan system. The Gaelic nobles who had measured their prowess by the size of their armies gradually adopted Sassenach values and became more concerned over the amassing of capital through 'improved' use of land. Ambitious sheep-farming, arable and fishing projects led to the relocation or removal of families and in Sutherland alone between 1809 and 1819 over 15,000 people left. Then came the infamous Highland Clearances of the 1820s when eviction was often accompanied by house-burning and even slaughter. Mass emigration ensued. Forests were cleared for sheep-grazing and fuel, and much of that vast denuded landscape from Cape Wrath to the Trossachs, traditionally thought of as 'highland', was created in a few brief years.

Today abandoned and barely habitable cottages are snapped up as holiday homes. 'They're the white settlers,' I was told by Dougie MacDonald in his tiny house overlooking Clashnessie. His father had been a crofter on Stoer,

Peat Cutting

but Dougie found little appealing in the life. 'I tried it but the land was sour –
there wasn't enough anyway. Two ridiculous acres! When I was a lad it
didn't seem so bad. Don't suppose it ever does. We always had a fine fire of
thick peats. My dad would cut 'em with the others over in the bog – he was a
dab hand with a tuskar, cut a thousand peats in an hour and kept on going all
day. I used to help him a bit. We'd come on back around five o'clock and
tackle my mother's pieces [flour scones with butter] before supper. Not
much meat, maybe once a week on Sunday. Breakfast was 'brose' – a
scooping of oatmeal with salt and milk. Salt herrings were good, though. It
was mainly our own stuff – tatties, turnips, oatmeal – same as now.' He
nodded towards a pan boiling on the stove. It was full of potatoes. In the sink
were more unpeeled potatoes and on the table, salt, pepper and margarine. I
saw no meat or eggs and no refrigerator. On the wall above the table was a
faded colour print in a frame of a sternfaced man. 'William Ewart Gladstone',
Dougie told me, 'My dad called him "the crofter's hero". Didn't make much
difference, though, in the end. Most of them had to do what I did – work for
somebody else. You couldn't do much else.'

6

Mists move in over Point of Stoer suddenly, sweeping across the sandy coves and headlands. The rambler will find majestic silences here. I walked from the point past the lighthouse at Cluas Deas down the track to Achnacarnin accompanied only by the occasional swirl of seabirds and the calls of red-throated divers and great skuas, venturing south from their colony on Handa Island.

Now deserted except for the occasional ornithologist, Handa Island was once a burial ground when wolves roamed the coastal forests. The rocky ground of the mainland often prevented deep burials and wolves hunted out the corpses until, as recorded on a stone set above the road to Glen Loth in Sutherland, a hunter named Polson killed the last she-wolf in the year 1700. According to the tale, he and two boys tracked the wolf and her six cubs to a defile in Glen Sletdale. The boys killed the cubs and left Polson to deal with the vicious female by winding her tail around his arm and stabbing her twenty times until she finally fell dead. Polson received several severe bites and almost died from his wounds. Even after his recovery it's said that people treated him warily, for when the moon was full 'he turned strangely queer and bared his fangs like the very creature he had slain so bravely'. Many scottish folk tales have this kind of eerie dénouement.

Equally wild are the moors and headlands beyond the Brae of Achnahaird and the secluded cove of 'Auld Dornie' harbour sprinkled with fishing boats. Care is needed here. Paths tend to be unreliable and often end in bogs or at marshy lochans on Rubha Mor. Yet for seekers of seclusion this is fine walking country – a place to rediscover your own peace.

I picked a clear day for my rambles here and lay back on a soft hillside basking in a warm sun. A curlew flung out its dismal warning somewhere behind me and meadow pipits and greenshanks chirped. Among the rocks, dappled with lichen and puffy with tufts of heather, were scatterings of starry saxifrages, butterwort and roseroot. Breezes off the ocean shook their leaves and bowed the brittle nardus grass. I thought of nothing really important. At one point I may even have been thinking of nothing at all, which is a rather difficult thing to do for any measurable length of time. Some obscure guru with a name longer than his beard once offered the thought to an impatient world that 'in nothing is everything'. The world as usual ignored him and the guru eventually disappeared into his own nothingness, claiming as he departed that he was now everything. I didn't quite under-stand at the time and I'm not sure I do now. It sounded like one of those Zen word-plays, infinitely complex and infinitely obvious, and a little too obscure for most western minds to grasp. And yet there are moments – tiny capsules of non-time – when the incessant chatterings of the mind cease. One is

Suilven

touched and exposed, and a link is made with something beyond the body. Most people are fortunate if they experience this kind of sensation a dozen times in a life. But each occasion can never be forgotten. Names have been given to the experience – spiritual awakening, a sense of the infinite, universal harmony. I had that sensation, a little shiver of awareness, on that hillside, on the very first day of travel – and it more than made up for the ankle!

The following day I climbed Suilven. You have to, really. I'd studied its northern slopes, green to the summit, from Stoer Bay where it forms the most prominent outline of a chain of ancient stumps – Quinag, Canisp, Cul

Mor, Cul Baeg, Stac Polly and Beinn Ghabhlach. Far beyond to the south rose the great crest of the Torridon range and to the east the gneiss-capped summit of 3,273 ft Ben More Assynt. I went through all the usual excuses – too far, too dangerous, too risky on the ankle, too tiring – and began the long haul, as I knew I would, from Glencansip Lodge early in the morning. It was a hard day with tough scrambling on the upper slopes below the summit. The actual height of 2,399 ft in no way reflects the effort needed to top it or the splendour of views in the late afternoon across the loch-splattered Coigach tundra far below, the still mirror of Loch Assynt and the pink sandstone peaks of the coastal mountains. It was only on the descent that my legs began their wobbling antics and the late evening was spent attending to blisters in the warmth of the camper. This time Fred showed a little more concern and tried licking them. You've perhaps never experienced the sensation of a cat's sandpapery tongue on a chronically sore spot, but one has an overwhelming urge to giggle and howl simultaneously. Howls won and Fred retired hastily to the rear of the camper pursued by a series of sharp epithets.

The next day I met Mrs Gibson. I'd spent the morning exploring Kirkaig Falls above Inverkirkaig and visiting the Achins' unusual weaving centre and bookshop tucked up a track near the bridge. The road here over to Lochinver is a narrow, sinuous creature, twisting through tiny glens littered with dwarf-birch. Occasional glimpses of rocky headlands, scattered islets and the open sea relieve the intensity of the scenery. Cautious driving is essential if one is to survive the antics of other impetuous motorists.

A small sign read 'Museum of Childhood – Lon Cuilk' and pointed up a narrow track. I followed it, through a gate and out onto open moors with vistas across Loch Inver. Ahead of me I saw a house in a sheltered dell and I parked in the yard, outside the side door. A spasm of high-pitched yelpings greeted my arrival with an even higher-pitched voice demanding silence. The door opened and out peeped a diminutive lady, hardly five feet tall, wearing a pom-pom hat. 'The museum?' she asked with a bright smile. I nodded. 'Go down. I'll get the key.' She pointed to a new building at the bottom of her garden about the size of a large garage. My feet were still tender from the Suilven climb and I limped slowly down the path. 'Now what on earth have you been doing with yourself?' The lady, who introduced herself as Mrs Gibson, trotted perkily after me, tut-tutting as I explained my predicament. 'Oh, you men. Always climbing something. Serves you right.' For just a moment I was a child again being rebuked by mother. 'Never mind. There's a chair inside. Sit down. You'll feel better.' She opened the door and we stepped in.

I'm not sure what I expected. The shed itself was a bare structure – exposed rafters, plain walls, simple windows. But the floor and raised displays were smothered in dolls of all sizes dressed in every style from Spanish flamenco to pre-punk contemporary. There were shawls too, christening dresses, cradles, miniature tea services, prams, teddy bears, a tiny sewing machine, display cabinets filled with childhood memorabilia – and an immense fluffy cat which turned out to be real. Mrs Gibson sat demurely to one side while I absorbed it all. I murmured something like 'amazing' and she took that as her signal to begin. 'Make yourself comfortable,' she said, pointing to a chair and began to explain about her collection, how she'd always wanted dolls when she was young but only ever had two, one of which she dropped and smashed on the same Christmas morning it was given to her. 'It just ballooned somehow,' she explained, gesturing helplessly at the display. 'And they're all different.'

When I arrived I knew nothing about dolls and cared even less. When I left almost an hour later I had the makings of an expert confidently able to distinguish an 1890 Curman-Steiner from an 1865 Armand Marseille and expound upon the unique aesthetic qualities of Kammer-Reinhardt's 'character' dolls and Jumeau's 'paperweight eyes'. I had learned that Britain was really 'not very advanced' when it came to doll-making in the nineteenth century and that mass-production techniques in the 1890s in France and Germany ended the 'true' era of doll-creation. I had (blushingly) peeped under crinolines and petticoats to examine the quality of body-structure (every material was used from papier mâché to metal) and had fallen completely in love with an 1860 Gesland 'Poupée Modèle' dressed immaculately in blue silk with lace trimmings. Admittedly she lacked the stature of some of the others, but from the way she looked at me I know she felt the same. Mrs Gibson was very happy. 'I think you picked the best,' she whispered as she turned off the lights and we left the shed. I peered in at the window for one last look. From the outside it was all different, rather eerie – a film-set for some supernatural drama. Two hundred faces, four hundred eyes peered at me from the darkened room. My favourite was hidden in the shadows somewhere at the back. Not a sound – just endless stares. Then something brushed by my leg and I leapt away startled. It was Fred.

Mrs Gibson smiled her farewells as I manoeuvred the camper out of the yard. 'She really was the best one for you,' she said quietly. I didn't know what to say, but I knew what she meant. Dolls is dangerous!

And Lochinver is lovely. Most peninsula settlements are straggling places, scattered hamlets of grey and white cottages with the occasional sombre church or school to suggest a nucleus. But Lochinver is different. I made the long, winding descent alongside an excitable stream, tumbling over itself to the long sea loch below. I was quite unprepared for the baronial bulk of the Culag Hotel towering over the pier against a backcloth of pines. Mellowed travellers putted in a large walled garden and a sign on the notice board offered the ghillie's service for brown trout, sea trout and salmon fly fishing. Fishing boats clustered around the harbour wall and seabirds hovered expectantly as couples wandered slowly along the jetty. Round the corner on the shallow arc of the bay were the stern highland houses, presbyterian grey and white, linked and yet separate. The local general store advertised smoked chicken and smoked venison sausages. Unfortunately they'd sold out of both.

Ardvreck Castle and Loch Assynt

I took the road round the head of the bay, across the Inver river bridge, and followed signs to the Highland Stoneware Pottery near Baddidarach. A small group of sheds and mobile homes clustered in a hollow below the road. Prince Philip had visited a few days previously and David Grant, one of the directors, was still glowing. 'We've had the most remarkable response ever since we began.' He pointed to displays of thick, grey-based pottery decorated with hand-painted flowers and butterflies. 'We based the process on Japanese techniques, the use of simple, single brush strokes. But it's not cupboard china. It's tough stuff!'

I peered into the workshop and watched designs being painted on the unglazed clay shells. One young girl created a complex motif of branches, leaves and blossoms in seconds, using her brush with the flair of a conductor's baton. Outside the window I saw Suilven again, rising out of the rocky plateau above Lochinver. Pinned to the wall by a work-desk and splattered with clay from a potter's wheel was a snippet from a poem:

> Amazed I gazed on grand Suilven
> As southward she seemed sailing
> With canvas spread, a mighty ship
> 'Gainst where the red sun seemed to dip
> With golden streamers trailing.

12

Drivers who find the backroads south of Lochinver a little hair-raising are advised to take the A837 alongside Loch Assynt back to Skiag Bridge. The road north along the coast through Clachtoll and Drumbeg is even narrower with alarmingly steep gradients. Nevertheless it has its compensations, not least the Stoer cliff walk described earlier and hidden sandy coves at Achmelvich and Drumbeg. But the inland scene is even wilder and more disordered, rising up to the craggy summit of Quinag. Today visitors relish the bleakness. The authors of *A Traveller's Guide Through Scotland* (1807) were less impressed:

> The country is everywhere deformed by rocky mountains, the sterile moor and the dangerous brown morass . . . The more inland parts are nothing more but a vast group of dreadful mountains divided only by deep and very narrow valleys, whose declivities are so narrow and steep as to be dangerous without guides.

The journey to the ferry at Kylestrome can be made in comfort within an hour, although far longer should be taken, with frequent pauses for such surprises as the Pictish tower or 'broch' at Clachtoll, the pink beach and waterfalls at Clashnessie, coastal walks near Drumbeg overlooking the island-splattered Eddrachillis Bay, and a detour south to the ruins of Ardvreck Castle on Loch Assynt.

This sixteenth-century stronghold-home of the Macleods of Assynt is remembered mainly for its guest, the Marquis of Montrose, who sought refuge here following an abortive attempt to maintain episcopalian church government in Scotland after the execution of Charles I. He was roundly defeated on the Hill of Weeping near Carbisdaie in 1650 and subsequently betrayed by Neil Macleod for the sum of £25,000, £20,000 or a mere £500 worth of oatmeal, according to conflicting historical accounts. Montrose was executed in Edinburgh but – once again it's a Scottish sting-in-the-tail tale – Neil Macleod had little time to enjoy his new-found wealth before the Restoration brought the troops of Charles II racing to Assynt to imprison him and occupy the Macleod lands for more than a hundred years.

Here at the castle and the hamlet of Inchnadamph the temptation to climb 3273 ft Ben More Assynt is almost irresistible, or at least to explore the Allt nan Uamh caves where 8,000-year-old human bones were discovered. The remains of lemmings were also found, which led to the remark by a thickly-bearded student in the Culag bar at Lochinver that lemmings and crofters had much in common. It had been a boisterous evening with Gaelic songs by the locals and free-flowing beer. The Spirit of the Highlands was an almost tangible presence. But abruptly the mood was broken and an ominous silence spread over the room. The barman paused in the middle of pulling a pint. Someone coughed nervously. The barmaid went pale. 'I wonder', began one of the singers, a burly man in a navy blue fisherman's sweater, 'I wonder if you'd care to repeat what you just said now.' No one moved. The student took the bait, apparently oblivious to the mood, and began to explain his thesis that highland crofters brought about their own destruction by refusing to cooperate with the landowners in modernising the marginal economy of the region. 'They were stubborn – bloody minded. They wanted their own patch of land and that was all. They didn't consider changing, most of them. They wouldn't listen even when it was proved they'd never last another generation – they'd all starve. They just went ahead and des-troyed themselves.' A moment's silence was followed by a thunderous uproar as a dozen men bellowed out rebuttals and the student began to realise what was happening. The barmaid had vanished. People began moving for the door and an old man passed me chuckling. He paused and whispered, 'I'd be getting back a bit laddie, if I were you. You're a wee touch too close sitting there.' He was right, and much as I would have liked to record the ensuing discussion, I decided I had a lot more travelling to do, and discretion, in this instance, was certainly the better part of valour.

'He's opened up a real wound wi' that one,' the old man remarked as we strolled alongside the fishing pier. He was still chuckling. 'M'be there's something in what he says. We're sticklers for tradition in these parts and I'm not sure that it's got us very far really. There's a few that carries on, but the old places are pretty much dead nowadays – it's all holiday cottages and outsiders trying to preserve everything like it was theirs. S'not bad here yet, but south round Torridon its hard to find anyone who's lived there for more'n few years. Some only come for a few weeks a year. Rest of the time their houses are empty. Applecross is the same. They opened a road up but it was too late. Most of them had gone. Now the houses are falling in or they've been snapped up by outsiders. Captain Wills [of the Wills tobacco family] is tryin' some new ideas, so I've heard, but he'll have a job on. Even round here,' he gestured at the village of Lochinver straggled along the bay in the moonlight and the fishing boats nestling against the harbour wall, 'the trawlermen aren't local, most of them come by bus from the east coast every week. They say property's too expensive. City folk have been buying it all.' The picture he painted sounded very bleak. I asked him how he thought it might all end and he chuckled again. 'Maybe a few more cheeky bastards like that one,' he nodded over at the bar where the hubbub still continued. 'At least it makes 'em think a bit.' His face tightened. 'They've all got families that've lived round here for God knows how long – for ever more'n likely. If they want to stay they'll stay. Some go off for a while and come back. Some you'll never see again. But it goes on you know – and they're still around to argue about it.'

We stood on the edge of the quay. A chilly breeze blew in off the loch and wavelets clicked against the seawall. 'You staying long?' he asked.

I said I had no plans. 'Best way,' he murmured, 'Best way.' And then, 'If you're around tomorrow I'll show you a few places, if you'd like.'

So I stayed.

It's the only way to travel.

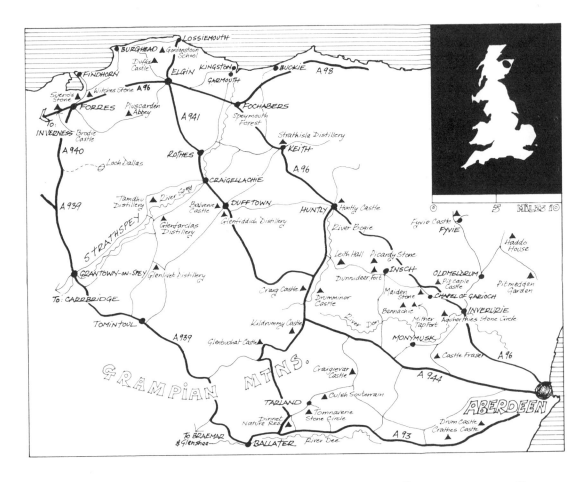

2. The North-Eastern Grampians

It was midsummer in the Grampian mountains and snowing hard.

Far below, a valley basked in mellow mists and the river Dee sparkled among meadows edged by cloaks of conifers. Unfortunately such views were brief – mere flickers through the roaring blizzard.

From a distance the white-topped hills had seemed a little peculiar, but putting it down to some trick of light in the highland massif I continued up the long Glenshee climb from Blairgowrie. About a mile from the summit I realised it was snow, but by then it was too late to turn back. The blizzard ripped across the moors, intensifying by the second. The entire road surface was white. Bracken fronds drooped disconsolately under their cold caps.

16

The camper skidded, lurched, did a fancy pirouette on the wrong side and reached the top of the infamous Spittal of Glenshee. Visibility was appalling. To pause would have been unwise, so on I danced around the Devil's Elbow, past Clunie lodge and down the long glen with those distant views of the summery Dee valley between trailings of sleet. The drama ended abruptly as I popped through pines into bright afternoon and paused to refresh myself at the baronial hotel in Braemar. The place was agog with tourists and for once I was glad of company. Through broad windows I could see the blizzard looking more like a gentle morning mist from my enveloping armchair by the fireplace.

'In't Grampians,' my informant had recommended, 'keep away from't Great Glen, Aviemore and Braemar an' tha'll have t'place to thi'sen.' He was a Yorkshireman from Birdwell just outside Barnsley who knew more of Scotland than most residents. We'd met in Blairgowrie as I prepared for my mountain explorations. 'Twenty-three years we've been coming,' he boasted. 'Twenty-four if I count 1949 but that were only a short 'un. Never got beyond Trossachs. Car broke. So call it twenty-three. Every year somewhere different north of Perth. I don't think Scotland starts till you get north of Perth. *She* doesn't either. She sleeps all t'way to Pitlochry.' A nod indicated his plump wife, sitting in a gleaming Armstrong Siddeley. 'Lovely machine that,' he murmured complacently. His wife smiled. 'Picked her up for a song and never a day's trouble. She's been everywhere – to't top of Sutherland, to Skye, around Loch Shin – everywhere and not so much as a murmur.' His wife assumed she was the subject of the conversation and smiled even more brightly. 'Last year we did t'Don Valley and there were hardly a soul. Castles, palaces – the lot. Went round a few whisky distilleries – proper ones y'know – enough highland malt in those vats to float QE II. Marvellous smell. Ten sniffs and you're floored. Found a commune place near Elgin where they grow forty pound cabbages an' that, talking to 'em, dancin' round 'em . . .'

I ended up with a list of most unusual places and an overwhelming urge to explore this secluded corner of the Grampians. The summer snowstorm had only intensified my curiosity and I left the tourist buses of the Dee valley behind, climbing over the low ranges north of Ballater into quieter country.

Prehistoric inhabitants of this region also doubtless experienced its freak climate and, erring on the side of caution, built their settlements, circles and souterrains on the lower ground in the north-east. Traces are abundant and more than sixty sites are described and illustrated in *Early Grampian*, an excellent booklet published by the Regional Council. Many are rather obscure and of primary interest to archaeologists, but I found a dozen places

Tomnaverie Stone Circle

well worth visiting. The stone circle at Tomnaverie across the valley from Tarland's demure church is particularly dramatic, haloed round a rocky hill and thought to date from about 1800 BC. To the west and south shadowy ranges rise up over the green valleys. The stones of the Aguhorthies circle west of Inverurie are larger but in a rather more sheltered site.

A few miles east of Ballater are the extensive Kinord sites, remnants of circular huts, fields, tracks and souterrains scattered around the glacial kettle holes and lochs of the Dinnet nature reserve. The odd island in Loch Kinord is an Iron Age 'crannog' – an artificial defensive mound of rock and wood. Nearby is the Kinord Cross, an intricately carved crucifix dating from the end of the Pictish era. Other more elaborate stones include the 10 ft Maiden Stone west of Chapel of Garioch with its Pictish mirror and comb symbols, the nearby Picardy Stone which once stood on a small grave-cairn, the four crudely-carved stones set in the east gable of Fyvie church and, most memorable of all, the great Sueno's Stone outside Forres, 18 ft high and writhing with animal-decorated vines and tumultuous battle scenes. Many archaeologists regard this as Britain's most impressive Pictish monument

18

while disagreeing on the significance of the gruesome carvings of soldiers, horsemen and piles of headless bodies.

More recent in origin is the granite Witches' Stone standing on the opposite side of the road. This is one of three erected to mark the equally gruesome death of three witches said to have inflicted King Duffus with a painful disease during a stay at Forres Castle. The unfortunate creatures were seized, speedily condemned, rammed into spiked barrels and rolled down the length of Cluny Hill. The stone is said to mark the spot where the barrels stopped. If so it must have been an extraordinarily long roll, possibly assisted by a vengeful populace.

By far the largest remnants of early civilisation in the Grampians are the forts at Burghead, the Mither Tap on the easterly summit of Bennachie, and the spectacular ruins of Dunnideer outside Insch. Much of the former has been absorbed within Burghead village, a charming seaside community, although the Burghead and Elgin museums contain important discoveries from the site including Pictish symbol-stones carved with bulls. Bennachie is an even more confusing remnant marked by massive screes of granite around a weathered tor. Tracks from Hillfoot (signed from the Maiden Stone) lead up through the thick skirts of forest on to the purpling moor. The main defence wall is still distinct 100 ft below the summit, as are traces of a parapet walk and an ancient entrance-way flanked by the ruins of protective walls. Best of all are the views over the gradual land fall to a coastline flecked with white villages.

The Dunnideer summit is lower but the hill far more abrupt, rising suddenly from the Bogie river to the broken walls of a medieval castle surrounded by three concentric rings of defence works. The original Iron Age vitrified fort was an effective defence-point against Roman incursions, and an abandoned brass sword or gladius suggests at least one abortive attack on the defiant Picts. Today the wind blasts across the summit, whistling round the remaining castle wall with its shattered window-hole.

At Culsh, just north of Tarland, one need never heed howling winds in the well-restored souterrain. This is one of the cosiest of Iron Age structures, and found throughout Britain, most notably at the Iron Age village of Chysauster in Cornwall. Basically it consists of a curved subterranean passage of variable height and width reinforced by drystone walls and a stone slab ceiling. Its precise function is uncertain, although even temperatures would have provided excellent food-storage conditions, and the narrow entrance-way, a perfectly defensible niche in times of attack. Exploration is advisable with a torch and the farmer in the adjoining house seems quite happy to loan one of his.

While the scores of antiquities in the north-eastern Grampians reflect its role as habitable territory as far back as 4,000 BC, the most prominent evidence of its continued popularity is the abundance of castles, in and around the valleys of the Don and Dee. While the Dee valley castles, particulary Braemar and Balmoral, are high-priority spots on the itineraries of Grampian tourists, the castles of the Don and Bogie rivers are far less well-known and from the hidden-corner hunter's point of view, much more enjoyable to explore.

Many of the ancient edifices are in a ruined state, and among these Kildrummy is king – 'the noblest of Northern castles' according to Dr W. Douglas Simpson who supervised excavation here for more than two decades. It was first established under Gilbert de Moravia in the early thirteenth-century and modelled on the Chateau de Coucy near Laon, France. Gilbert, who as well as being a baron was also Bishop of Caithness, insisted on the inclusion of a chapel in the massive structure and had it built slightly out of alignment with the castle walls to ensure accurate east–west orientation. In 1306 Robert Bruce's wife and court ladies narrowly escaped a siege here by the future Edward II while remaining Scots defenders were betrayed by one of their own who fired the fortress and claimed his reward from the English. In yet another gruesome Grampian tale, the traitor, having been promised all the gold he could carry, was literally filled to the brim with the stuff by the victors who poured the molten metal down his throat. The castle was rebuilt and continued to play a major part in regional history well into the eighteenth century when it was abandoned to the elements. A new 'castle-hotel' now stands beside the ruins catering for the more discerning highland travellers.

Notable ruins with occasional restorations exist at Duffus, Balvenie, Huntly and Glenbuchat, but most memorable are such typically Scottish-Baronial castles as Craigievar, one of eight major properties owned by the National Trust for Scotland in the Grampians. The style is unique, owing its strong verticality to the scarcity of structural timber and its fairytale tower and turret decorations to the French, with whom Scotland maintained close 'Auld Alliance' ties between the thirteenth and sixteenth centuries. This particular edifice, secluded in woods at the end of a long estate drive, is an exotic creation dating from 1626 and built for 'Danzig' Willie Forbes, a prosperous Scottish merchant. Yet for all its soaring walls and festoon of gables and chimneys, the place possesses a domestic intimacy as it peers out, slightly tongue-in-cheek, over the velvety Braes of Leochel-Cushnie. Inside is an extravagance of decorative plaster ceilings, enormous fireplaces, canopied beds, a grand staircase leading to the Great Hall, abundant heraldic

Craigievar Castle

motifs (including Willie's own crest and motto: 'Doe not Vaiken Sleiping Dogs') – and yet all the lived-in feel of a real home.

A second creation by Craigievar's architect, I. Bell, is the 1636 tower of Castle Fraser set in a formal court and approached down a long tree-lined drive. Construction commenced in 1575 under the 6th laird, Michael Fraser, but Mr Bell's later work transformed the place into another splendid example of the Scottish-Baronial style. A popular poem celebrated his architectural achievements here:

> Cast your eyes
> On Fraser's glorious pile
> which southward lies
> Whose fame, whose structure
> is by none excelled . . . etc.

Subsequent residents cluttered the simple rooms with Victoriana. The great hall, now restored to its original exposed granite and white plaster, contained a gigantic organ obliterating most of the west wall and set in a warehouse of antimacassars, chaise-longues and ponderous mahogany tables. Some of the smaller rooms wear their Victorian trimmings a little more comfortably, notably the colourful smoking room and the Trophy Room dripping with the forlorn heads of ibex, bison, tigers, deer and two stuffed dogs, both family pets. To the delight of romantics, the structure is a warren of hidden rooms and narrow spiral staircases, and possesses a 'Laird's Lug' – a cramped niche between the floor of the 'Worked Room' (full of needlework displays) and the vaulting of the Great Hall beneath. A trapdoor in a cupboard gives access to steps leading into this musty space, thought to have been a safe deposit. Sir Walter Scott preferred to see such hideaways as spy-holes and made dramatic use of them in his *Fortunes of Nigel*. A second spy-hole giving a clear view of activities in the courtyard can be seen near the tiny tower chapel.

On my visit here the courtyard buildings contained an excellent exhibition on the Grampian Castles, at least twenty of them, and enough to keep an enthusiast active for a fortnight. Even more overwhelming is the Grampian Regional Council's booklet, *'The Castle County'*, which gives details of sixty-seven separate structures, many ruined and most not open to the public.

Crathes, Drum, Braemar and Balmoral along the Dee are all a little over-crowded during the summer. William Adam's classical Haddo House, Muchall's Castle and the Great Garden of Pitmedden were too close to the

Aberdeen suburbs for my liking, and the splendours of Brodie Castle near Forres and Midmar Castle outside Echt were not then open to public gaze. So I picked the refined Leith Hall, a short way beyond Teacher's distillery at Insch, and spent a couple of hours being introduced to the history of the Leith-Hay family by a charming lady guide with an encyclopedic knowledge of almost every object on display.

'I've only been here two weeks,' she told me modestly before launching into lengthy descriptions of Bonnie Prince Charlie's miniature writing set presented to Andrew Hay on the eve of Culloden, the Jacobite pardon granted by George III to the same Hay, Napoleon's sash given to the family by a 'grateful lady', and the elephantine armchair designed to seat females in crinolines. We moved in a leisurely way from the formal rooms to the four low-ceilinged chambers in the oldest part of the hall, dating from 1650. Later additions created an internal courtyard and a flowering of turrets and towers on the corners of an otherwise plain structure. My guide pointed out the flock of goat-like Soay sheep brought from the island of Hirta in the St Kilda group where they still run wild. A string of ducks landed in explosive disarray on the lochan created from a patch of swampy ground by one of the Leith-Hays earlier this century. Nearby was a walled garden with arbours, ponds and rockeries and further in the distance, the eerie 'Secret Path' or Henrietta's Walk carved like a tunnel through a dense spruce plantation. One could easily spend a day here exploring the paths through the 240-acre estate, but after a quiet walk near the bird-watching hide I left to continue my rambles through this castle-studded region.

Mrs Burges-Lumsden opens her nearby fifteenth-century Pitcaple Castle to the public on a regular basis and visitors delight in the tale of Mary Queen of Scots dancing under a thorn tree here after a banquet in 1562. Craig Castle near Lumsden is a warlike pile unadorned except for slit windows and gunloops, and the cosy fifteenth-century Drumminor Castle, a mere fragment of a once vast edifice, still contains the 'Happy Room' (so named by King James II) and an unusual round-stair tower entrance. I was told that two elderly ladies looked after the castle and 'entertained visitors if they felt in the mood'. Unfortunately no one was at home when I called.

Fyvie, 'that crowning glory of Scottish baronial architecture' according to Sir Herbert Maxwell, was also closed to the public. So I contented myself with a distant view of its south façade, over 150 ft long and dominated by a towering central gatehouse, and recollections of the seventeenth-century oh-so-Scottish tale of Andrew Lammie and the miller's daughter. Andrew was Lord Fyvie's trumpeter and dearly loved by Agnes Smith, daughter of the local miller. The miller's family reacted cruelly to the news and while

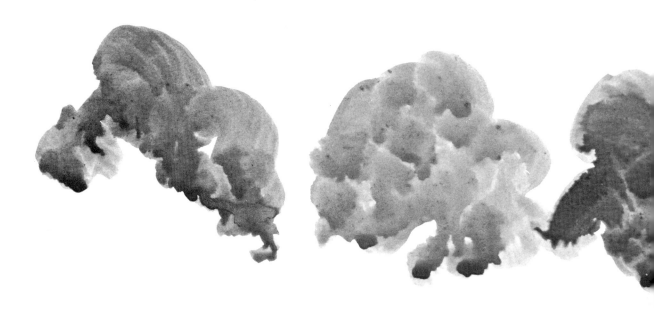

Castle Fraser

Andrew was away buying the wedding dress in Edinburgh, beat her to death:

> Her brother strake her wondrous sore,
>   Baith cruel strokes and many,
> And brak' her back at the ha' door
>   For likin' Andrew Lammie.

Agnes's memorial stands in Fyvie churchyard, erected by public subscription in 1859, and a sculpted Andrew still blows his trumpet from the castle roof-top in the direction of the now ruined mill.

'Tales like that, they drive you straight to the bottle.' Alex Doughty downed his dram in one gulp and waited impatiently for the barman to refill his glass. The tap room of the pub in Huntly was filling with the Saturday crowd. He banged his glass on the counter. 'You cannae call this place your own on wikends,' he mumbled through a broad moustache, loud enough for

a gaggle of pink-haired youngsters to hear. Their single earrings shook menacingly but they said nothing. That could come later as it invariably did on Saturday nights in this rigid little town of grey granite streets, grid-ironed round a formal square with clock tower and fountain. Through the window I could see the craggy ruins of Strathbogie Castle, one of the ancient homes of the Gordons, its huge heraldic doorway lurking behind trees at the end of main street.

Alex selected his brand of malt carefully from more than twenty on the back-bar. 'This one you drink more slowly,' he told me, admiring its pale gold colour. We'd been discussing what everyone discusses in this part of the highlands – whisky. He sipped it like vintage claret, savouring the bouquet and running the sharp-smooth liquid around his tongue. 'Did they show you how to do it right then?' I nodded. I'd just returned from wanderings in the whisky country around Dufftown, Tomintoul, Grantown-on-Spey, Rothes and Keith – a small area on the map but a universe of experience for the dedicated malt-drinker.

25

Alex Doughty

Tourists have recently discovered the attractions of 'the only Whisky Trail in the world' and make ritual stops at the five distilleries for their potted-presentations and 'wee drams' to send them on their way. Yellow AA markers (not Alcoholics Anonymous as one American suggested) lead through the gentler valleys around Keith's Strathisla distillery to the broad moors and glens beyond the Glenfiddich plant at Dufftown. The model village of Tomintoul, the highest in the highlands, is a convenient half-way point where every second shop is a whisky emporium offering scores of brands, some over forty years old, others exceeding 100° proof. 'Fresh Haggis – shot this morning' signs suggest a rather un-Scottish humour, and pamphlets provide interesting glimpses of the whisky-economy: 'At the Glenfarclas distillery 25 men produce 10,000 hogsheads (five million bottles) of whisky a year'; 'British Excise Duty accounts for 85% of the price of a bottle of whisky'; '60 of Scotlands 110 Malt Whisky Distilleries are located in the Grampian region'; 'At one time there were 400 stills in Glenlivet alone – it was the most profitable way to sell barley – and pony trains carried the

26

ankers or ten-gallon casks south to Braemar and Perth.' Today the only distillery left in Glenlivet is Glenlivet with a 150-year-old licence and a large plant steaming quietly in the valley. A little further north around Speyside is Glenfarclas on a bleak moor below the 2755 ft peak of Ben Rinnes, and the less well-known Tamdhu distillery.

Somewhere along the way, near Carrbridge, I stumbled into the final night of a week-long ceilidh, one of those gatherings of traditional Scottish entertainers in the Highlands. The pubs and hotels were throbbing to pipes, fiddles, accordions and drums. Out in the streets impromptu reels whirled scores of enthusiasts around the lamp-posts and folk singers moaned at the full moon. Two local ceilidh bands vied with one another by the river and a great ginger giant of a man complete with kilt (one of the few I saw worn in the highlands) tumbled backside first into the water and vanished leaving only a hand clutching a whisky bottle above the surface. After an extraordinarily long immersion he rose up like Neptune, poured what was left in the bottle down his throat and continued his lusty singing of an ancient ceilidh folksong, drowning out the fiddle players with sheer gusto.

I completed the loop-tour and, turning right by Telford's famous Craigellachie Bridge, came again to crisp, pristine Dufftown dominated by its castellated clock tower. As Rome was founded on seven hills, so the tourist blurb goes, Dufftown was founded on seven stills, and a riverside walking tour from Fife Street alongside Dullan Water and back via Mortlach Church and Princess Royal Park passes most of them, ending at the famous Glenfiddich distillery below the ruins of Balvenie Castle. I felt much refreshed by the exercise. The Dullan chattered through its wooded glen, pausing in pools and cascading over river rocks. The water was a rich, clear brown, the peaty water so essential to high-quality malts. Peat is also used to fire the kilns in which the malted barley is dried, whence the distinctive taste of whisky. I paused to watch the silky strands of the Linen Apron Fall and wandered above the steep rock ravines carved by the river to join the B9009 Tomintoul road leading back into town.

In common with many 'model' Grampian towns laid out by local lairds, Dufftown was the creation of a local laird, James Duff, 4th Earl of Fife, who leased building plots and three grazing areas to each family at nominal terms to encourage settlement. The great family of Gordon developed Huntly as a woollen manufacturing centre adjoining their castle and had a local weaver here design the 'sett' of the tartan for the newly established Gordon Highlanders in 1794. (This gave rise to the erroneous idea that the Scottish clans had always been distinguishable by the sett of their tartans – an idea dismissed as 'utter fraud' by Sir Walter Scott but enthusiastically endorsed by tartan manufacturers.) Other model communities included the 4th Duke of Gordon's village of Tomintoul where farmers were granted 'shielings' for their cattle on the Braes of Stratharon, and great cattle migrations took place every summer; the town of Keith where the Earl of Findlater's 'new' town sits harmoniously alongside its older counterpart; and tiny Monymusk where Sir Archibald Grant transformed a 'wild and dreary moor' into rich agricultural land enclosed by verdant woods. I paused here one morning during my search for prehistoric remnants and was given remarkably informed advice by a young man working the cash register at the local shop. I happened to mention this to the verger outside the twelfth-century church across from the village square, and was told proudly that I'd been speaking with 'our young laird'. He pointed out a large building behind trees as Monymusk House, parts of which, he told me, were built from a twelfth-century Augustinian priory, long vanished.

'We had Christians here far earlier than that, though. Around the sixth century they say that some of St Ninian's missionaries came up from Whithorn [see Chapter 4]. Culdees they called them.' He pointed to the ornate ninth-century Pictish stones standing just inside a small door at the base of the sturdy church tower. 'Those were carved by some of the converts.' Above were photographs of a famous reliquary, the Brecbannock, which contained relics of St Columba and was given for safe keeping to Malcolm de Monymusk in 1315 after the battle of Bannockburn. For centuries it remained at the Old Hall and is now in Edinburgh's National Museum of Antiquities. He pointed to the pure Norman chancel arch. 'All that was covered over after the reformation. It was 1932 before we saw it.' I asked if the story of Prior Elphinstone's conviction for murder here was true, and he nodded solemnly. 'It was a fiery place, that old priory. Religion wasn't so peaceful then and there's many tales left to be told yet.' Unfortunately he couldn't recollect any – unlike Alex in the pub at Huntly who was now well into his sixth dram and bawling out half-truths about the town and its history with the eloquence of an Irish leprechaun and the ingenuity of a Yankee tinker.

He noticed my somewhat sceptical expression. 'Now laddie, don't you be so canny till I've told you about the Horseman's Word and then we'll see what you think.' The babble of voices surrounding us at the bar ceased abruptly and a dozen pairs of eyes focused on Alex who was slowly finishing his drink, studiously ignoring the impact his remark had made. 'Aye now, that's a tale for you' he whispered, pushing his glass across the counter for a refill. 'That's something for you to think about.' The silence continued, a most unusual occurrence for a Saturday night, until a stout middle-aged man with a leathery complexion nudged Alex gently but firmly on his elbow. 'Ach, you needn't be tellin' about that nonsense, Alex. It's all over now and forgotten, and you know that well.' Alex laughed loud enough to shake the glasses. 'Aye, it's finished right enough, Ernest, it's finished. So who cares if it's told or not – specially if it's the nonsense you say it is?' 'Leave it alone,' said Ernest calmly. 'It's best left alone, Alex.' Alex turned and looked at the smaller man by his side. He was smiling as broadly as ever but something passed between them, a flicker of a meaning, something seen by the silent observers gathered round the bar. Another pause and then Alex swung back to his empty glass. 'Am I to have this filled or not?' The barman reached for the bottle of malt and Alex coughed slightly. 'It's all nonsense – it is – so we'll talk about something else. Tell me, laddie, have you seen Kildrummy yet, now there's a place for you . . . ' The babble began again, Ernest drifted away and whatever Alex was going to tell me was forgotten in another tangle of tales.

Forgotten by him, that is, not by me. I eventually found the story of the Horseman's Word in an obscure book on Grampian folklore and understood why Alex may have changed his mind. It appears that secret societies with pagan links have been a feature of the highlands for centuries and the Horseman's Word was one such organisation deriving its support initially from farmhands around Huntly. Its activities were particularly rife during the late nineteenth century when almost every man linked with the land is thought to have been initiated as a 'made horseman', learning incantations, reading passages of the Bible backwards to invoke the Devil, worshipping Cain, the 'first Horseman', and shaking hands with 'Auld Hornie' the horseman's 'De'il'. Each member swore absolute secrecy: 'Hell conceal, never reveal; neither write, nor dite, nor recite; nor cut, nor carve, nor write in sand.' According to some outsiders its activities were harmless and mainly involved the propagation of ancient knowledge about the control and management of horses. To others it was a sinister clique of satanists dabbling in witchcraft and other dastardly activities. A few alarmists even claim its continued existence today in remote highland valleys. That's the problem with secret societies – you never really learn the truth in a maze of innuendo and 'understandings'. But there's obviously some power still left in the name, and Alex never mentioned it again.

The following day, after an appropriately tumultuous Saturday night in Huntly, I rolled downhill from the upland moors and valleys out onto the coastal plain. Fringed by the tranquil Speymouth forest I found Fochabers, yet another Gordon-sponsored model town. In this instance the family decided that the original village of estate labourers and tenanted farmhands was in the way of planned extensions to Gordon Castle and so demolished it,

29

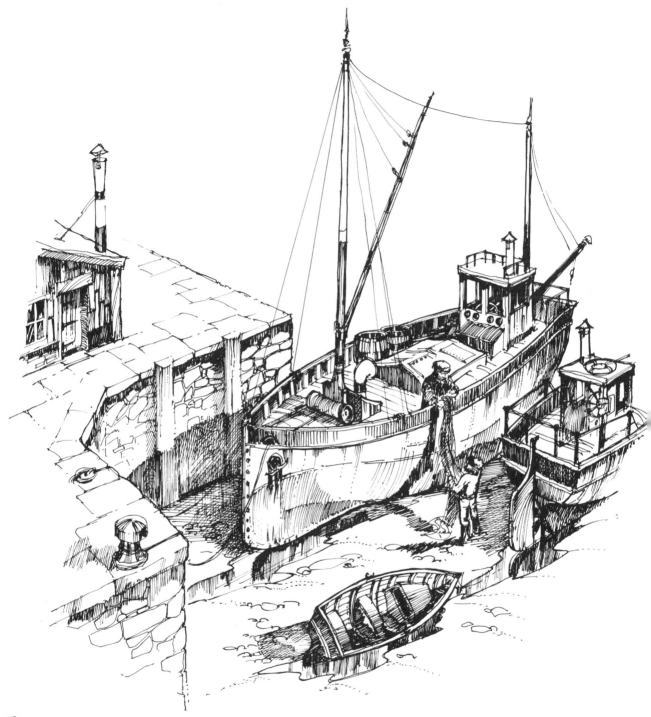

Fishing Boats at Buckie

leaving only the market cross with its 'iron collar' to which small-time criminals were shackled. The new village, a restrained masterpiece of Georgian town planning, was designed on two prime axis-lines, the first the Aberdeen to Inverness coastal road and the second aligned with the castle itself. Both axis-lines met in the formal market square dominated by the Doric-porticoed Bellie parish church. The castle axis was later interrupted by an Episcopalion chapel at the end of Duke Street and made finally redundant by the demolition of the castle in 1955. Outside the village one of the lucrative economic bases of the region, the Baxter foods factory, proudly exhibits its Gordon tartan trademark in memory of the company's founder, ironically not actually a Gordon, but one of their gardeners whose wife had a knack for making fine jams.

I wandered slowly westwards taking country lanes at will, across broad green sea-meadows and through the Speymouth and Monaughty pine forests. Walking trails were signed and led off into the deep resin-scented darkness, cut by rapiers of sunshine. The silence buzzed and the paths had the bounce of a good mattress. I could hear hollow bird-calls but saw nothing until, turning a bend by a mossy boulder, I came face to face, or rather face to rump, with a large red deer. He appeared most indignant at the interruption and trotted off, head high, into the gloom.

At Kingston, landing place of King Charles II in 1650, I found a sleepy scattering of white and grey cottages around a silted river meandering through marshes. A high shingle bank made excellent coastal walking and gave views back over the plain and the purple Grampians. Seabirds floated in warm-air spirals and a tiny boat laced through the shallows by the stick-stiff reeds. Three swans galleoned in its wake and disappeared into tall marsh grass. I roamed further through this little land, cosy with cows by the seaside. Some of the towns, particularly Lossiemouth, have adopted a distinctly resort-like appearance. Others like Buckie and Burghead possess less-commercialised charms and peer contentedly over the Moray Firth.

Elgin and Forres on the hectic A96 are used to the constant flow of traffic and tourists, yet have managed to maintain much of their history and character. Elgin's massive thirteenth-century cathedral stands in ruined splendour at the edge of the town park next to the sixteenth-century 'Bishop's Palace' (actually the Precentor's mansion). A walking tour of Old Elgin centres on the marvellously Scottish main street (a stern, harmonic mixture of dourness and dignity dominated by the classical bulk of St Giles's parish church) and meanders down some of the granite side streets passing Thunderton House in Thunderton Place, once the most noble of Elgin's mansions, and the church of Greyfriars Monastery on Abbey Street with its medieval interior.

The high street of Forres is equally notable for its splendid clock tower and cross, the adjoining Falconer Museum, and its links with Shakespeare's *Macbeth*. Cawdor Castle is only a few miles to the west and it was just outside the town, on the 'blasted heath' of Hardmain Hill, that Macbeth and Banquo met the three Forres witches busy at their incantations. Witch-love permeates the region. I mentioned earlier the Witches' Stone outside Forres (near the ornately-carved Sueno's Stone) marking the spot where three witches were rolled to their deaths for conspiring to kill King Duffus. His castle, now a ruined pile, is a few miles east near Gordonstoun School, alma mater of Prince Philip and of Charles, Prince of Wales. At sleepy Burghead, every 11 January at 6 o'clock in the evening, a 'Clavie King' lights the tar-barrel on a shaft which is carried round the town in blazing fury to Dourie Hill and cascaded down the slope. The scorched pieces, known as 'witches', are carefully prized and said to protect their owners against all spells and evil influences.

Hidden-corner explorers will delight in the surprises of the adjoining countryside. Pluscarden Abbey, for example, nestles below a wooded range of hills in a quiet valley between Forres and Elgin. Although only a segment of the nave is still used as a church and monastery, it contains many noble architectural features of the thirteenth-century transitional style.

A few miles away off the A940 Forres–Grantown road is a secret valley road signed to 'Beachans' leading past abandoned homesteads and water-falls to Loch Dallas. Fishermen know the place well and a few of the other thirty or so lochans scattered in this quiet upland area, but most travellers hurry by on the main roads, oblivious to its charms.

Most memorable of these local surprises is the Findhorn Foundation just outside the once-important fishing port of Findhorn. Originally a secluded enclave of devotees living in old caravans at the edge of a military airfield, today this pioneering centre in group-living is known throughout the world for its durability (many communes tend to collapse after the initial period of euphoria) and its willingness to share concepts through a remarkable array of publications, seminars and guest programmes. Origins were humble in the extreme. In November 1962 Peter and Eileen Caddy along with Dorothy Maclean suddenly found themselves no longer in charge of the baronial Cluny Hill Hotel in Forres but out of work and living in a tiny buckled caravan on the Findhorn Bay dunes. Rejecting all fears of looming-doom they began a life of self-sufficiency, creating a garden in the sand, 'putting light into everything we did' and tapping the 'life-force' of the plants and

Part of the Findhorn Garden

vegetables they grew. To cynics all their talk of plant 'Devas' and 'nature spirits' seemed to reflect a divorce of minds from everyday reality, but they persevered, expanding the garden organically, praying to the plants and cajoling them into growth and abundant fruition. Tales of 40 lb cabbages created instant local folklore and attracted the curious. Gradually it became apparent that other individuals and groups throughout the world were discovering similar principles for tapping 'life forces' within plants and also within human beings, and a commune of like-minded individuals began to establish itself here. The publication of *The Findhorn Garden* focused attention on their activities and today, almost twenty years later, the Findhorn Foundation is an extensive spiritual community of 260 members working closely in cooperation with nature and with themselves.

I spent a day here. Outsiders are welcome and I was taken on the 'two o'clock tour' with six others to see the gardens, the spanking new University Hall, the printing shop, the caravan-homes, and the Sanctuary where community members gather to meditate together and plan activities. I intended to write extensively on what I'd seen, but changed my mind. Words are clumsy and capable of misinterpretation when used to describe spiritual ideas and ways of life. Suffice it to say I sensed the caring here, the love that members seemed to have towards one another and the overwhelming enthusiasm and determination in everything that was being done.

It was a perfect place to end the journey.

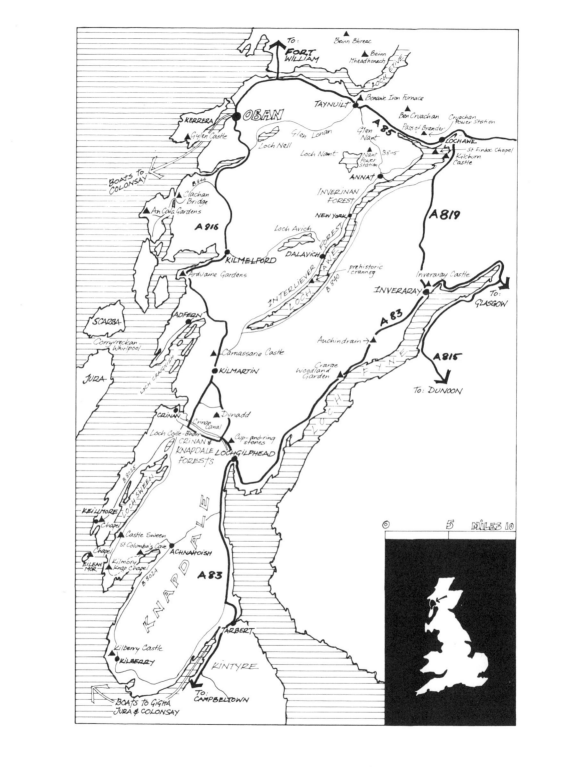

3. Loch Awe and Knapdale

'And all owing to a wee song.'

The small, wizened man mowing the grass at the Old Bonawe Iron Furnace left his machine and joined me on my rock. It was a cold seat but drier than the grass. I could see past the thick granite walls of the long-empty limestone and charcoal sheds out across the ferry point on Loch Etive to the elephant-hide slopes of Beinn Bhreac and Beinn Mheadhonach.

'Before that nobody much went down to Campbeltown. The herring boats had gone. They once had thirty-two whisky distilleries. There's only one left now, m'be two. Hotels were closing. But that Beatle chap changed all that. He and Tom Wilson. He was Pipe Major wi' the Campbeltown Piper Band and they got together and recorded that "Mull of Kintyre" song in a barn somewhere and next thing everybody's coming to take a look at the place. Can't blame 'em either. There's only one road but it's a fine drive.'

He was right. It is a pleasantly scenic journey with the ocean on one side and gentle hill scenery inland, ending with a rigorous scramble over the bleak Mull itself, on the edge of towering cliffs. But around Campbeltown the tourists were a little too numerous for my liking and I returned up the east coast of the peninsula in search of rather more secluded places in this corner of Argyll. Fortunately I found them in abundance.

The first was this odd iron foundry at Taynuilt looked after by my friendly informant with his lawn-mower. 'Sometimes I wonder why they put it here,' he told me as we strolled round the massive stone sheds built high above the loch. 'We had good charcoal, but fancy carrying iron ore all the way from Cumberland! Even today it would be a bit daft. In the 1750s I can't think it made much sense at all.'

The iron foundry was actually one of several projects in the region during that period reflecting a desire by landowners to industrialise the Oban coast and utilise the abundant cheap labour following the infamous 'clearances' of the late eighteenth century. Most failed, although Bonawe, built to last a thousand years, struggled on making cannonballs and pig iron moulds until 1873 when production could no longer compete with the industrial towns of England. 'By that time this was a sad place,' the ground-keeper said, looking over the ruins of the blast furnace. 'If you go back in the hills you'll see. People left by the hundred and the land just died.'

So I went into the hills around Lock Awe (at $25\frac{1}{2}$ miles the longest loch in Scotland) and discovered the silent valleys and the abandoned homesteads – and the kind of peace people seek in remote Grecian islands. True, the roads

Kilchurn Castle and Loch Awe

are narrow, mere paved strips for the convenience of the few residents, hidden away behind rocky bulges in the marshy moorland. I followed one through desolate Glen Lonan past lochans and scattered highland cattle whose shaggy coats and immense horns reflected the ancient wilderness of the hills. They stood motionless, as old as time, watching the antics of occasional intruders from dark eyes hidden under thick manes. Cattle, curlews and golden eagles are the true inhabitants of these remote regions. I travelled for ten miles and met no one on this lonely road (which is perhaps just as well as there were no passing places and the edges tended to be marshy). The demure Loch Nell provided solace at the end of the drive.

A second, more dramatic road, this time with occasional passing places, took me south from Taynuilt to the quiet shores of Loch Awe near Annat. The lake was calm and dappled with soft grey ripples. To the north, below the immense bulk of Ben Cruachan (3,689 ft) and the Cruachan power station, is the Pass of Brander where the MacDougalls were routed by Robert the Bruce in 1308.

Glen Nant is altogether a more gentle valley. I passed the entrance to the Nant power station and peered down on the narrow loch, serpenting between forest-cloaked hills under silky clouds. Remnants of castles reflect its role as a natural barrier protecting the Campbells of Inverary from their enemies. The most notable is Kilchurn at the northern end of the loch, built in 1440 by Sir Colin Campbell of Glenorchy and occupied by his descendants until 1740. On a nearby island and accessible by boat from Lock Awe village is the tiny thirteenth-century chapel dedicated to St Findoc with ornate carved slabs in the burial ground.

But the real pleasures here are the walking trails through Inverliever Forest along the whole of the loch's western shore from Annat to Ford. The information centre at Dalavich village (those prefabricated timber 'villages' so loved by the Forestry Commission always appear as uncomfortably alien in the natural landscape as their hard-edged forests) has trail guides, although these are often unnecessary as the routes are well marked. One walk ends up in New York, of all places, actually a tiny hamlet with a lakeside pier. A second climbs high above the loch and looks down on a prehistoric crannog, an artificial island in the lake built to support a communal dwelling safe from predators and marauding tribes. A third provides an eagle's view of the loch from a rocky eyrie above the Inverinan, and a fourth leads over the tops through pine forests to tiny Loch Avich, secluded in a high valley and surrounded by sheep-cropped shores. This round trip trail is five miles and I cheated, driving my camper on the narrow road from the turn-off near Dalavich to Kilmelford. Again I met little traffic and enjoyed one of the finest scenic drives in this secluded countryside south of Oban. The peaks of Ben Cruachan and the southern Grampians peered over the lower rocky hills and two sparrowhawks spiralled slowly, waiting for lunch.

My lunch was equally effortless. I merely walked into the cosy pub at Kilmartin, ordered a sandwich and found myself in the middle of an impromptu ceilidh. Two Americans guitar-strumming their way around the world had been joined by some of the locals, a barman with a remarkable tenor, and a young girl with all the blushing highland sweetness of a Stevenson heroine. And off we all went chorusing through a score of folk ballads from Mull to Maine while the peat fire blazed and beery froth rolled down pint glasses. Outside mists were creeping in from the Sound of Jura and the sun shone through a silvery haze. Inside we caroused on until the landlord reluctantly pulled the bell chain at closing time. The two guitarists sang a last chorus of the 'Skye Boat Song' and we all tumbled out together into a sparkling afternoon.

The village was quiet and I wandered across to the church on the opposite side of the road. Inside I discovered restored fragments of sixteenth-century crosses with distinctly twelfth-century-style carvings of Christ crucified and Christ in majesty. Outside, a group of ornate gravestones resplendent with armed knights and heraldic shields lay together overlooking the slow slope to the shores of Loch Craignish. Watery sunshine flickered on the waves.

These hills were once part of the sixth-century kingdom of Dalriada founded by Scots when they journeyed here from Ireland, a mere twenty miles away. Ancient remains are abundant – the largest area of cup-and-ring marked stones in Britain (up a track to Achnabreck Farm north of Lochgilphead), burial cairns, a glebe cairn at Kilmartin itself in the field below the church, a stone circle and large standing stones – all provide an appropriately mystical setting for the great fort of Dunadd, seat of the first Scottish kings. The flat-topped hill rises abruptly from the marshy flats of Moine Mhor. The climb is steep, leading to the imprint of a human foot said to be that of King Fergus, and a bowl cut in the bed rock. Close by is a graceful line-carving of a wild boar, possibly marking the place of royal investiture and the nucleus from which the great Celtic kingdom of Scotland emerged. The spot is not well-signed and most of the boat-lovers frollicking around the locks of the nearby Crinan canal seem unaware of the importance of this little highland corner. Many also miss the quiet walks in the Crinan and Knapdale forests to the south of the busy harbour. Once again trail books are available and well-signed paths pass alongside inland lochs, the seventeenth-century clapper bridge at Achnamara, an ancient graveyard at Achadh NaCille marked by fragments of carved stone, and the Iron Age fort of Druim an Duin.

My favourite walk begins at the Loch Coille-Bharr information centre and meanders around oak and birch shrouded shores, past woodlands carpeted with blaeberries. Their succulence attracts roe deer, along with badgers, foxes and occasional wildcats, the prime inhabitants of Knapdale. The ruined corn mill of Coille-Bharr was once an important centre for tiny settlements scattered over the peninsula and stands in trees on the edge of the loch. Nearby are grassy foundations of the deserted Kilmory Oib hamlet and an ancient holy well marked by a carved stone. Economic decline began here as early as 1739 when a new settlement was established for Knapdale residents at Cape Fair, North Carolina. Ever-stricter clearances culminated in the terrible potato famines of the 1840s and the total abandonment of the area was complete by the end of the century. Mounds of stones mark the remnants of old walls and the surrounding forest waits to move in.

Compared with the Mull of Kintyre and the Dunoon peninsula, Knapdale is a reclusive area of sandy coves, ancient castles and tiny chapels. Keillmore was once a shipping point for Jura cattle brought over on wherries, wide-beamed boats lined with heather from which the unfortunate creatures were thrown to swim to the jetties. Close by is a thirteenth-century chapel surrounded by excellent examples of medieval tombstones. The site is dedicated to St Abban mac ui Charmaig, a seventh-century Christian who founded a school here and a retreat on Eilean Mor, a craggy little islet out in the Sound of Jura. Boats can occasionally be taken from Castle Sween or Crinan to the sanctuary cave and a medieval chapel, once an ale-house visited by John Paul Jones on a raiding cruise during the American War of Independence. It's a lonely spot with views of Islay and the Paps of Jura across often-snarling seas. Visible to the north are the outer currents of the Corryvreckan whirlpool, a notorious tidal race between the northern tip of Jura and tiny Scarba island. On still days the fury of these waters can be heard for ten miles and small craft venture there at their peril.

On the opposite side of Loch Sween are the remnants of twelfth-century Castle Sween, said to be the oldest stone fortress on the Scottish mainland and destroyed by Sir Alexander Macdonald in 1647. A few caravans occupy the adjoining land and the place has an eerie quality when fogs roll in from the sound and a thick white silence descends over the drooping conifers – hardly a place for the faint-hearted, especially if you end up by mistake, as I did, in the rock-shelter below the west walls among a collection of eerie prehistoric relics.

A couple of miles further south is the thirteenth-century Kilmory Knap chapel, similar in design to Keillmore and possessing its own collection of medieval gravestones. A third, very like the other two, stands by the secluded St Columba's Cave on a side road off the delightful Lochgilphead–Tarbert–Kilberry loop around the main Knapdale peninsula. (A road connection with Kilmory Knap was never made, but I gather the walk is rather bracing.) There are actually two caves here, the first with a rock-shelf altar, primitive font and scratchy crosses carved in the rock. The second, smaller, cave on the left is very plain with the merest outline of a cross on the rear wall. Further south the sign to Kilberry House Farm leads to a shelter containing medieval and earlier gravestones, most of which have been collected from bridges, stiles and abandoned cottages in the area. The adjoining castle, home of the Campbells of Kilberry for 500 years, is an odd mixture of seventeenth century and Victoriana and rarely open to the public.

But for all the chapels and castles in this corner of Argyll it's the silence one remembers most, sitting in rocky coves looking out over the Hebrides and the Sound of Jura, watching seabirds skim the surf, skipping flat stones over mirrored sea-lochs. And the food. At Adfern I found an inn serving the best seafood I'd tasted in the highlands, and I ate a Danish dinner at the hotel near Annat on Loch Awe.

I was also introduced to a few local delicacies by an old fisherman near Tarbert who regaled me with tales of teeming herring fleets that once filled the port, as he crashed pots and scraped frying pans on an ancient cast-iron stove. We happened to meet at the harbour and he invited me to look through his collection of old photographs of Tarbert back at his butt-n'-ben cottage. Somehow, as it always does in this kind of situation, afternoon turned quickly into evening and he insisted on 'makin' a wee bit of tea' as I sketched his frenzied activities. 'I like company,' he told me, waving his arms to indicate the plethora of cooking utensils scattered around the store and sink. 'Family comes every Sunday. My wife was the cook, she did it all. She died two and a bit years ago. I learned her recipes and the family come just like they used to. She made me promise that.' Steam billowed round his wrinkled bald head, and pans sizzled. 'It's nae but a warm-up from yesterday,' he said modestly as we settled down to a tea of 'Cullen Skink' (a fish chowder of cod, onions, milk and diced potatoes), a chicken stew which he

Fisherman at Tarbert

called 'Stove Howtowdie', and an enormous dish of 'Rumble-de-thumps', a kind of bubble-and-squeak mixture of cabbage, potatoes, onions and butter. It was late before I left to a farewell of 'You're sure, now, you'll nae stay for supper?'.

A handful of travellers to coastal Argyll seek out even quieter places than Lock Awe and Knapdale, catching ferries to Gigha, the fertile 'Isle of God', from Tarbert or Tayinloan (on Kintyre) with its flourishing Achamore Gardens, or the more isolated Hebridean island of Colonsay reached by boat from Oban and Tarbert. This is still a 'real' island of farmers with an active social life (a dance at Kiloran village hall should be avoided by those with weak hearts), and a long history. St Columba is said to have paused here en route to Iona and banished all snakes. On the tiny island of Oransay, linked at low tide to Colonsay by a strand, are remnants of a sixth-century monastic settlement around a fourteenth-century priory. Velvet-smooth grass meadows cropped by Oransay's shaggy wild goats slope down from Ben Oransay to white-sand beaches deserted except for the occasional grey seal

41

Kiloran Bay · Colonsay

arriving for a change of scene from the offshore islet of Eilean-nan-Ron. Larks, ring plovers, fulmars, red-throated divers and gannets are among the 150 species of birds recorded regularly.

Colonsay House with its rhododendron gardens is a focal point for most visitors, while only the more adventurous enjoy Balnahard beach littered with cowrie shells, the prawn-filled pools on the strand, the sand-dunes and caves of Kiloran Bay, and free fishing on Loch Sgoltaire. It was here I tickled my first trout. I'd heard of it being done by hungry hikers and back-to-basics enthusiasts but never tried it until I found this lochside pool, surrounded by rocks and heather roots, below a small cascade. There were at least three fish, shadowy flickers in the shallows at the base of the splashing water. I lay down on the rocky edge and slowly immersed my arm until it lay on the pebbles and sand at the bottom. The fish were facing away from me as I moved my hand to a position immediately under the closest one. Still no reaction, so gradually I allowed my arm to rise, holding my hand in a shallow cup until it was directly below the trout's light coloured belly. Then ever so

gently I curled my upturned fingers along its silky underside stroking very softly. The fish ignored the whole procedure and its tail flicked rhythmically in the current. I continued stroking until my hand was actually enclosing its belly. Slowly I eased the fish upwards, its dorsal fin rippling like a sail, to an inch or so below the surface. One last stroke, a quick flick of the wrist, and the blue-brown creature curved gracefully out of the pool to land on the bank by my feet. I couldn't believe it – I'd caught a trout barehanded without a hook! I felt a sudden surge of backwoodsmanship – a feeling I remember as a boy after netting my first newt or climbing my first man-sized tree. The trout failed to share my euphoria and thrashed indignantly on the short grass. I'd been so engrossed in the process I never considered what to do with the fish if I caught it. I certainly had no appetite to eat it but was reluctant merely to throw it back. So I compromised and hastily photographed it before easing it into the loch where it flashed away in a streak of silver, doubtless issuing frantic warnings about this nut with the sexy fingers.

The boat to Colonsay from Oban passes alongside the island of Kerrera, which is linked to the mainland by a short ferry. This is rugged walking country. It took me most of a day to complete the six-mile trail from Horse Shoe Bay, where King Haakon of Norway assembled his fleet in 1263 for the battle of Largs, past the tall ruins of the MacDougalls' Gylen Castle, through a rocky interior long abandoned by crofters, and back to the tiny one-teacher school. I had the island to myself and dawdled away the afternoon, almost missing the last boat back across the channel at 6 p.m.

Better known than these few secluded places are the coastal gardens of Argyll basking in Gulf Stream mildness and resplendent with rhododendrons, azaleas, magnolias, tumbling waterfalls and rock gardens. An Cala, across the famous Clachan Bridge from Oban (a 1792 Telford creation 'spanning the Atlantic' between the mainland and Seil Island), is followed by Arduaine (north of the hilltop ruins of Carnassarie Castle), the Carradale House Gardens (on Kintyre), and my favourite, the unusual Crarae Woodland Garden on the western side of Loch Fyne.

Equal care has been lavished on the grounds and maintenance of nearby Inveraray Castle, home of the Dukes of Argyll (heads of the great Campbell family), though this 'major bastion of our heritage' is scarcely hidden-corner territory. Tourists pour through Inveraray's pristine streets and past the massive classical façade of its church, admiring this notable example of planned eighteenth-century townscape – easily the most attractive in the highlands. Even the tartan 'n' whisky 'n' haggis shops, a mobile fish and chip stall by the pier and the cacophony of foreign accents echoing from its white walls fail to diminish the dignity of the community and its neo-Gothic castle peering fairytale-like over the loch from sloping lawns.

One sombre note was struck, however, as I wandered through its great pale pink and blue rooms, festooned with plaster and painted garlands, thick with armour, sober with portraits. A few miles to the south, almost exactly half-way between Inverary and the Crarae Garden, are the primitive remnants of Auchindrain, a group-tenancy farm on Argyll land, in a bare valley set back from Loch Fyne. Here at the same time as the Duke of Argyll was lavishly decorating his new castle in the latter half of the eighteenth century, ten families, more than seventy people, scrabbled for a subsistence existence of oats, turnips and potatoes below the bare hillsides in conditions that had changed insignificantly for more than 300 years. While such contrasting scenes had been a feature of economic life throughout Britain and Europe for centuries, rarely have circumstances led to the preservation of this evidence so strikingly as at Auchindrain. Throughout my journeys in Scotland I'd seen scores of abandoned crofting communities, but here the deterioration

44

Auchindrain — Crofter's House

has been held in check to provide a clear picture of life in the eighteenth and nineteenth centuries.

A small museum gives a basic introduction to local farming techniques and instruments, and a path winds up from the rear door across the Infield to the seventeen barns, thick stone-walled cottages and sheds scattered over the slope. Cruck-framing was used in one of the cottages and cross-beams consisted of untrimmed tree trunks. Birch branches padded with moss provided the basic roof structure which was then topped with reed thatch held down by weighted stones. Barn and house were one, all rooms leading directly off a single passageway with a central parlour-cum-kitchen-cum-bedroom providing the focus for family activities. One of the rooms has been furnished with box beds, a spinning wheel, butter churn, peat-box, huge black kettles on a huge black cast-iron fireplace, and even a milldewed copy of the 1889 *Hazell's Annual.* There's evidence in another of the late eighteenth-century dwellings of an open fire placed centrally in an earth floor, with a ventilation hole in the roof – a feature common to Iron Age dwellings!

Life was hard, but photographs in the museum suggest that leisure was not altogether uncommon. Shinty played with hockey-like sticks was a popular pastime along with regular bouts of dram-drinking and the telling of rambling Gaelic tales by the peat fire in the parlour. But the faces tell other stories of endless winters, disastrous crops, short-lived children and tedious lives of no expectation. Nevertheless Queen Victoria was said to be 'quite impressed' by conditions here when she was given a conducted tour in 1875 by the Duke of Argyll, who drew her attention to the commune-like system of multiple tenancies introduced by his family.

There's something about the place that brings young enthusiasts; mostly volunteers, to work on difficult restorations here – some expected to take years. I talked to one of them, a student of Glasgow University, who came to the site most weekends. 'People get indignant, really mad sometimes, about the conditions they lived in here. Actually, for Scotland, they weren't bad. Single crofters in the islands had it much worse and most had given up by the late 1800s. This place still had six tenant families in 1930 making some kind of life here – they worked together, as a team, a kind of small commune. That's what makes this place so special. They didn't actually own the land but the rents weren't much and most of what they made was theirs. They were independent, they were self-sufficient and they got things done. There's a lot of people today wouldn't mind trying to live along those lines – if things continue the way they are, we may not have much choice!'

It's a thought, although I think I'd pick somewhere a little less bleak than Auchindrain.

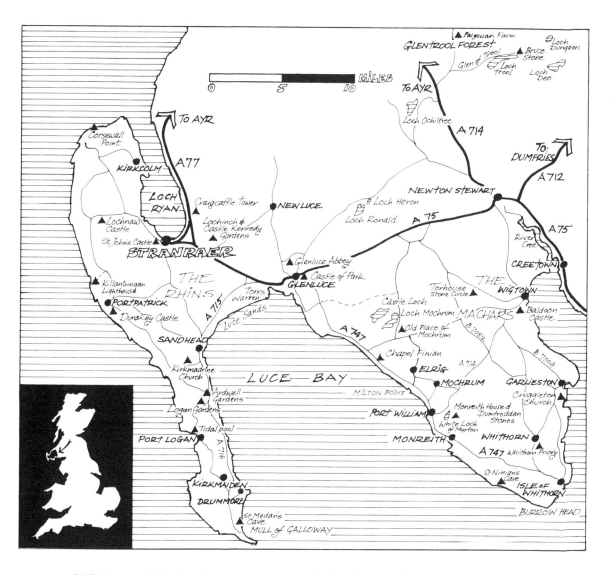

4. The Rhins and Machars

The two shepherds sipped champagne warily from thin-stemmed glasses. A bottle of Moët and Chandon lolled in a silver ice bucket on the beer-splattered pub table and the farmer sat next to them holding his glass confidently, taking gulps of the frothing wine between gales of laughter. Raunchy jokes chuckled out from a huddle of men at the bar in tweed jackets, deerstalker hats and long boots. The two shepherds were silent, seemingly

47

The Glentrool Wilderness

unamused by the tales. Their eyes peered down at the table, studying the beer spills. Their cheeks were brilliant red – they were blushing furiously. The farmer, oblivious to their discomfort, poured more champagne from the dripping bottle into their glasses which sent them both squirming deeper into their seats. He toasted them and they quietly toasted him back. It had been a good sale. Midday Thursday at the Newton Stewart sheep auction and they'd sold everything for one of the best prices of the morning. Next time they may not be so lucky but this was a special occasion and it was worth the celebration!

A babble of men and sheep enveloped the narrow streets around the market pens. Inside the high-roofed octagonal auction room it was boiler-hot. Farmers, shepherds, farmhands and plump girls were down to bare arms and open necks. Only the auctioneer maintained decorum by wearing jacket and tie as sweat streamed down his face and stained his collar. His sandpaper voice rasped out bidding prices at machine-gun pace, ending sales only seconds after the sheep had been driven into the central arena. They were Blackfaces, one of the finest Scottish breeds, from one of the finest breeding regions.

The Newton Stewart auctions are renowned throughout the sheep-

48

farming world. The bidders and observers, all clutching freshly printed sales catalogues still smelling of ink, pressed in closer. Every man connected with the business carried his own horn-handled crook or walking stick and bidding consisted of a complex series of stick-wiggling antics comprehensible only to the auctioneer. High above the hullabaloo the W&T Avery Shadowless Dial Scale peered over the crush of bodies as it had done for more than half a century. Pubs across the street welcomed the weary and were as crammed as the auction rooms. Luncheon menus featured fresh Cree salmon, the smallest and sweetest of Scottish salmon, and venison pie. Here they all stood – deerstalkers, tweeds, boots, brogues and crooks – pint-happy and salivating at the rich aromas curling through the pipe smoke.

By 4 p.m. it was all over. Purple-faced they rolled out on to the main street, blinking in the strong afternoon light. It had rained briefly and the road was a mire of mud and dung. Land Rovers, Range Rovers, Volvo estates and one horse and trap all rumbled out for the hills or the plains beyond the pristine town.

To the south are the Machars, the lowland flats along Wigtown Bay. To the north the vast loneliness of the Glentrool and Carrick moors, an unroaded region of hidden lochs and peaks topped by the bulk of Merrick (2,766 ft).

During the summer Glen Trool and Loch Trool become a focus for ramblers exploring the Galloway Forest Park. A working hill farm at Palgowan gives an insight into the shepherd's moorland life. Paths splay out into the wilderness from the end of Loch Trool near the famous Bruce Stone, a memorial to the Scottish king who initiated his campaign for independence with a victory here against the English in March 1307. Most visitors venture only a short distance on to the moors. Merrick is a popular day-long climb but much of the remainder – the Rhinns of Kells, Loch Dee, Loch Dungeon – is empty territory, the haunt of golden eagles and hidden-corner seekers.

From a heathery hill near Loch Dee I peered out over the Stranraer and Wigtown peninsulas, the Rhins and Machars, stretching into the grey blueness of the Solway Firth. The land looked old and worn. Above the flat fields of the Machars ran a rock and gorse spine sprinkled with lochans and peat bogs. Around the Mull of Galloway, high cliffs rose vertically from Luce Bay and the land writhed northwards, a narrow wrinkled finger. It's a region with a long history. Prehistoric circles and burial mounds are scattered over the landscape, some dating back more than 4,000 years. Ancient churches, a saint's cave, and the remnants of a fifth-century settlement reflect the emergence of Christianity in southern Scotland after the arrival of St Ninian at Whithorn in 397 AD. He built a tiny chapel here and later a small monastery, the Candida Casa (White House) and his popularity was such that he occasionally had to seek solitude in a slit of a cave by the ocean, three miles away (well worth the walk). He travelled widely throughout Scotland converting pagans and founding churches. Whithorn became the cultural and religious centre of the Celtic world, and, although somewhat overshadowed later by St Columba's colony of Iona, remained an important place of royal pilgrimage until such observance was made illegal by Parliament in 1581. It was once thought that ruins at the nearby Isle of Whithorn, a rambling village of warehouses, craft shops and colourful cottages round a rocky harbour, were St Ninian's original church and that the present twelfth-century chapel was built as a commemoration. However, recent discoveries at the ruins of the priory in Whithorn – foundations, rings, patens, chalices and croziers – tend to confirm this as the site. An archway off the colourful main street leads up The Pend to the priory and its museum containing inscribed stones and other important relics.

The region is rich with ecclesiastical remains. Nearby on the coast south of Garlieston is the compact twelfth-century Cruggleton Church, one of the few cohesive examples of Norman architecture in Galloway with a hefty round arch separating the nave from a small chancel cell. Fragments of a castle stand alone on nearby cliffs. This is the parish of Sorbie, noted for its

The Pend · Whithorn

unusually high rainfall and the uncanny ability of its residents to predict weather changes by the appearance of the 'weather gaw' a vertical shaft of light, rainbow-like in colour, often seen over the Kirkcudbrightshire hills.

On the opposite side of the peninsula, above Port William, are the foundations of the tenth-century Chapel Finian founded by the Irish saint, Findbarr, on a sandy rise above a coastline of shark-teeth rocks. A few miles further north, just outside Glenluce, are the far more substantial remains of twelfth-century Cistercian Glenluce Abbey set in cow-studded river meadows below woods. A museum provides details of its original size and architectural refinements, showing the emergence of the pointed style from the heavy Romanesque era. The delicately-vaulted chapter house, completely intact, is a masterpiece of fifteenth-century work with Decorated windows. I was told by the curator of the abbey's association with Michael Scott, a notorious borderland wizard whose antics were immortalised by his namesake, Sir Walter Scott, and who is said to have enticed the thirteenth-century Black Plague into the abbey vaults and sealed it there for ever. Of equal fame was

51

Alexander Peden, the seventeenth-century 'Covenanter's Prophet' who ministered at New Luce Church, a few miles up the road from the abbey, before his expulsion by the Episcopacy. Covenanters' graves mingle with prehistoric cairns and standing stones on the moors above the village.

The most revered relics of earliest Christianity are the three fifth-century inscribed stones displayed in the porch of Kirkmadrine Church. They bear the names of early Celtic bishops – Viventius, Mavorius and Florentius. The cross and loop symbol carved in the tall, undressed slabs is one of the earliest faith-signs of the Roman-Christians, and the site is a favourite haunt of archaeologists. Less known is the nearby boulder hidden in woods by the entrance gate to the Ardwell Estate, inscribed with the single word: MURDER. According to legend, it marks the place where one of the MacDoualls of Logan was killed by a gang of Gordon loyalists as he attempted to rescue a fair damsel kidnapped by Gordon of Clanyard. Supposedly it was a love-fight. Both men intended the girl as their bride although no record was made of her feelings in the matter. It was merely one more fracas in the endless feudings of Galloway families.

Whether prehistoric settlers on the two peninsulas ever involved themselves in such conflicts is not clear. But there is abundant evidence to suggest a distinct fear of invasion by sea. Cliffs and coves throughout the area are littered with remnants of ancient forts of earthworks. Particularly interesting is the Iron Age fort on the Isle of Whithorn promontory and the coast around Burrow Head (south of Whithorn – access by foot off a backroad) where motes and defence works abound to the trained eye. Further inland one discovers isolated cairns, burial chambers and, most notably, the great stones of Dumtroddan and the Torhouse Circle. The former consists of three standing stones a short walk from the north lodge gate of Monreith House and further rocks with cup-and-ring markings in an adjoining field. The Torhouse Circle is more impressive (and easier to find) – a distinct circle of nineteen boulders surrounding three larger stones, two at each end of a lower stone and all of uncertain significance.

I approached the site the long way from Chapel Finian, turning along a narrow backroad up on to the desolate moors of Loch Mochrum and I passed a sinister-looking castle – the Old Place of Mochrum – lurking behind trees on the edge of the wilderness. This is one of the most unusual structures in the region, consisting of two independent towers built fifteen feet apart in a large courtyard and with no apparent means of communication above ground level. Its isolation emphasises the utter bleakness of these uplands, and recent afforestation of the fringes does little to reduce the feeling. A damp haze hung above the island-littered lochs. I knew that only a few miles to the east were the fertile pastures of the Machars, sliding out into Wigtown Bay, but up here I saw only browning bracken, furious explosions of gorse bushes and dangerous stretches of black bogs. Nothing disturbed the stillness except the cry of a curlew. It was an ideal setting for some of the more heinous incidents in Sir Walter Scott's novels – a place loved by seekers of wild seclusion.

Gavin Maxwell, author of those famous otter-books, *Ring of Bright Water*, *The Otter's Tale* and *The Rocks Remain*, lived at nearby Elrig as a boy. He was born into a family of rank, related to the Duke of Northumberland and his grandfather was the famous archaeologist-politician, Sir Herbert Maxwell of Monreith. He seems to have been a shy boy given to solitary pursuits. As he grew up he undertook unusual adventures and projects, at one time purchasing the Isle of Soay, famous for its primitive sheep, and establishing a short-lived shark-fishing industry there. His book, *Harpoon at a Venture*, brought him some acclaim and he launched out as a professional portrait painter in 1949 before travelling among the marsh Arabs of southern Iraq gathering material for *A Reed Shaken by the Wind*. On his return he lived in a small cottage on the western highland coast observing the lives of otters which inspired his most popular series of books.

'Very quiet. Reclusive I suppose you'd say. A polite lad though.' I met an old woman living in one of Elrig's neat terrace-cottages. 'He couldn't have chosen a better place.' She pointed at the wind-blown trees fringing the loch and hiding Elrig House: 'Very lonely out there, specially in the long dark days.' Across the road a worn sign over the door of a house read, 'A. Kie Flynn. Licensed in Tobacco.' It seemed to be the closest thing to a shop in this bleak hamlet on the edge of the moors. 'I've never read his books, y'know. I know tha's bad but I cannae find them when the library comes once a week. Someone else always borrows them. And me living so close – and liking reading too!'

Other writers found the region conducive to literary endeavours. Sir Walter Scott loved its folklore and its lonely houses; Baldoon Castle, a mile south-west of Wigtown, was the setting for his novel, *The Bride of Lammermoor*. John Buchan used parts of the area in his *Thirty-Nine Steps* and the indefatigable Robbie Burns rambled and frolicked through the cliffs and glens to the north and east, 'exploring every den and dell where I could suppose my heroic countrymen to have sheltered'. For travellers who don't mind Tam O'Shantering with other tourists there's a Burns Heritage Trail linking some of the more important places around Ayr, Tarbolton and Mauchline, centred on the lavish Land o' Burns Centre at Alloway.

Myself I prefer the quietude of the Rhin cliffs and the loneliness of the

Lochnaw Castle

southern Galloway moors. And it was this same loneliness that long ago encouraged the construction of those high, thick-walled castles, slit-windowed and turreted – bastions against attack from the sea. A few, such as Dunskey Castle at Portpatrick, remain sturdy shells, tough as the cliffs on which they stand. Others, most notably the 1570 Craigcaffie Tower north east of Stranraer, the sixteenth-century St John's Castle in Stranraer itself, Glenluce's castellated Castle of Park, and the bold bulk of Lochnaw Castle, have been preserved more or less in their totality. The latter, hidden up a rough track on the edge of its own loch, is a particularly interesting diversion now used as a Commonweal Club hotel, craft centre and restaurant. It is an ideal place to pause, as I did, for tea and homemade scones by a cavernous stone fireplace in the old kitchen. On a small island in the loch are ruins of an eleventh-century fortress. Stone from there was used to construct the present fifteenth-century edifice, ancestral home of the Agnews, the ancient Sheriffs of Galloway. A branch of the Agnews resides in Australia and at the time of my visit the place echoed with down-under accents and lively *bonhomie.* The smell of baking bread filled the ancient dungeons, now used as the craft shop, and outside a herd of rare four-horned Jacob sheep ran free in the meadows, watched over by three very large, shaggy and bad-tempered goats.

Lochinch Castle, home of the Earls of Stair, is a very different kind of bastion, built more as an expression of power and affluence than for defensive purposes, and surrounded by the famous Castle Kennedy Gardens laid out in Versailles-inspired magnificence by the 2nd Earl. The 200-species pinetum, an avenue of monkey-puzzle trees, rare shrubs, azaleas and rhododendrons are the main attractions here for visitors en route to the Stranraer Irish ferries, or the increasingly popular Gatehouse of Fleet and Kirkcudbright coastline.

The moderating influence of the Gulf Stream drift offshore has created an ideal environment for such botanical extravaganzas, and while Castle Kennedy certainly is the most impressive in terms of scale, the smaller Logan Garden south of Stranraer contains a far more varied display of exotic flora and fauna. In the palm-shrouded walled garden one feels transported to some oasis from the *Arabian Nights.* Shafts of limpid sunlight filter through palm fronds like sand through a sieve on to mossy trunks and velvet lawns. Streams gurgle under cabbage palms, lily-topped pools reflect a tranquil stillness, and bird calls echo in purple clouds of *Hydrangea villosa* bushes. Outside the walls, footpaths meander off alongside Gunnera Bogs and up into tropical woodlands and fern gardens. The ruggedness of a rock gulley contrasts with the drooping lushness of a tree fern mound, and the martial dignity of a thick beech hedge. It was here I discovered the head gardener immersed in a complex pruning exercise. We chatted and he told me he'd been at Logan for more than twenty years. 'Ah, but I'm just one of scores of people who've worked here. The ones you should really talk about are the McDoualls, especially those sons of Mrs Agnes – they travelled all over the world collecting specimens for this place. They created it, really. Family'd been here since the eleven hundreds, right up till the end of World War II. It needed a bit of restoration then but one of the worst times was just recently, that winter of 1978–9. We lost more than 300 species, didn't stand a chance against that cold. It's looking better now but after those frosts, it was enough to make you weep. Luckily we'd plenty of stock at the Royal Botanic in Edinburgh so we soon got things going again. But I wouldn't want any more winters like that one, thank you. One a lifetime is quite enough – especially for a gardener.'

The 1978–9 winter was indeed a freak experience for residents of the Rhins and Machars. They are used to relatively mild weather all year round and considered the frosts and snows an infringement of their God-given rights. Not that the people are soft in these parts. On the contrary, their history shows them to be a hardy, determined lot. The area was a hotbed of covenanting in the seventeenth century when loyal presbyterians rejected all attempts by Charles II to reimpose 'wretched episcopacy' and worshipped at remote 'conventicles' rather than attend Church of Scotland services. Such gatherings were declared treasonable by Act of Parliament in 1670 and many tales are still proudly told of suffering and martyrdom under the repressive persecutions of the government. Most notable, almost of legendary status, was the plight of the Wigtown Martyrs commemorated by a great obelisk on the hill overlooking the town square and simple gravestones in the churchyard above the old cliffs. A well-worn path leads up past the ruins of a church dedicated to the sixth-century St Machitis and alongside the 1853 parish church to an iron railing enclosing three white-painted stones. One records the hanging of William Johnston, John Milroy and George Walker 'for their adherence to Scotland's Reformation Covenants' in 1685. The other two memorialise Margaret Wilson (aged 18) and Margaret Maclachlan who were tied to stakes on the beach below the town and drowned in 1685. Woodrow's *History of the Sufferings of the Church of Scotland* gives the gruesomely heroic details of their deaths.

> The old woman's stake was a good way in beyond the other, and she was first despatched, in order to terrify the other to a compliance with such oaths and conditions as they required. But in vain; for she adhered to her principles with an unshaken steadfastness . . . she sang the 25th Psalm from verse seven, downward a good way, and read the eighth chapter to the Romans with a great deal of cheerfulness. While at prayer, the water covered her – but before she was quite dead, they pulled her up, and held her out of the water until she was recovered and able to speak; and then by Major Windram's orders, she was asked if she would pray for the king. One deeply affected with the death of the other said, 'Dear Margaret, say God save the King, say God save the King. . . .' Most deliberately she refused, and said, 'I will not, I am one of Christ's children, let me go.' Upon which she was thrust down again into the water, where she finished her course with joy.

Generally, travellers in the Rhins and Machars choose solitude, quiet villages, and the surprises that always accompany hidden-corner exploration. It's not a place for rushing. One should wander at will on the narrow country lanes, pausing to stroll down paths to coves below precipitous cliffs, enjoying high teas and 'suppers' at harbourside hotels, listening to Gaelic folk songs on local radio stations, or wandering such wild dunes as the Torrs Warren beyond Sandhead at the northern end of Luce Sands. Few people explore the coastline at Corsewall Point north of Kirkcolm where Robert Louis Stevenson's father built the lighthouse. Those who do will be rewarded with immense vistas of the Kintyre, Arran and Cumbrae mountains, and a glimpse of the nearby Corsewall estate. Here was the home of Sir John Moore, whose woodlands were planted in the same formation as the British troops at the battle of Corunna.

Further to the south I followed signs along a cattle-grid track to the Killantringan lighthouse, open to the public 'at the discretion of the lighthousekeeper', and scrambled down cliff paths to a rocky cove, skimmed by gulls and surf-silent. Beyond Glenluce I followed backroads past Loch Ronald and Loch Heron into the wild open country of Loch Ochiltree where sheep-shaven turf forms a cushiony resting place for afternoon reveries and long gazings at the Glentrool hills.

Most delightful are the old coastal ports slumbering by silted harbours. Port Logan is simply a line of white fishing cottages and a pub peering over the raised road around Portnessock Bay. On the opposite side is a most unusual tidal pool, built in the 1790s, where visitors can watch the twice-daily feeding by hand of pollack and cod which arrive, tame as puppies, whenever the bell is rung. Portpatrick is an altogether larger place with its golden hotel peering down on a compact harbour from cliff-tops. Narrow streets edged by colourful terraces meander up the hill beyond an ancient ruined church with a round tower. Before the dominance of Stranraer this was the main port for Ireland on the Scottish coast and little seems to have changed since those days. The creaking general store still contains its racks of biscuit tins. Coffee is freshly roasted and ground here and delicious aromas roll down the street to the clustered fishing boats.

On the rock-fringed west coast of the Wigtown peninsula sits demure Port William, a creation of Sir William Maxwell of Monreith in 1770. His adjoining estate contains the White Loch of Myrton, now an important nature reserve with an ancient Celtic cross on its shores. The tight-walled harbour was once the scene of many smuggling incidents, and regulars at the Monreith Arms across the road pride themselves on their knowledge of local escapades. 'The canniest,' began one old man who claimed to be a disowned member of the Maxwell family (an amused shaking of heads by his cronies), 'the cheekiest was in 1852 when a couple of luggers arrived off the port crammed with men, tobacco, and spirits and were just about to row it in on the longboats when a damned excise man rolls up with thirty or so soldiers and tells them they're all goin' to be arrested. The Captain, I forget the name – Robertson was it, maybe Macleod – I don't rightly remember – anyway he was a gre't big jock of a man, came sailing over in his boat and bold as a harpie told the excise man

Port Logan

and his soldiers that if they didn't move out very hastily they'd get a broadside from his guns. Aye, but he was a canny man too, y'know. He said that if they moved off quickly as made sense he'd maybe leave a few gallons of spirit for them by the quay and they'd all part friends. And they did. He went back and carried on unloading. The excise man and his troops vanished and came back a few hours later to pick up their reward just like the captain'd said. Now tha's a cheeky man for you!'

I've left my favourite haunt until last. I drove south from Drummore, past the big white farms, out towards the Mull of Galloway and the promontory at the tip of the peninsula. It's wild here and sturdy shoes are often needed for the clifftop walk to the lighthouse perched 250 ft above an always-snarling sea. Views on a clear day are superb across the ranges of Galloway and Dumfries to the hills as far away as the Lake District, the Antrim coast of Ireland, the Isle of Man and, 100 miles to the north, the great Paps of Jura in the Inner Hebrides. Closer are the rocky islets of the Scares in the middle of Luce Bay, home of thousands of guillemots, kittiwakes, razorbills, shags, fulmars, and seals. North of the narrow peninsula neck is St Medan's Cave hidden in the cliff where excavations in 1872 revealed an ancient statue of the Virgin and pilgrim-badges. Medan is thought to have been a ninth-century

Irish princess after whom Kirkmaiden parish is named.

On the crest of the peninsula just south of the neck are hollows of ancient dykes. They are the work of Picts driven south by the marauding Scots, and legend tells of two survivors, father and son, who made a last stand here against the enemy. Robert Louis Stevenson's poem 'Heather Ale' describes how, after being captured, they refused to share the secret of that wonderful Pictish concoction made from heather and honey and were hurled to their deaths over the cliffs. Yet one more example, it would seem, of the stubbornness and independence of the populace.

Which reminds me of one final incident. You remember those two embarrassed shepherds in Newton Stewart trying to sip their champagne and not enjoying it one bit. Well, I didn't finish the story. After making valiant efforts one of them turned to their boss, the farmer, and quietly but firmly told him they didn't think too much of the fizzy stuff and if he wouldn't mind they'd rather celebrate their successful sale with a dram of the usual. The farmer looked hurt but the shepherds were resolute and pushed their glasses away. A moment's silence was followed by a bellow of laughter as the farmer ordered fresh glasses and a bottle of whisky for the two of them. Honour was satisfied and once again the independent Galloway spirit had triumphed!

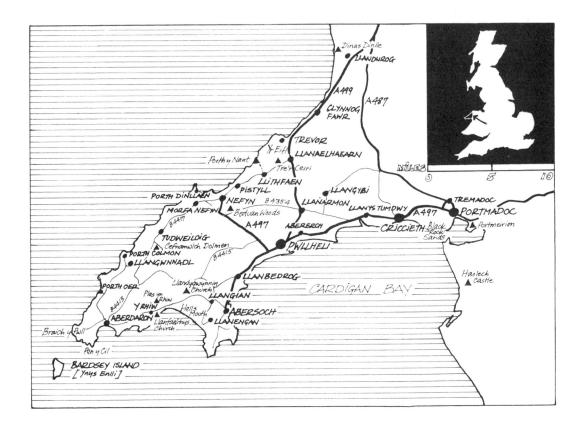

5. The Lleyn Peninsula

Dark dawn clouds cracked open over Cader Idris and the sun yolked out spraying the mists with fresh yellows. Even cows noticed and peered across meadows bleary-eyed. The stillness was buffeted by breezes from the ocean, tumbling over the gorse and up the flanks of Lleyn's mountain guardians, Yr Eifl (the Three Rivals). Colour rolled out across the valleys like an opening carpet.

I am normally unaware of dawns, preferring the cocoon of my bed until the sun warms things up, but this particular morning something stirred me around 5 a.m. An hour later I found myself, still yawning, high on the eastern peak of the Rivals above the village of Llanaelhaearn in an erratically-shaped enclosure 1,000 ft long surrounded by turf and stone walls. I shared the solitude with a handful of sheep huddled in a corner at the far end of the sloping site. All around were the stumpy foundations of circular huts, more

60

Yr Eifl

than 150 of them, remnants of the Iron Age 'Town of Giants', Tre'r Ceiri – the Knosses of Wales. I'd been told at Llandwrog's Harp Inn (the only pub I saw in Britain with a plaque outside the door advocating temperance!) that views from these heights were spectacular in the early morning. I'd noted the comment half-heartedly and gone on listening to tales of the slate mines and saints that seemed to be the prime constituents of local folklore. But the idea of an early rise had planted itself somewhere between conscious and sub-conscious and here I was, shivering slightly, watching the world fill with majestic forms – layer upon layer of purpled ranges stretching across Lleyn, up from the jumbled dune coast of Harlech, up past the lower peaks of Rhinog Fawr, Y Llethr and Diffwys, into the high bastions of Snowdonia and Cader Idris. To the north across Caernarfon Bay lay the gentle ripplings of Anglesey. A little closer I could see the Dinas Dinlle, a prominent 100 BC hill-fort on the coast near Llandwrog. To the south-west stretched the whole length of Lleyn, a solitary arm jutting out into the Irish Sea from the muscular mainland shoulder. At the far end, peeping through sea mists, was the hump of Bardsey Island 'like a basking whale', once an important outpost of Christianity and reputed burial-place of 20,000 saints.

The northern shores of the peninsula are fringed with steep cliffs. In places whole mountains tumble directly into the surf. Ahead the land eased itself out, meeting the sea in the long sandy strands and dunes of the south coast. The interior was dotted with farms in a green quilt of meticulously walled meadows, and lanes arched by high hedgerows wriggled aimlessly, reluctant to reach anywhere. A bracken and gorse hill rose abruptly as a reminder of Lleyn's ancient wilderness. Wind-shaped copses, smooth as snail shells, clustered along the cliff tops.

A Welsh poet described Lleyn as 'a Land apart – a place where the spirit finds peace'. Obviously he was not referring to the more popular resorts of the south coast – Pwllheli, Criccieth and Portmadoc – but to the quiet interior of the peninsula, the little-known coves and cwms of the north coast, and the towering headland cliffs of Braich y Pwll. These were the places I had come to explore. 'Lleyn is more Welsh than Wales,' I'd been told by an enthusiast in Chester. 'They're very keen on keeping the language and suchlike. Anything in English tends to get painted out, so best learn a few words quick. Very important. If you need a public convenience look for a "Cyfleusterau Cyhoeddus". It's a mouthful, but you best get used to it.'

What struck me first as I rambled along empty lanes was the profusion and richness of Lleyn's churches. I'd expected grey chapels, dour bastions of Nonconformism, scowling over valleys. Instead I found examples of ecclesiastical architecture from earliest Norman to the most refined Perpendicular

St. Beuno's Chest

along the north coast and around Abersoch. Equally varied were their dedications to such Welsh saints as Engan, Pedrug, Aelhaiarn, Denio, Cian and Gwynin. Bardsey Island was once an important centre of pilgrimage (two trips to Bardsey were of equivalent spiritual value to a Rome pilgrimage) and the main routes across the peninsula to the embarkation point at Aberdaron are dotted with holy wells and adorned with way-churches. St Beuno's at Clynnog Fawr is one of the finest, a large airy structure, predominantly late sixteenth-century Perpendicular, with a huge east window facing the road. This is the reputed burial-place of St Beuno, one of Lleyn's most notable saints whose principal miracle-working skills seem to have consisted of reassembling decapitated and dismembered bodies and blessing birds, in particular a curlew who found his book of sermons inadvertently dropped in the mud while crossing the Menai Strait to preach in Anglesey. God apparently got the saint's message and subsequently safeguarded all curlews' nests by making them virtually impossible to find.

Beuno is thought to have arrived in Clynnog around 635 AD and his original cell (at one time used as the local lock-up) is preserved as a chapel next to the church and linked by a dark cloister roofed in massive stone slabs. In the nave stands his impregnable oak chest hollowed from a tree trunk and bound in iron (hence the phrase 'as impossible as breaking St Beuno's chest') into which the early equivalent of tithes were paid by any local farmers whose calves or lambs possessed slit ears at birth, the mark or 'Nod Beuno' of saintly property. This custom continued on into the eighteenth century, as

63

did the healing ceremonies associated with his burial-place. These required paralytics and others first to wash in his nearby well (not far from the 'dolmen' relics of an ancient burial mound visible from the main road) and then to spend the night sleeping on top of the altar-shaped tomb. Obviously the number of miraculous cures was sufficient to maintain the legend and the church, which was subsequently expanded and enriched by the Tudors. Even Lord Newborough's excavations in 1793 which found neither coffin nor bones under the tomb in no way diminished its attraction as a healing source although it did revive ancient disputes as to the exact location of the saint's remains. The parishioners of the nearby twelfth-century Pistyll church, a secluded single-cell structure on the edge of a deep cleft to the ocean, claim that the bones of an unusually tall man beneath the altar are the true relics of St Beuno and that the two other St Beuno churches on Lleyn were supplied with empty coffins when the complex burial proceedings took place. Apparently there was so much anguish raised by the question of his burial-place that his disciples dispatched three identical coffins and corteges to three different churches to hide the identity of the actual place of internment. Many believe Pistyll is the place, although it's hard to imagine a more modest haven compared to the elegant traceried edifice at Clynnog Fawr.

I visited the tiny church one evening at dusk and sensed a distinct pagan atmosphere in the remnants of an ancient ash grove, the lepers' window, and the strange fragments of a mural on the north interior wall opposite a Celtic font. The font was decorated with chain-patterns and symbolic writing thought to depict life without beginning or end. What made the tiny place even more peculiar, and somewhat eerie in the half-light, was the profusion of dead and dying flowers, rushes, and leafed branches strewn throughout the nave and across the altar. An ancient piano was shrouded in fronds, others dangled from the thick rafters which were marked by rope holes used when the roof was thatched. Coating every surface was a thin film of dust. To complete the scene, a circle of candles in tiny silvered trays stood round the lip of the stone font as if in preparation for some mysterious rite. I learned later that the church is lavishly decorated in this manner three times a year at Christmas, Easter and Harvest and that, as far as my informant knew, all ceremonies here were perfectly Christian in nature!

The tower-less three-aisle church of Llangwnnadl is unimpressive externally but possesses a spacious interior sensitively restored in 1850 by Henry Kennedy. The octagonal font bears some odd carvings, one resembling a king's head, the other a coolie with a straw hat (actually a representation of Bishop Skeffington of Bangor). On the wall by the door hung the ancient doorkey 'used at weddings when no ring was available' and nearby was a pile of bilingual books labelled 'Butlin's Holiday Camps – An Order of Divine Service'. On the other side of the peninsula, housed behind barbed wire in an old admiralty training camp near Pwllheli, is one of those remarkable establishments attracting holiday-makers by the thousands every week of the summer. I never found out what their books were doing at Llangwnnadl.

Other churches worth visiting in this secluded part of Lleyn include St Engan's at Llanengan where the sound of the surf at Hell's Mouth Bay rumbles like a goods train in this refined sixteenth-century structure complete with misericords and Tudor screens. Nearby is St Maelryhys medieval church at Llanfaelrhys close to the ocean with box pews and ancient font, and the miniature Llandygwynnin church on the winding lane to Botwnnog possessing an unusual 'pepper pot' tower, box pews, a two-level pulpit and an all-white interior (including the floor).

But the ecclesiastical climax is St Hywyn's of Aberdaron, the 'cathedral of Lleyn', set tight in a hillside cemetery above the broad sweep of a bay. Ever since the sixth century, Bardsey-bound pilgrims have assembled here to await embarkation to the island. Rarely, though, have I seen a less cathedral-like building. The windowless walls suggest a barn of some kind and only the pure Norman doorway hints at its real function. The interior, illuminated by large sea-facing windows along the south wall and supported by thick round pillars and a hammer-beam roof, emphasises the power and significance of this most important of Welsh churches – once a place of sanctuary for Gryffydd ap Rhys, King of Deheubarch, during his escape from Henry I in 1115.

'We still get a few real pilgrims during the summer, but most just go out there for the ride.' I was talking to a young man who had strolled across Aberdaron's sturdy single-arch bridge and was standing patiently on the sea wall waiting for the Ship Inn to open. 'There's not much to see, really. I helped with the boats once. It's about five miles out there. Best part is when you get in those currents, sweep you all over the place, they do, if you're not careful.'

An old Hovis Bread sign hung lopsided on the wall of a slate cottage and three brown ducks waddled nonchalantly in a line across the road to the stream. The seaward-facing doors of the inn were buttressed by dozens of tiny sandbags, actually hessian moneybags, all stamped 'Property of Barclay's Bank'. Behind us the broad bench arced out to distant cliffs. 'It's quiet enough tonight,' remarked the young man as we stared out over a pink-flecked sky and maroon ocean. 'Some days we get the big tides and there's water everywhere, running up the streets and all over. It's a hell of a mess. Enough to make you move out.' There was a click behind us and the pub

Aberdaron

door opened. We continued our chat over a pint of beer and I asked about other places worth seeing in the vicinity. 'Try the Keating place,' he told me. 'Lovely ladies they were. Made this garden all by themselves they did.'

The story of the Misses Keating is rapidly becoming a piece of contemporary Welsh folklore. I drove up the long slope from Aberdaron to the rocky tiara of Y Rhiw and then began the descent to the Keating house, Plas-yn-Rhiw, hidden in a jungle-like wood above the great sweep of Hell's Mouth Bay. It was a perfect summer evening, wine-clear and sparkling. The whole of Lleyn stretched out before me, framed by distant ranges across Cardigan Bay. I almost missed the entrance and braked suddenly on the steep hill, turning into a leafy avenue beside sloping meadows. A small dedication plaque by a gate signified my arrival at the estate. The house was completely shrouded in lush vegetation, in stark contrast to the windtorn moors only a few hundred feet up the hill. Unfortunately, Honora Keating, the last remaining of the three sisters, was not at home. A Welsh-speaking gardener seemed the only occupant. My hope had been to meet one of the minds behind this exotic creation, the slow rebirth over fifteen hard-working years of an abandoned Regency mansion set in tiny sloping terraces, brimming with rhododendrons, fuchsia, rosebushes and rampant scatterings of bright flowers. What makes the place so memorable is the tenuous balance between the surging wilderness of the surrounding woods and the delicately controlled environments of tiny lawns, walks, caverns, grottoes and secret arbours filled with birdsong and the chucklings of hidden streams. The family, originally consisting of an ailing mother and her three daughters (the architect-father died at the age of thirty-nine), purchased the property in 1939 with 'brambles in the bedroom and a stream running through the hall'. After all their efforts of restoration they donated the property to the National Trust and opened the grounds to visitors by appointment during the summer.

Some of Lleyn's villages are less than memorable places – sprinklings of plain slate and granite cottages reflecting the hardy life of the residents and characterised by 'names longer than their main streets'. Others, however, possess distinct charm and are well worth seeking out. Abererch, Llanarmon and the quiet waters of Llanbedrog, for example, are all within easy reach of Pwllheli. Even Abersoch, with its creeks and sand-dunes filled with avid yachtsmen and sun seekers during the frantic weeks of midsummer, is for most of the year a delightfully uncommercialised place and an excellent centre for exploring the southern peninsula. Llangybi, on the other hand, is always quiet and few people know about the remnants of St Cybi's well hidden in the tiny valley behind the church. At one period during the

Porth Dinllaen

eighteenth century it was developed as a healing spa, but all that remains today below the beech woods is a ruined cottage-size building with walls four feet thick. Summer nestles here among the quiet lumpy bundles of sheep. Porth y Nant, reached from Llithfaen, is a ruin on a far grander scale – an abandoned quarry village of terraced houses, quarry-manager's house, school, chapel and lone letter-box. The place exudes a sense of splendid desolation, a dead community full of its ghosts. The windowless buildings are still largely intact and in the past have attracted such itinerant residents as communes of flower-power people and cliques of leather-and-chain Hell's Angels (fortunately at different times). A far earlier resident in the same cwm was said to be Vortigern, the high-king of Britain, accused of treachery and sent here to die by his successor Dinas Emrys.

Old quarries are a familiar sight around this part of the coast, along with tiny hard-scrabble farms where families pick and prod a living from rocks and a weary earth. The high-quality granite mined at Trefor is used in the manufacture of curling stones and the building of calvinistic chapels whose stern façades are an integral element of almost every community in this early nonconformist region.

Porth Dinllaen is another village constrained by changed fortunes. It sits beneath the cliffs at the end of a track across the Nefyn golf course, a line of white cottages and a pub dozing peacefully with all its great dreams gone. According to the MP William Madocks, promoter of the gigantic land-drainage and seawall schemes at Portmadoc, Porth Dinllaen was the ideal site for a major Welsh port and harbour for the London–Dublin boats. Never one to waste time when motivated, Madocks set up the Port Dinllaen Turnpike Trust and built a plumb-line-straight road across the peninsula linking this sheltered bay with Pwllheli, Criccieth, Portmadoc and the main London road. His model village of Tremadoc was laid out as a miniature masterpiece of nineteenth-century town planning complete with theatre, town hall and spacious market square. Madocks's villa, Tan-yr-allt, was situated on the outskirts and provided a temporary home for Shelley and his wife Harriet, before an unfortunate shooting incident sent the poet scampering off to Venice. Lawrence of Arabia was born at nearby Woodlands in 1888.

The range of projects constantly increased – the building of the Portmadoc harbour for exporting slate, the construction of the Ffestiniog railway (now a popular tourist attraction) to speed the transport of slate from the mountain quarries, and plans for the new town of Porth Dinllaen on the cliff tops possessing all the flair of a Wren-inspired scheme. Then, just when it seemed he had successfully lobbied complete support for his ideas including a £600 investment by the Royal Family, the crucial vote was taken on the

London–Dublin route and Holyhead was chosen instead by a majority of one vote.

David Lloyd George admired Madocks and his boundless ambitions, although his power came a generation too late to influence the outcome of such schemes and prevent the entrepreneur's continual flirtation with bankruptcy. The fiery Welsh prime minister was born in Manchester in 1863, 'a sturdy, healthy, little fellow with fine curly hair,' wrote his father, who died when David was two. Richard Lloyd, a shoemaker uncle living in Llanystumdwy, undertook the responsibility of bringing up the child at his modest terraced house on the edge of this charming Welsh village. After a lifetime of political and social prominence, Lloyd George returned here to be buried round the corner in a tiny cwm.

'He knew everything he wanted. "Nothing fancy," he said, "None of those trumpets and angels. Just a circle and a stone".' The plump middle-aged lady in a large purple apron paused from washing the steps to her terraced cottage, a few yards down the road from the memorial, and we chatted about the famous man. 'He'd come down from the big house.' She pointed up the steep hill, the back road to Criccieth. 'You'd hear him coming with his stick talking to everyone and laughing, he had a lovely laugh. He'd go as far as the bridge, maybe walk to the cottage, you know, depending how he felt, and then go back up again. Later on when he wasn't too good they'd send a car down, but I don't think he liked that much. He loved the Pennant Valley and his bit of wood!' She nodded at the shady copse above the stream. 'There was a favourite piece of poetry by Eifion Wyn, about Cwm Pennant. He had a marvellous memory for an old man, lovely voice for singing, too. I don't remember it exact but it was something like "Lord why did thou make Cwn Pennant so beautiful and the life of an old shepherd so short?" He really loved his Lleyn you know.'

Lloyd George alternated between his moorland home near Churt in Surrey and the house on the hill above Criccieth, occasionally strolling the town's manicured lawns overlooking the ocean, beneath the ruined bulk of an ancient castle. The crisp white hotels and neat gabled terraces still possess a totally Victorian charm, a sedate seaside resort unimpressed by contemporary fashions, confident in its composure.

But whereas Criccieth and the string of resorts along the south coast suffer from summer throngs, Lleyn contains more secret places such as Lloyd George's Pennant Valley cradled in mountains with narrow sheep-tracks leading to the summit of Meol Mebog, 'the hill of the Hawk'. Further to the west in quiet fields near Tudweiloig is the massive Cefnamwlch dolmen, remnant of a Bronze Age burial-place. Best of all, though, are the tiny coves

71

Cefnamwlch Dolmen

and cwms of the north coast – Porth Colmon with its hamlet of white-washed cottages, Porth Oer of the 'whistling sands' (the piercing shrill of quartz granules rubbing together in dry sand), the long clifftop walks at Morfa Nefyn near Porth Dinllaen, the Cornish-flavoured beach cottages at Nefyn, and a dozen other nameless places approached by cliff paths and bumpy tracks. The beautiful Boduan Woods on the Pwllheli road out of Nefyn are normally a quiet sanctuary, as are the towering wind-lashed cliffs and moors of Braich y Pwll and Pen y Cil, the Land's End of Lleyn, towering over Bardsey Island Sound. This is real walking country, a place to lose yourself for hours among the heathered slopes high above the furious surf and a perfect place to end this exploration.

Only I didn't. Instead I almost 'ended' in the middle of dinner in my camper parked out on the hard flat sands of Black Rock, near Portmadoc. On hot summer days this lovely place is uncomfortably crowded, but after 7 p.m. on the evening I visited, the tourists had returned inland to hotel dinners and pubs, leaving the vast strand and the sunset to me. I toasted my good fortune with an extra glass of wine and a cigar. Fred joined in the celebration, demanding a second bowl of catfood. I was contemplating whether to spend the night here when splish-splashy sounds trickled

through the window disturbing my mellow mood. I peered out and to my consternation found the camper surrounded by water, half way up the wheels. The tide was coming in and coming in fast. I leapt out, drenching myself in the rippled waves, and felt my feet sink in the no-longer firm sand. All the advice of steel-nerved world-explorers stuck in jungle swamps and sandy wastes came rushing back – don't panic, move the vehicle slowly, no jerking, try reverse first, keep a straight line, maintain even revs. I did everything wrong. It was almost dark and the creature wouldn't budge. I could hear the tyres squelching deeper into the mud. To hell with it! I did what came most naturally, put her into first gear, revved hard, released the clutch with a whallop and jack-rabbited out of the deepening trench, off in a tight arc through the waters onto the firm sands beyond.

I turned round to see what kind of mess all that erratic motion had created in the camper. Fred was sitting on the table staring at me haughtily, wondering why I'd chosen to interrupt his bonus dinner, now liberally strewn all over the floor. He shook his head slowly as if the whole affair was beyond his comprehension and began preening himself as we moved off slowly into the night.

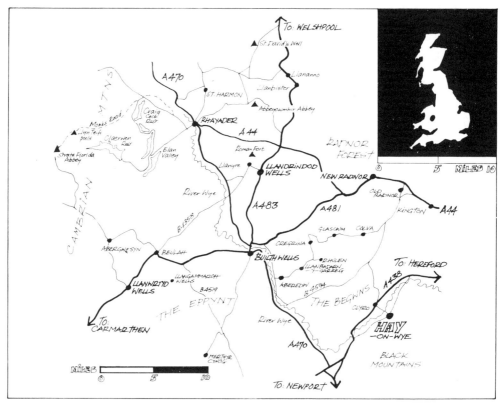

CH. 6.

6. Kilvert's Border Country

I began in a town of books, a cosy tangle of streets and shops below the remnants of a Norman castle and a seventeenth-century Jacobean mansion. Everywhere I turned were bookshops – counter-culture, science and natural history, art and antiques, history and heraldry, children's, 'the cheapest bookstore in the world'. Windows brimmed with books. The talk in the pubs was all books. A British Museum Library silence cocooned the racks. The cinema was a converted bookstore, as was the fire station and the work-house-like Frank Lewis House below the Swan Hotel.

The little market town of Hay-on-Wye, population 1,500, has been trans-formed from a dying community of empty shops and crumbling charm to the

74

world's largest repository of antique and second-hand books primarily by forty-three-year-old Richard Booth and a cadre of like-minded enthusiasts. The charm still exists – the narrow alleys tumbling downhill to the ornate clock tower, the old market, the ruined castle, flickers of the lazy Wye between trees – but now the streets are bristling with activity as book-buyers from all over the world make pilgrimages here in search of elusive titles from a stock of over one and a half million. Booth is so delighted with the success of the revitalisation that he and his pub-elected 'cabinet' proclaimed independence for Hay and the creation of an anarchistic kingdom. 'In January 1977 it was decided that action must be taken to stem the forces of inertia and incompetence that led to decay, and to revitalise Hay by ensuring the livelihood of its inhabitants and restoring the town to its former prosperity.' He has no time for the bunglings that allowed the town to decline and dismisses government bureaucracy as 'a very efficient way of giving highly educated fools jobs in offices'.

The town is so busy prospering that there's little time for the frimperies of government. The Minister of Agriculture couldn't attend a cabinet because one of his cows was calving and the Minister of Social Security was too busy trying to get a second job. When the initial cabinet meeting was held in the castle, wrote Mr Booth, 'Norman Radcliffe had so much to drink he could not remember whether he was supposed to be Prime Minister or Minister of Defence and a blond lady called Vivienne, who happened to be around, kept the minutes, but these were subsequently lost.'.

The literary associations of Hay are fitting introduction to the rolling hills of old Radnorshire north of the Wye. This is Kilvert Country, a little separate land whose charms and customs were recorded by the Reverend R. F. Kilvert, Curate of Clyro from 1865 to 1872. Regrettably much of his work has been lost. When he died shortly after his marriage at the age of thirty-eight he left twenty-two notebooks full of his observations and often blunt opinions on the appalling conditions in which his parishioners lived. William Plomer at Jonathan Cape published selections in three volumes. Tentative plans to release the complete works, however, had to be dropped after it was discovered that most had been given away or mislaid, including Kilvert's extensive studies of Radnorshire folklore and legends. So Kilvert enthusiasts (and after a long TV series their numbers have increased dramatically) must content themselves with following his footsteps along the paths and lanes around Clyro and relishing what remains of his richly evocative prose:

Monday 1st May 1876
. . . the weeping willow still drooped like a green shower and the boundary brook

of Cwmrafor came leaping and foaming down the beautiful goats' dingle under the green shadow of the sunlit weeping willows and silver birches swiftly flashing.

One of the many aspects of Radnorshire life that fascinated the diarist was the local Devil-cult which permeated every aspect of rural life and, according to the poet William Probert, unleased an unnatural enthusiasm for 'darkest gloom and the wild and horrible dingle'. Wizards and warlocks abounded in the secluded valleys. The occasional 'white witch' hired to counteract the spells and incantations of the 'evil ones' had an uphill (though often lucrative) struggle. Kilvert mentions the wizard 'Jones the Jockey' who possessed a book full of spells one of which involved the slow death of a toad to discover who had stolen his wife's washing. He also described the 'burning of the bush' in wheat fields on New Year's Eve as protection for crops, the retention of Yule log ashes after Christmas festivities as a charm against the Devil, and the hanging of withered birch twigs outside cottages 'to keep the old witch out'.

But most of all Kilvert seemed to enjoy his pastoral wanderings in the Black Mountains and The Begwns close to his residency at Ashbrook House in Clyro. The village today consists of a clustering of cottages around the Baskerville Arms, a rather dull church approached through a lychgate and yew tunnel (the enormous black and green safe in the middle of the nave is one of its most memorable features), and a small pottery that welcomes visitors.

Far more intriguing churches can be found to the north along the twisting switchback road from Aberedw to Old Radnor. The substantial thirteenth-century Aberedw church perches dramatically above the Edw riverlet, torrenting down to the Wye Valley, whereas the white-washed single cell of Llanbadarn-y-garreg church is set by itself in a sunlit buttercup field. A stream flickered behind bushes and a flurry of ducks circled in a pool as I pushed open the mossy gate and ambled across the grass. There was no porch – just a yew tree and a small bell-cote. The door was stiff and covered with dozing flies. Inside was utter simplicity, a stone floor, plain pews and pulpit, an altar-like Jacobean dresser, an office swivel-chair for the priest and a hollowed chunk of rock for a font – all bathed in shafts of sunlight reflected from white walls. Decoration was minimal, consisting of a memorial plaque to three generations of Evan Evans and a rather overbearing royal coat-of-arms (a 1644 canon law obligation in Welsh churches).

At Rhulen church all the basic accoutrements seemed to have been carved out of a solid cave-like interior. The east wall had no window and light

Rhulen Church

trickling through two small panes on the south wall created a womb-like cosiness. Again decoration was limited to a small harmonium and a simple octagonal font on which I found the following hand-written note:

> The people who worship in this tiny church are so very touched by the generosity of visitors that to show their gratitude they would be pleased if you would care to take away one of the small gifts placed in the font as a memento of your visit.

Arranged in and around the font were bottles of home-dried herbs, small paintings on thin sheets of grey slate, small bouquets of dried flowers, book-markers, and pots of home-made damson jam.

Outside, once eyes became accustomed to the brightness again and the additional brilliance of the external whitewash, you notice what an odd little creation this place is with its lopsided west wall, the huge yew tree at the east end (which may explain the tiny chancel and the lack of an east window), the ponderous black bell-cote, a large porch with stone seats, and a worn 'sanctuary ring' on the door. Even more unusual is the circular churchyard thought to indicate a pre-Christian graveyard. The place was totally charming so I sat down on the grass and sketched it with frequent bites of damson jam sandwiches.

Beyond the stone cottages and well restored thirteenth-century church at Cregrina the area becomes wilder with peaty streams tumbling through tight wooded valleys. Hills rise steeply, and beyond St David's church at Glascwm, founded in the sixth century with major thirteenth and fifteenth-century additions, the road reaches the high open tops, a mixture of moorland and scattered pastures. At Colva I walked up a sloping path between ancient yews, under the enormous beamed porch and into a spacious thirteenth-century church lit by oil lamps, each with its tiny reflecting mirror. Again the simplicity of the interior, containing school bench pews, harmonium and royal coats-of-arms, was typical of churches in the region – with the notable exception of St Stephens in Old Radnor. Here the modesty of most Welsh valley churches is abandoned for the splendours of a fifteenth-century decorated edifice, complete with beacon turret, peering out over Radnor Forest from its hilltop. Inside all is space and light through clear windows under a lavishly decorated roof. A lace-like screen separates the nave and two aisles from the chancel. At the west end a massive boulder of igneous rock, thought to have been a Bronze Age altar stone, is used as a font. The organ casing, carved in intricate linen-fold patterns around 1500, is the oldest in England.

Another equally impressive display of wealth dominates the entrance to New Radnor in the form of a 77 ft memorial to Sir George Cornewall Lewis. This hard-working politician, 'Radnorshire's most distinguished son', held many high offices under Lord Palmerston's two administrations and at the time of his death in 1863 was Secretary of State for War. As a close friend of Queen Victoria he was so impressed by the extravagant memorials to Albert that he suggested John Gibbs, the famous monument-architect, should design his edifice with all the trimmings. Today, travellers gaze awe-struck at its octagonal pinnacled finery, its rich tiled friezes, Gothic canopies dripping with ornamentation, the griffin-like gargoyles, the heraldic shields, the statues of Justice, Truth, Oratory and Literature, all ending in a richly carved cross atop the spire.

The village itself is a pleasantly modest collection of cottages around a hotel and inns under the shadow of an ancient castle mound. Behind is the great unroaded dome of Radnor Forest. Footpaths follow wriggling streams up wooded dingles in its flanks. On a map the area seems rather small, but walking or horse-riding one moves through a seemingly endless country of hidden woodland pools, ancient wells and such delicate waterfalls as the Water-Break-Its-Neck cascade above New Radnor.

Equally wild walking and driving country is the remote mass of The Eppynt west of the Wye Valley. Much of the marginal architectural economy here was eradicated during the Second World War when the army turned the area into a training ground and firing range. Today abandoned farmsteads dot the empty hills. Near Llangammarch Wells on the B4519 I passed the ruins of the Drovers Arms Inn, once a popular resting-place on the cattle-road to London. Further down at Upper Chapel I met Aneurin Jones whose parents had lived at nearby Merthyr Cynog before being moved out in 1939. 'I was nine when we left but I can remember a bit about what things were like then. My father raised ponies, real mountain breeds, sold them at the markets. He once took thirty all the way to Llandidloes because he knew he'd get a better price there. Mostly, though, he sold them to Anglesey folks. Sometimes the Irish would come in this far, but normal times they bought ponies when they'd got to the coast. Best fair was at Llangammarch Wells in October – biggest in Wales. Hundreds of horses and ponies. They closed down the town for a day, except the pubs, mind – I only went twice but I remember it clear as last week. We sold forty-five ponies one year and came back with all new suits and a brand new clothes washer and a fancy umbrella for my mother. She cried for two days.'

To the north of the Eppynt are the even more remote Cambrian Mountains and the lovely string of man-made Elan Valley lakes west of Rhayader, the

Monk's Road across 'the Desert of Wales'

'Lake District of Wales'. Long before the tourists discovered the region and filled the summer lanes with wheezing traffic, the nineteen-year-old poet Shelley and his wife Harriet settled at a small house at Cwm Elan and wrote delightedly to friends: 'A ghost haunts it, there are several witches in the neighbourhood and we are quite stocked with fairies.' The remains of the house can still be seen in the lake waters of Caban Coch. Soaring crags here lead up to the barren moors beyond the valley. Clusters of oak and birch are the remnants of once-extensive upland forests, now replaced by dark swathes of sitka spruce. Narrow, sheep-tracked side valleys, wild and over-grown, hide old lead mines and shepherds' huts. Then the road turns and ahead is the gigantic 184 ft end-wall of Claerwen Reservoir and almost five miles of water stretching back to the Cambrian Mountains watershed.

Hardy walkers will relish the twelve-mile hike on the ancient 'Monks Road' from the head of Craig Coch reservoir to the ruins of the Strata Florida Cistercian Abbey at Pontrhydfendigaid, across the appropriately named 'Desert of Wales'. (An alternative track follows the edge of the Claerwen

Reservoir.) John Leland, appointed King's Antiquary in 1583 and sent off to produce the first inventory and guidebook on Britain, was uncomfortable in this bleak territory of Moruge or Ellennith: 'All about and a great mile off towards Stratfler is horrible with sight of bare stonis, as Cregeryri mountains be' (i.e. like Snowdonia). I was fortunate on my ramble. Early clouds and mists cleared and I headed west in a sparkling morning across the barren moor broken by sudden rock outcrops, odd gorge-like clefts, and frustrating patches of bog. The worst was around the trout-filled pools of Llyn Teifi which Leland described in his wonderfully convoluted English 'Of all the pooles none standeth in so rokky and stony soile as Teifi doth, that hath within hym many stonis.'

A storm the previous day had left the ground like a waterlogged sponge. I sloshed through peat and alongside an odd clefted passageway in the rock known locally as the Shoefit, thought to have been the place where the drovers fitted shoes to the feet of their cattle in preparation for the long trek south. The whole moor was deserted. Coot and heron flew over the tiny ponds and lakelets in the distance, and browned moor tops rolled away to an empty horizon. It's not a place one would choose to cross on a misty day and the bare, unadorned ruins of the twelfth-century Cistercian abbey at the end of the trail only serve to emphasise the bleakness of the area.

A second route across the 'desert' from Llanwrtyd Wells to Strata Florida is suitable for driving, although conditions on the last fifteen miles can deteriorate rapidly in poor weather – in which case stick to the main valley roads and visit the old spa town Llandrindod Wells, cloaked in Victorian respectability above the river Ithon. Although the town's eighteenth-century origins were rather shady with tales of illicit gambling and debauchery in the hotels and 'lounges', a fresh start in the 1860s complete with railway, new hotels and pump rooms, brought this tribute from an enthusiastic society journalist of the time:

> Effacacious as its excellent waters are, one discovers too the indescribable purity of the air and exhilarating atmosphere and the bright reflection of its cheerful buildings. Its dry streets and elevated position arrest the notice of visitors immediately they emerge from the railway carriage. The jaded society belle, the weary man of business, the over-taxed student all return home after only a short lapse of time, with brightened eye and rejuvenated complexion and healthful countenance, to the merry whirl of fashionable society life, or the busy hauls of commercial activity.

And it's all still here today, if a little worn at the edges. I strolled through the faded green and gold interior of the rambling Hotel Metropole, complete with skylit chandeliers and a mural of Venice with real Venetian lanterns. Next door is the town museum and an extensive array of local Roman finds, many from the Castell Collen fort just across the river at Llanyre. I sampled waters from the Free Chalybeate Spring in the glen beside a rocky cascade. ('You'll see the Llandrindod Ghost if you drink too much of that stuff' mumbled a tiny drunk Welshman wobbling down to the Pump Room.) Many of the old cast-iron shop fronts remain – Morris, Pastrycook and Confectioner, in rich black and gold. Even the Job Centre office has an elegant Art Nouveau door and one can still see ancient ladies hidden in furs being assisted from Bentleys by chauffeurs and crisp white nurses.

Above the town a lake enclosed by woods is a popular haunt of children and lovers. The more adventurous follow the path up through the trees to Bongam Bank to catch a glimpse of Llandrindod's buzzards and rare kites hovering over the open ground, and return via the golf course at Little Hill with broad vistas over the Wye Valley and the Cambrian mountains.

The Glen. Llandrindod Wells

I ended my border country ramblings at Abbeycwmhir among the sparse remains of an enormous Cistercian abbey founded in 1143 and possessing one of the longest naves in Britain, surpassed only by York, Winchester and Durham. The decapitated body of Wales's last independent prince, Llywelyn, was buried here after his death at Builth in 1282. Conifer forests shroud the surrounding hills and a silvery mist eased itself over Camlo Hill into the quiet valley:

The air blew sweet from the mountains and tempered the heat of the sun. (Kilvert)

I had a choice of moving on or resting awhile in the nearby Happy Union pub with its sign showing a cheerful Welshman riding a goat. The decision wasn't too difficult.

83

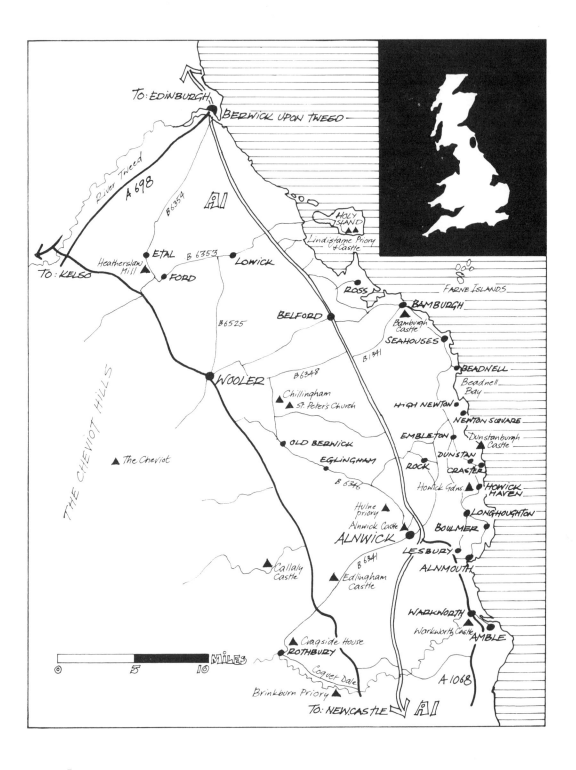

7. The Northumbria Coast

I came down from moorlands and high forests into a still summer day, trees wrapped in heavy-honeyed sunlight. Last night a bullying wind had punched the coast from Alne to Berwick, smashing fishing shacks and bringing havoc to the cornfields. Today early breezes swept up the torn bits and pieces and left the land fat-flushed with green, and seething with sappy juices.

In this magical day below silk-sack clouds I explored a quiet coast unvisited since childhood. I expected the worst and found it all untouched by the crass commercialism of the resorts. There were possibly more people, weary like me of the hullabaloo and candy-floss stands elsewhere, but I found my old niches – the placid Victoriana of Alnmouth, the brittle sea-cottages of Boulmer, the white sands of Beadnell Bay and the duney infinities of Ross – all as they had been almost thirty years before. It was a happy, grateful, older child now, billowing with bucket-and-spade fantasies, retracing paths on that soft summer's day by the seaside.

I began at Warkworth, a fairytale village below a proud, angular castle, the first of six major castles along this ancient coastal defence-line. Battles raged in these borderlands between the English and Scottish armies, and feuds between local lords continued for centuries until the late 1500s. Small villages, churches and even farms still have their ancient, windowless pele towers, the last resort of the peasantry; church records tell of frequent raids from north of the border and the 'loss of tithes again, gone to the enemie'. Warkworth is within a mile of the coast and yet feels separate, looped by the broad river Coquet after its wrigglings down Coquet Dale.

From the picturesque medieval bridge and gate tower the tree-lined main street climbs steadily past the market cross in Dial Place to the rocky hilltop bastion. The first castle was founded by Robert de Mowbray, Earl of Northumberland in the late eleventh century, with radical reconstruction during the Norman era and late fourteenth century. Kings have slept here, Hotspur spent his boyhood here, inspiring Shakespeare's somewhat disrespectful use of the locale for both parts of *Henry IV* ('this worm-eaten hold of ragged stone'). Turner painted it gleefully and artists today sketch its towering outline from the river shallows flecked with rowing boats.

Since the fourteenth century the Percys have owned the castle, hence the huge Percy lion on the tower in the courtyard (an apparent combination of griffin and lamb distinguishable only by its rod-straight tail). Over the bridged moat the bold remnants are a confusion of ruined outbuildings laced with dungeons, cellars, brewhouse and kitchens leading to the keep, and

Warkworth Castle

broad vistas over the Coquet valley. Anyone laying siege to the castle would have been in for a long wait. The capacity of the underground larders and other storage facilities were adequate to keep a sizeable army happy for months. And God would doubtless have given favourable ear to the case of the occupants because of the extraordinary accumulation of chapels within the compound, plus a delightful one in the keep itself with arched piscina and sedilia.

Visitors to the castle often miss two other notable places of interest in Warkworth. First is St Lawrence's church, one of the most complete Norman churches in the north, with a chevron-patterned vaulted chancel. The delicate grey-gold stone, the effigy of a crusader with his heart in his hand, and the graceful fifteenth-century south aisle, all add to the interest of the place, encouraging slow exploration and pensive walks in the quiet, copper-beech-shaded churchyard by the river.

Continue walking (or boating) a mile or so alongside the river above the castle and you'll find the tiny Warkworth Hermitage, founded by the Percys in the fourteenth century as a priestly retreat. Records of 1531 show that the chaplain was rewarded with '20 marks yearly, pasture for 12 cattle, one bull and two horses, also two loads of wood and a draught of fish every Sunday' in exchange for daily prayers 'for the good of all such noble blode as now levynge and for the soules of such noble blode as be departed'. And this was no mere soggy cave carved in the river cliffs. On top of the precipice were the religious man's orchard and pastures. Below, in addition to a rock-hewn chapel and sacristy complete with carved pillars and vaultings, was a substantial kitchen with oven, a hall 15 ft by 18 ft with fireplace and window, a solar over the hall, and evidence of other pleasant conveniences. An elegant niche indeed, although inmates may not have thought so if the Latin words of a psalm once painted on the chapel wall were any indication: 'My tears have been my meat day and night.'

Alnmouth is a delightfully secluded haven, a cosy, slightly Victorian village, stretched along the banks of the river Aln where it weaves out to sea. On the south side of the estuary, dunes and silver sands merge into a hazy distance inviting lonely rambles, even in the height of the summer season. Black, tar-crusted fishing shacks huddle in the lee slope among marram grass below prim boarding houses. Drybrough's Beer signs indicate modest pubs on the high street. Little alleys run off into odd little collections of back-cottages, slightly dowdy and shame-faced. An ancient bus wheezes downhill to the Hope and Anchor and lets out a long hissing expletive.

The old harbour here has long been silted up and the town relies upon small craft, loyal summer visitors and golfers to keep its marginal economy

Craster

alive. It never feels hectic. People soon merge into the dunes leaving broad swathes of shimmering beach unoccupied. One wonders at the tirades of John Wesley against the boisterous, boozy mariners who supposedly inundated the little port during the late eighteenth century. Maybe he misinterpreted the thick, occasionally indecipherable, local dialect, all sing-songy and slurry. I chatted with a couple of older residents, both retired seamen, and understood nothing of our conversation. It didn't seem to matter. We just chuckled and aah'd and watched the river splashing out across the sparkling sands and the little Lowry stick-figures silhouetted against the sea.

Boulmer, in contrast, is a lonely place, a sea-blasted line of low cottages once a notorious smuggling niche. 'Aud Bob Dum of the Forest,' goes the song, 'He's riding to Boomer for gin.' Denims and overalls flail on washing lines and a holed dinghy rots on the shingle. The women keep out of sight and the men have the wind-whipped faces of long-time fishermen. They cluster, all shoulders and boots, around the bar in the Fishing Boat pub deep in rumbled musings below the painting of a lifeboat launching. This time the women are out in force, tugging the boat into flailing seas. You can hear the howl of the wind. Many of the men of the village have been lost in dangerous rescue-attempts in this treacherous strip of ocean and the painting is a memorial of sorts. The polished turtle shell, the swordfish snout, the nets

and other nautical bits and pieces dangling from the walls seem over-decorative for such a place, a bit of tarting-up for strangers.

Longhoughton, back from the coast, was another smuggling centre with pack trails spanning out to the Cheviot passes and into Roxburghshire. Even the vicar was part of the plot, hiding contraband in the fortress-like church behind walls five feet thick. A narrow road leads down from the village to the secluded beach of Howick Haven. The first layers of the Whin Sill, sheets of ancient lava, begin to rise out of the sea. From here northwards the sills become more pronounced, running out like platforms into the waves, turned upwards into seaward cliffs at Cullernose Point, and long inland crags. The quartz-like stone was once highly valued as building material and small coastal quarries were linked by jetties and aerial ropeways carrying out to the waiting ships.

Today the silence has returned. A lane runs through woods and wind-swept copses to Howick Hall and acres of sheltered gardens open to the public. Hidden deep in the rhododendrons beyond the delicate bridge is the family church, a recent masterwork of stone craftsmanship cleverly adorned in Romanesque details.

Then the lane tumbles abruptly through a whinsill cliff, now a nature reserve, down into the Cornish-flavoured fishing village of Craster. The circular harbour of this once-important herring fleet centre no longer contains its brilliant blue cobbles. North Shields boats deliver cargoes of the fish instead for kippering up in the smoking sheds. The aroma fills the little bay. Mr Robson gave me a short, concise course in kippering. 'You split the herring, clean them out and soak them in brine strong 'nuff to float a potato. Then you hangs them out to dry, and when they're ready, you line them up and smoke them for twelve hours over oakwood sawdust, pull them out and eat them.' Simple – and delicious.

Walks splay out from the village. On the Arnold Reserve among the whin-sill protruberances one finds puffins, cormorants, razorbills – and lovely sheltered silences. In the opposite direction is a grassy walk along the edge of the beach to the eerie 'fangs' of Dunstanburgh Castle ruins set on a prominent cliff. Built by the Earl of Lancaster in the early fourteenth century and strengthened by John of Gaunt, the castle saw extensive action during the Wars of the Roses when it exchanged hands on four separate occasions. Compared to the majesty and intricacies of Alnwick Castle a few miles inland, there's not much here other than atmosphere (a wild spirit expressed by Turner in a number of paintings) and tales of the ghost of Sir Guy the Seeker. According to legend the brave knight was led by a giant on a stormy midnight into the recesses of the castle and shown a sleeping princess on a crystal bed. He was told to choose between sword and horn to awaken the enchanted lady and thereby enter paradise. The poor fellow chose the horn which had no impact at all and was fated to walk the walls for ever cursing his misfortune. The princess presumably still sleeps somewhere in her subterranean vault.

Through Embleton, a cosy village with an ancient dove cote on the southern fringe, a lane swings away to the right and trickles down through High Newton to Newton Square. This unexpected three-sided terrace of cream cottages complete with pub, tiny shop and windsurfing centre, is a charming little niche for long beach days. Behind the pub are excellent examples of contemporary holiday cottages built with old cut whinstone. A lane in the other direction from High Newton leads to the great empty sweep of Beadnell Bay and brilliant sands edged by dunes. Relish the silence here. At Beadnell begins a more hectic stretch of coastline.

I say 'hectic' advisedly, for even on the busiest of summer weekends Seahouses manages to retain the Cornish charm of its tough, grey-stone harbour. Up in 'high-town' is a half-hearted attempt at a plastic bingo-disco nucleus edged by neon-bright fish and chip shops. But down below is all intense bustle as the fishing fleet comes in at 6 p.m. prompt. A bevy of brightly painted boats and Northumbrian cobles bump and jostle for places alongside the quay while trucks wait for the boxes of cod and haddock to be hauled up and clouds of gulls whirl and scream among the masts. The young fishermen in dungarees and yellow weather-proofs bawl and heave. Small fish are scattered on slippery wooden decks, others slide out of boxes as they ride high on pulleys and gulls snap them up before they hit the water. The old salts watch quietly, some wistful, others curious and critical, unconvinced by all the babble. One man rigged out in boots, blue jersey and sou'-wester stands at the quayside surrounded by an ogling group of visitors, explaining the activities with the eloquence of a local Dylan Thomas. 'Isn't he marvellous!' gasps one of the party. Her husband, a thin, pale man still dressed for the office, nods sadly with a far-away look in his eyes. Above, at The Olde Ship, pint-happy customers watch all the activity and study the nautical displays of knobs, clocks, maps, lamps and photos of Farne Island wrecks. In the distance the ancient line of coastal castles stand proud on their buttes with Bamburgh Castle the most prominent of all when viewed from the dune-lined road north of the town.

Ferries offer trips out to the Farne Islands, famous for their puffins and seals, and the red and white tower of the lighthouse on Longstone Island. It was here on 7 September 1838 that the lighthouseman and his daughter, Grace Darling, undertook that legendary rescue of passengers from the luxury steamer *Forfarshire* after its grounding on Big Harker rocks half a mile away. Fact and fiction are mingled irretrievably in the tale. Poets, songwriters, artists and promoters of all kinds (soup and chocolate manufacturers – even bonnet makers inspired by the hat she is supposed to have worn) had a field-day with the incident. The rather shy Grace became the classic brave heroine risking all for the sake of those less fortunate than herself. A London music hall impresario offered her a small fortune to row her 26-foot cobleboat twice nightly across the stage. Although she modestly chose to remain at the lighthouse, her death four years later from consumption provoked a new surge of 'Darling-delirium' and a revival of the tear-jerking songs:

> Twas on the Longstone Lighthouse
> There dwelt an English maid
> Pure as the air around her, etc.

Those familiar and not-so-familiar with the legend will relish the tiny Grace Darling museum brimming with memorabilia in Bamburgh. Her ornate Gothic-arched memorial stands in a railed plot in the churchyard.

The region abounds with tales of miracles and mythological creatures like the enormous 'Bamburgh Worm', who turned out to be a daughter of the

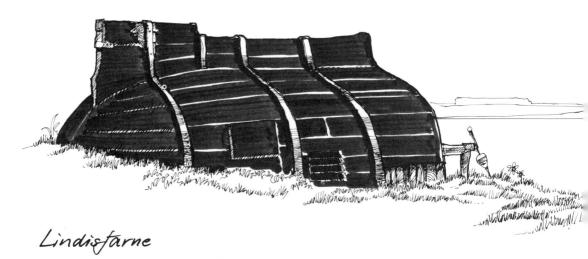

Lindisfarne

King of Northumbria transformed by a wicked witch. The witch in true Snow White style was actually her jealous stepmother-queen who, as soon as the princess regained her stately shape (rescued by her brother, the Childe of Wynde), became a slimy yellow toad. She is said to sit today somewhere below the castle in a cave whose doors only open every seventh Christmas. A complex series of sword-unsheathings and horn blowing, plus an actual sticky kiss, will restore the wicked queen, although why anyone should wish to undertake the task is open to question. She's perhaps better left where she is.

On Holy Island (Lindisfarne) the folklore is equally rich with tales of 'storms and fiery serpents' signifying attacks from external enemies. Labourers building the priory were said to be fed on bread made from air and refreshed from a bottomless cup of wine. Even today newly-married brides leap a Petting Stone in the churchyard to ensure good fortune and symbolise their blissful bounding into a new life. The only problem in yet one more magical place along this coast is the increased tourism of recent years which

makes exploration of the priory ruins, the castle and the Scottish-flavoured village rather less enjoyable than it once was. A facsimile of the richly decorated Lindisfarne Gospels ('a whirlpool of Celtic, Germanic and Scandinavian motifs') on display in the museum attracts almost as many admirers as the nearby Lindisfarne Mead plant and tasting room.

Nevertheless Holy Island is a place that retains its character against all odds – the long causeway drive across the tidal flats, the unusual upturned boat-huts of the fishermen backed by the castle on the rocky butte of Beblowe, fresh-made crab sandwiches from one of the cottages, and the bold Norman arching of the ruined priory. Come out of season if you can – but come. And after visiting all the guidebook features, wander off along the eastern edges of the island, and into the nature reserve lands and the silent dunes of the north beaches, a favourite winter resort of godwits, oyster-catchers, turnstones, knots and dunlins. Seals occasionally come into the shallow sandy coves for a frolic. There are traces of kelp pits where seaweed was once burned and used in the manufacture of soap and glass, but nothing remains of the numerous wrecks which brought sudden wealth to islanders

The Cheviots near Wooler

in past centuries. A Roman Catholic missionary reported in 1643 that 'the common people do pray for shippes which they sie in danger . . . they pray not God to suave you, or send you to port, but to send you to them by shipwreck, that they may gette the spoile of her'.

If Holy Island's charms prove a little too popular, there's an area of dunes I discovered at Ross, a cul-de-sac hamlet at the end of a narrow lane between Bamburgh and the island turn-off. Here one can wander for hours among silvery wastes with only gulls and the hiss of an incoming tide for company. Receding into the hazy distance once again are the shadowy castles on their mounds and the whole place seems lost to the world, silent in its own tranquility.

Away from the coast is the same silence along lanes, past surfing corn-fields and copses, and below the round, green Cheviots. I found tiny vil-lages, ancient pele towers, priories, and all the mellowness of a countryside shaped by a long intertwining intimacy of landscape and man.

Ford is one of those model estate villages, a little twee perhaps, reflecting

94

the tastes of its romantic patron, Louisa, Marchioness of Waterford. Following the death of her husband in a hunting accident in Ireland she moved into Ford Castle in 1859 determined to devote her life to good works and the welfare of her tenants. She began with the castle by removing the ghastly Gothic 'modifications' of earlier tenants and restoring the original façade. Then she had the village rebuilt complete with horseshoe-shaped door for the blacksmith and a 'Jubilee cottage' in honour of Queen Victoria. Ruskin-inspired critics found the place idyllic, but others were less impressed. Beatrix Potter visited here in 1890 and resented the petty regulations enforced upon the tenants – 'No cocks or hens are allowed . . . just peacocks strutting about. If I had lived here I should have let loose a parcel of sighs.'

But Louisa was not to be deterred. Encouraged by Landseer and Rossetti, she began the major task of decorating the walls and rafters of her village school with Pre-Raphaelite-style biblical subjects, painted on watercolour paper mounted on canvas and stretched in frames. The task took twenty-two years. She used residents as models and created a sequence of works of art remarkable in their power and grace. She died in 1891 and is buried in the churchyard by the hall, next to a more recent grave of the Joyceys, subsequent owners of the estate.

The church itself, a Victorian restoration, is rather dull except for an unusually hefty bell turret, but the views over to the west are magnificent. In the far distance is The Cheviot, green and gentle in a summer sun. A group of trees on the lower northern flanks marks the site of the camp of King James IV of Scotland before the battle of Flodden in 1513. His troops captured the defence tower in the grounds of Ford Castle and the fourteenth-century castle at Etal, an attractive partially thatched village nestled below the overgrown ruins.

Between Ford and Etal is Heatherslaw Mill, a 120-year-old water-driven corn mill on a site used for milling since the thirteenth century. The river Till wriggles by the large stone building. Inside, a grant from the Joycey family has permitted the reconstruction of the water wheel and gravity-feed milling system with millstones, elevators, grain-dressers, dust extractors and a confusing array of pulleys, belts and shafts. Photographs and diagrams make the whole process thoroughly clear to anyone with the patience to follow each stage. Some give up and enjoy tea at the adjoining café instead.

Beyond Wooler, a base for rambles into the Cheviots, the famous White Cattle of Chillingham roam the Earl of Tankerville's estates. These burly creatures, long-horned and quick-tempered, are the direct descendents of the aurochs and wild oxen and were trapped within the 600-acre estate after its enclosure sometime in the early thirteenth century. When alarmed the creatures adopt an ancient form of defence with cows in front, calves in the centre, males behind, and the single 'king' bull in the rear.

Travellers here often miss St Peter's church, a much-remodelled Norman structure containing the memorials of the Grey family and set in a sloping churchyard shaded by estate trees. Most notable is the Grey altar tomb in the thirteenth-century south chapel. The alabaster figures of Sir Ralph Grey and his wife Elizabeth lie surrounded by tabernacles, canopies, saints, and shield-bearing angels and all the fanfare befitting a fifteenth-century knight who died bravely in the Wars of the Roses defending Bamburgh Castle.

Returning slowly to the coast, I discovered two more churches worthy of detour. The first at Old Berwick was founded in the twelfth century by Queen Matilda, wife of Henry I, and possesses one of the finest Norman chancels in Northumbria. Beyond Eglingham, a charming scatter of cottages, I came across the hamlet of Rock. A single row of stone cottages faced on to a green, with a school and another Norman church. The revival of this once almost-abandoned community was largely due to Charles Bosanquet,

Governor of the Canada Land Company and notable philanthropist, who is buried in the churchyard. A 'truly valiant and loyal gentleman', Colonel John Salkeld, is another notable local memorialised here for 'serving King Charles I with a constant, dangerous and expensive loyalty'!

I ended my ramblings in that bastion of Northumberland culture and civility, the little cobbled market town of Alnwick. Again, one must share its delights with others and local guidebooks provide endless details of its castle, churches, schools, priories and parks. And yet for all the publicity there are aspects of the town missed by many visitors. On the western outskirts, for example, hidden in the vast Hulne Park, one can climb the Gothic Brizlee Tower for views over Alndale and the coast, then continue on to the ruins of the Premonstratensian Abbey of the White Canons and the Carmelite Hulne Priory. The remains of the nave here with its slender lancet windows are typically thirteenth-century in their simplicity, although a little overpowered by the high wall and tower built for defence in this volatile borderland country. The park is an idyllic place for woodland strolls and silent musings by the Aln (permits are usually needed from the Castle Estates office).

Alnwick once boasted almost seventy inns and alehouses along its cobbled streets and narrow alleys. Today most are gone, including the Post Boy, the Beehive, the Angel and the Turk's Head, famous for its roasting spits and cock-fighting ring. But the proud White Swan remains with its Olympic Room, a ballroom transferred intact from the sister-ship of the *Titanic* salvaging in 1935. The Black Swan is here too, and once entertained the wide-roaming Robbie Burns. So is the Old Cross displaying an upside-down cross on the wall, supposedly stolen from the abbey following Dissolution and erected by ale-happy masons. The window full of spider-webbed bottles and encrusted dust has been untouched for decades, but I'll leave the landlord to tell that tale of sinister superstition.

You can sense the town's long history as you ramble up Bondgate Hill around the free-standing market hall. Looking back along cobbled, tree-lined Bondgate, the fifteenth-century Hotspur Tower blocks off the vista with its massive stone bulk, and narrows the road to a one-lane ginnel. Just outside, dominating the southern approach to the town, is a fluted monument 83 ft high, erected in 1816 by tenants grateful to the Percy family for reducing their rents in a period of agrarian decline. The stiff-tailed Percy lion surmounts the column, known locally as 'The Farmer's Folly'. Apparently, the Duke was so astounded that his tenants could afford to finance such an ornate edifice that he promptly raised the rents again!

The remarkable fourteenth-century castle, stronghold of the Dukes of

The Hotspur tower. Alnwick

Northumberland and still a well-used home, hides modestly behind the market-place. The full grandeur can only be appreciated from the river paths and grounds landscaped by Capability Brown. Long walls stretch across the mounded site, graced by round defence towers, and rising to the high barbican trimmed with life-size statues of guards, heralds and archers perched on the battlements like decoys. Visitors are invited to delight in the Renaissance-style state rooms, the Roman museum, the armoury, the Tintoretto and Titian masterpieces, the library, and the endless array of Percy portraits celebrating the family's prominence in England since the Conquest. I spent a whole afternoon here before returning once again to the quieter charms of little Alnmouth.

Most of the day-visitors had left and the empty sands were pink against a mauve ocean. A breeze blew across the dunes rattling the grass, and two elderly ladies walked a puffy pekinese past the lacey eyes of the boarding houses. Fred paid no attention. He chased a tiny crab into the sea and I romped after him.

8. The Cumbria Coast

Millom looks lost, a clutch of red sandstone and slate terraced houses on a bluff above bleached marshes. Sand flats and sea merge in green-greyness, and tar-black skeletons of iron mines rear up above the marram grass. Gulls hover over glistening rooftops screeching at clouds. Shops close early and a smell of chips mingles with the ozone.

The lakeland poet Norman Nicholson has lived in Millom most of his life. 'We're told we're not a "viable" community. A hundred years ago Millom was a little boom town. Now we're told we're too remote, too far away.' In 1968 the Millom Haemetite Ore and Iron Company closed and 800 men were idled overnight. Subsequent efforts to attract light industry were only moderately successful and a company with a novel idea for producing mini-hovercraft eventually folded even after its employees had worked without pay for weeks. National newspapers became curious about this tiny determined community, but, in the words of the *Guardian*, found 'a proud history and very little else'.

Yet somehow Millom will just not fade away. A museum of local history opened up recently with an enthusiastic group of volunteers showing visitors the mock-up of the old Hodborrow ore mine, a nineteenth-century worker's cottage, a slide show of the town's history, and an ever-expanding miscellany of smaller exhibits. 'There's a tremendous community feeling. People just don't want to move out,' my young guide told me, eyes gleaming behind thick spectacles. The museum brought tourists – a handful at first – tired of crowded Lakeland lanes, looking for something a little different. Just outside town they found the tiny eleventh-century church with its unusual Fish Window and tomb-bedecked Hudleston Chapel nestling in the shadowy remnants of Millom Castle. At Haverigg with its pebble 'cobble-duck' walls and gaily painted houses they discovered miles of untramelled dunes and sand. To the north they wandered the quiet lanes over Stoneside Hill or explored the bleak wilds of Black Combe, Norman Nicholson's favourite hill, watching like a 'dark, parental presence' over Millom.

> Home at last to the known tight streets,
> The hunched chapels, the long canals of smoke –
> And now, from my own doorway, between gable and chimney,
> That harsh, scarred brow, entirely stripped of snow,
> Impending over yard and attic sky-light,
> A dark, parental presence.

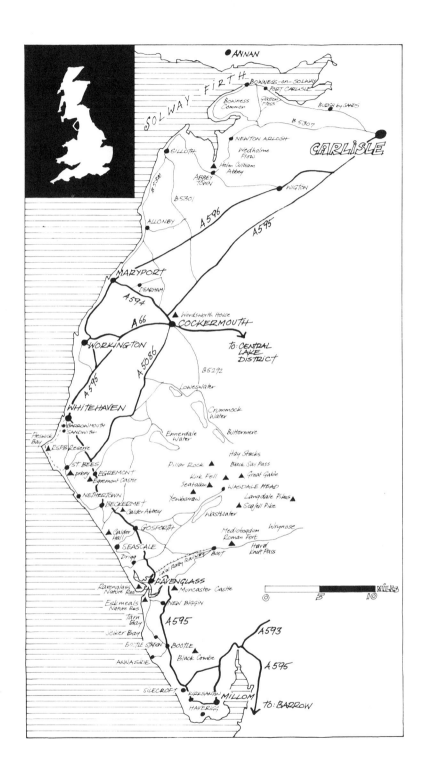

The lone hill is always there. 'My grim Neighbour, huge Black Combe', Wordsworth called it in a letter to Sir George Beaumont in 1811. 'When you can see Black Combe it's going to rain. When you can't, it's raining' goes the droll Cumbrian saying. Yet the Combe is hardly Lakeland stature. Fifteen miles to the north rise the peaks of Great Gable, Scafell Pike, and the Langdale Pikes in a brittle, scree-littered landscape blasted by gales and shrouded in mists for much of the year. But here the scenery is greener, less dramatic, a place for quiet rambles in lonely countryside and on empty beaches. Except for the intrusion of Calder Hall's cooling towers near Seascale, little has changed along this coast in centuries. Tumuli and stone circles remain unmolested in quiet valleys. Near Kirksanton is the Giant's Grave marked by two huge boulders fifteen feet apart. At Ravenglass and Hardknot Pass are impressive remains of Roman occupation during the first century AD. Churchyards contain fragmentary evidence of the earliest Viking-Christian faiths. St Bridget's at Beckermet, a tiny village surrounded by old iron ore mines near the Windscale Research Centre, has a thousand-year-old Viking grave, and Darham outside Maryport boasts a twelfth-century church with a Norse cross and various carved stones from the same period.

At Gosforth Church near Seascale is the sapling-thin, fourteen-foot-high Gosforth Cross unravaged by the elements and smothered in such mythological figures as the Norse god Loki and his wife Sigun, from the Norse poem *Voluspa*. Trinity symbols bedeck the cross itself but the lower shaft represents the pagan world-ash Yggdrasil supporting the universe. This is the largest and best-preserved ancient cross in Britain. (Regrettably, a second specimen nearby was deliberately lopped in 1789 and converted into a sundial.) Inside the church, two massive hogback tombstones originally covering the graves of Norse chieftains are shaped as houses of the dead, one depicting a tiled roof, the second thatch. The heads of two more crosses are built into the wall above the tombs.

But it's the beaches, those endless tracts of sand and dune, which bring explorers back to this undiscovered region. The flats near Haverigg, where heath and sand merge, are ideal for sand-yachting, while other coastal hamlets boast of their crabs. 'They get sweeter the closer you get to the Solway' I was told. (Egremont has a crab fair in September which combines gustatory indulgence with the World Gurning – face-distortion – Championship and the Biggest Liar Competition.) Annaside, Tain Bay, Bootle Station, Selker Bay and other secluded 'non-places' are ideal for pensive rambles among the shallows. A firing-range occupies part of the area but access is usually permitted unless the red flags are flying. Watch out, too, for road-flooding in unusually high tides. Silecroft and Drigg can become a little

Gosforth 'Viking' Cross

over-active on weekends, but near New Biggin is the quiet Eskmeals Nature Reserve, a 125-acre promontory of sand dunes on the south side of the Esk estuary famous for its resident natterjack toads and profusion of bird-life – oyster catchers, cormorants, black-headed gulls, kestrels and sparrow-hawks. Normally dunes are associated with spiky, leg-scratching marram grass and little else in the way of vegetation. Here, however, unusual micro-climate conditions have encouraged the growth of lady's bedstraw, birdsfoot-trefoil, sneezeworth, biting stonecrop, heartsease, pansy, adder-stongue and the resilient sea holly. The only problem is that to reach the dunes, visitors must first cross a broad stretch of squelchy saltings which during certain periods of the year can be extremely wet.

Most of the coast between Millom and Nethertown is flat and relatively featureless, criss-crossed by high-hedgerow lanes reminiscent of Cornwall. Then at St Bees the walker faces towering sandstone cliffs, blood red, and the prospect of a spectacular walk to Whitehaven. I paused first at the twelfth-century St Bees Priory, a mile or so inland from the beach, to admire the Norman west door with its three orders of columns, and an adjoining example of Norse art in the turbulent 'Dragon Stone'. No one is quite sure who St Bees was. A medieval legend suggests she was Bega, a holy princess who had fled from her father's Irish court and lived as a hermit in this quiet cove around 700 AD. She then moved to the court of the King of Northumbria where she was made the first English nun by St Aidan and later established the Whitby monastery. The story has many equally unreliable variations, but the Normans found them convincing enough to establish a Benedictine priory here in 1120 for six monks, dispatched reluctantly from St Mary's Abbey in York. It was never a very important or popular place. In 1379 only four monks were in residence and frequent Scottish raids were a constant harassment. At the Dissolution the buildings covered a mere 1½ acres and were rapidly dismantled to expand nearby farms and provide convenient stone for the adjoining St Bees School, founded by Queen Elizabeth I in 1583. Lead was stripped from the roof of the priory, the timbers rotted and the tower collapsed. The structure was left in an abysmal state until serious restoration work began in 1817 when Bishop Law of Chester founded a theological college here to train clergymen for the rapidly industrialising towns of the north.

Today the Priory is a modest remnant of a modest past, which is more than can be said for the pink-stone stumps of Calder Abbey, sitting forlornly in river meadows a mile or so east of Calder Bridge. Officially the site is not open to the public, but a rather odd young man, sitting like a pixie on the ball-finial at the entrance gates reading a very tattered book of poetry, told me he rented a flat in the adjoining mansion and I could inspect the remains with pleasure. This I did, accompanied by a curious goat and a peacock who seemed the best of friends and as interested as I was in the Gothic fragments of the transept and the weather-worn tombs of local knights. I thanked them both for their company and they nodded their farewells in unison. The pixie at the gate had vanished.

Back on the red cliffs of St Bees I took a three-hour clifftop walk to Whitehaven along perfumed paths, beside gold-flowered gorse bushes, with great wind-blown vistas of ocean and lakeland mountains. A short valley detour led into hidden Fleswick Bay, circled by worn sheets of sand-stone and littered with pebbles and occasional semi-precious stones. It was the height of summer and I was alone here. The grumbling sea ground the round pebbles and gulls skimmed the surf. I lay back on a patch of sand and dozed, becoming part of the gentle rhythm of the place for a short while. When I left the sun was edging its way around the headland, casting long shadows across the beach. I continued north past the RSPB Reserve, the third largest colony of sea birds in England, and the only breeding habitat of the black guillemot. I passed along the fringe of Sandwith, with tight terraced houses tumbling downhill, around the remnants of a nineteenth-century alabaster works at Barrowmouth and the sprawling Marchon Chemical works, into the colourful Georgian heart of Whitehaven.

A market was in full swing. Frantic scrabblings at the vegetable stands signified the evening sell-off bargains. Rock music blared from cheap, over-tweetered speakers at the record stalls. A dairy stall featured rare Maller-stang cheese. At the next were Tattie pies and thick coils of Cumberland sausage full of rich seasoning. Women argued at the dress stand. By the shirt stall an elderly man in a muddy raincoat swore blind he'd given ten pounds and only received change for five. The stall-owner had heard it all before. 'You was here last week wi't same tale. I remember you, same time. . . .' 'It weren't me. . . .' 'Hey Ronnie, there's this fella again, same as last week, with his bloody ten-quid lark. . . .' 'It weren't me. . . .' A small boy with a school cap watched open-mouthed as the bawlings intensified and I remembered those stringent medieval regulations once governing the conduct of fairs and markets of Olde England . . .

> That no man do pick any quarrel matter or cause for any old grudge or malice to make any perturbation or trouble.
> Also that no manner of persons do bear any Bill, Battle Axe or other prohibited weapons.
> Also that all manner of men repairing to this market do bear and keep the Queens Peace upon pain of £5 to be forfeite and their bodies to prison.

104

For all the bustle and brouhaha of the market-place, Whitehaven's fortunes have declined dramatically since the days when Sir John Lowther developed the coalfields here during the eighteenth century. He also expanded the shipbuilding industry and encouraged the creation of a stately town, inspired by Wren's plans for rebuilding London after the Great Fire of 1666. Trade with American colonies boomed during the slave days and the town is proud of its links with that country. Mildred Warner Gale, grandmother of George Washington, was buried in St Nicholas's Church in 1700 and John Paul Jones, 'The Father of the American Navy', was apprenticed to a Whitehaven ship-owner at the age of twelve. His later antics when he unsuccessfully tried to destroy the shipping here by fire in a surprise attack during the American Revolution only increased his local reputation.

But all that was long ago. Mining today is largely uneconomic, even though great reserves lie up to seven miles beneath the ocean, and the town has experienced an economic doldrums which reduced its growth and cocooned much of its character. Travellers normally anxious to avoid industrial centres will be pleasantly surprised by the colourful dignity of the town, the elegant residences in Lowther Street near the Civic Hall, the Georgian church of St James, various industrial archaeology monuments to the mining era at South Beach and the lively Rosehill Theatre on the outskirts. Whitehaven also provides a most convenient centre for expeditions into little-known 'clefts' of western Lakeland – the tranquil shores of Ennerdale Water, Crummock Water, Loweswater, and the thick black shadows of the Wast Water valley.

This mysterious finger-lake, the deepest in England, is bounded on its eastern flank by huge sheets of scree. To the north rises the pyramid of Great Gable and to the west the huddled peaks of Seatallan, Yewbarrow and Kirk Fell. The lanes from Gosforth rise gradually from the green coastal plain to bracken-covered undulations broken by rocky outcrops. Wind-bent pine and scrub-oak cluster by the roadside. The lake itself is elusive, wrapped in silence and hidden in its cleft. This is real walking country. To appreciate the silence one must abandon the car and wander off along sheep tracks, pausing at the water's edge below ribboning clouds torn by the peaks. Even on the quietest of days there are crackings and rumblings on the scree as the slopes of broken rock constantly adjust themselves and move – infinitely slowly – outwards into the lake. The hamlet of Wasdale Head is a welcome haven in this wilderness, a centre for climbers and a place of final rest for those who have died in the fells. The gravestones at the tiny church are evidence of the ferocity and power of the grey-green hills at the head of the valley.

High Fells above Crummock Water

In complete contrast, the small and little-known lakes of Ennerdale Water, Crummock Water and Loweswater lie quietly in their mountain bowls, fringed by forests. Here the landscape has an openness, a generous dignity, tempting to the novice walker. Smaller peaks such as Mellbreak, Lanthwaite Hill, Great Borne and Brackenthwaite Fell offer pleasant day-long rambles. Only the upper reaches of Ennerdale, beyond the lake and inaccessible by road, can be classed as true Lakeland territory. Serious hikers relish this long scramble alongside the river Liza past the 2,927 ft Pillar Rock precipices and the Hay Stacks, through Black Sail Pass to Great Gable, towering over minions, its crown wreathed in clouds. This is one of the finest walks in the Lake District and should not be undertaken lightly. Alfred Wainwright's excellent route-books on Lakeland hikes are invaluable companions on expeditions of this calibre.

Back once again in the lanes of the plain, I wandered slowly seeking out snippets of history and folklore. In tranquil Georgian Cockermouth I spent an afternoon at the birthplace of Dorothy and William Wordsworth, a refined mansion set back from Main Street with a riverside terrace. Wordsworth's father was granted the house in 1766 along with the stewardship to Sir James Lowther, entrepreneur-extraordinary, who owned a large portion of the Cumberland coast and most of Whitehaven's industry. A contemporary of Wordsworth's at the local grammar school was Fletcher Christian, leader of the mutiny on the *Bounty*, whose birthplace, Moorland Close, is a farmhouse on the southern edge of the town.

At Egremont I discovered an attractive market town with a typical trumpet-shaped main street, a gradual widening of the thoroughfare originally designed to provide room for stalls and the bustle of market activities. The weathered remnants of a twelfth-century motte castle stood in a park at the lower end of the town where the rivalry of the De Lacey brothers was immortalised in Wordsworth's 'The Horn of Egremont Castle'. The horn, so the legend goes, was suspended outside the main gate and could only be blown by the rightful heir to the estate. During the Holy Wars the two De Lacey brothers, Eustace and Hubert, were involved in conflict against the infidel. At first they fought well together:

> Side by side they fought (the Lucies
> Were a line for valour famed)
> And where'er their strokes alighted
> There the Saracens were tamed.

But Hubert, the typically jealous younger brother, arranged for Eustace to be

Arthur Liggett

killed and then returned home triumphantly claiming castle and lands. Although he was unable to raise a squeak out of the horn, no one seemed much concerned until one night, when Hubert was comfortably ensconced in bed, the horn gave out a mighty blast and sent him scurrying from the castle cursing his luck. His brother Eustace had somehow escaped death and returned to reclaim his rightful property. Poor Hubert wandered around the Lake District for years, fearful of his brother's vengeance, but was eventually pardoned and ended his days in a monastery.

'I know a much better one than that!' An elderly character in thick fisherman's sweater at Ravenglass slurped his pint in the front room of the Ratty Arms and grinned at his captive audience – myself and two hikers. 'You can put that book away,' he told me through frothy lips. 'I'll tell it you proper.' I'd been admiring Robert Orrell and Peter Caldwell's delightfully bouncy history of this old seaport, now drowsing behind dunes at the junction of the Esk, Irt and Mite rivers. 'You'll not know much about the Penningtons . . .' he began, leaning across the beer-splattered table conspiratorially, 'but any

Ravenglass

number of strange tales have come out of that old castle.' He jerked his
thumb in the direction of Muncaster Castle on the edge of Ravenglass. This
grey Gothic pile built round an ancient pele tower has housed the
Pennington family since the thirteenth century and is now open to the
public, complete with animal park and garden centre. Regrettably I had left
my tape recorder in the camper and after ten minutes or so of the old man's
rambling monologue was lost in a maze of tales about family feuds, Lord
Muncaster's efforts to abolish the slave trade, a hired jester whose humorous
antics included the decapitation of the castle carpenter, the smuggling activities of local residents, and the legend of 'The Luck of Muncaster'. The 'luck',
he explained, is a seldom-seen glass bowl ornamented with gold and white
enamel. It was presented to the family by Henry VI in gratitude for hospitality following his defeat at Hexham in 1464 and prior to his capture a few days
later in Lancashire. The King emphasised that as long as the bowl was kept

unbroken, the Penningtons would enjoy good fortune, or, to put it in the language of a plaque in the Muncaster chapel, 'whykkys the famylie shold keep it unbrecken thei shold gretelye thrif'.

Our storyteller downed the remnants of his pint, licked the froth from his lips, and pushed his glass into the middle of the table. One of the hikers offered him a refill which he gladly accepted. I said I'd like to sketch him at which point he whipped out a very worn pipe, stuck it between his teeth and, pointing to a very gnarled growth on the end of his nose, told me, 'don't forget mi wart'.

Arthur Liggett, it turned out, didn't live in Ravenglass although his father had been the fisherman here before the port silted up. But he knew the place well and pointed out a few of the village 'characters', J. A. Pharoah's Boot and Shoe Making shop, the Pennington Arms and the pink dunes across the river which formed the Ravenglass Nature Reserve (The Gullery), a famous

111

centre for 10,000 pairs of black-headed gulls. Unlike the adjoining Eskmeals Reserve, it is closed to the public during key breeding periods.

I was entranced by this diminutive coastal village rising castle-like out of the sand flats pierced by small windows, its back turned to the sea, its walls worn and dour. On the inside, gaily painted cottage-fronts and cobbled courts face each other across a single bowed street, narrowing at each end. Boats, nets and buoys lie scattered around, suggesting that the village has an economic base other than the trade of summer tourists who come to travel up Eskdale on the narrow-gauge La'al Ratty railway. They also buy the freshly ground flour from the nearby Muncaster Mill and visit the massive remnants of the Roman baths, evidence of Ravenglass's importance as a coastal fort. 'Used to call it Clanoventa or something like that,' Arthur told me as we stood gazing at the thick arches. 'Clever lot, those Romans,' he mused, 'they'd got it all here, central heating, hot water, glass, air vents, the lot. More than most places have got today up on't fells.' He nodded towards the lonely farms scattered across the bleak hillsides beyond the village. 'I lived in one of them as a young 'un and it weren't funny.' His wry comments didn't surprise me. I'd recently taken the 'Mountain Goat' minibus on one of its daily trips across the Lake District's two infamous mountain passes, Hard-knott and Wrynose (only recommended for steel-nerved motorists). My purpose had been to visit the impressive remains of the Mediobogdum Roman fort on Hardknott. But I was equally moved by the wildness of much of the landscape and the sight of tiny farmsteads, smoke curling from chimneys at the end of trackless valleys and hollows, where a few families still manage to make a living from hardscrabble acres and a score of sheep scattered over barren fells. 'People forget, y'know, when they come touristin' and treckin' over't hills,' Arthur commented, 'that there's them that really belong here, them that's lived here as long ast' Penningtons, m'be longer. They're as tough as rocks. They've got t'be to put up wi' it.'

The vivid image of those isolated farms contrasted sharply with the decorous Edwardian ambience of Seascale, perched on a trimmed-turf slope above a broad beach, oblivious to the nearby nuclear power station. Even the Furness Railway Company paid homage to the dignity of the place by constructing its 1860 water tower in authentic Scottish-Baronial style, a respect for environment all too obviously lacking in the subsequent ticky-tacky scatterings of tract-developers on the edge of town.

A similar spirit of calm dignity can be found much further to the north at Silloth, a perfectly preserved Victorian resort on the Solway Firth set well back from pine-fringed dunes across wide green parkland. I had travelled along inland lanes to Allonby, an attractive craft and gallery village alongside

112

a sweeping bay, once visited by Charles Dickens and Wilkie Collins on their "Tour of Two Idle Apprentices". Then I followed the flat wind-smoothed coastline north into the heart of this attractive little town. The white terraces of Criffel Street ease themselves out on either side of Silloth's parish church. The road is laid with granite sets and short side streets contain colourful rows of smaller houses, crisp as new bank notes. Nothing is out of place. Even the diminutive amusement arcade at the far side of the putting green possesses quiet composure from a distance, and the cheeky seaside postcards are kept in a hidden rack behind the souvenirs counter. 'It's a family place, y'see,' I was told by a lady of the local chemist shop. 'We don't want to do anything to attract the other elements. It's so nice the way it is.'

I'd been led to believe by Arthur that some kind of summer festivities were always being offered by the town. He wasn't sure but thought they might include exhibitions of Cumberland wrestling and hound trailing, a sort of fox hunt without the fox in which hounds compete in following specially laid aniseed-scent trails, up to ten miles in length. As it turned out, he was mistaken, and I found instead that all Silloth could offer during my visit was a small circus (unavoidably detained elsewhere for at least another week), a disco ('you're too old for that', I was informed by a local shopkeeper) and a couple of reputable pubs that kept strict hours.

So after a breezy ramble on the town beach and golf course I headed inland, and at Abbey Town, discovered the sturdy Holm Cultram Abbey, a twelfth-century Cistercian centre once nine bays long and now substantially reduced in size but still containing rich Norman remains. In common with much of the Solway region, it was subjected to regular raids by the Scots and a major sacking by Robert the Bruce in 1319. Offering hospitality to its defenders, in particular King Edward I and his troops in 1300 and 1307, only exaggerated the abbey's plight by depleting its coffers and necessitating a special order from the Pope granting indulgences to those penitents visiting the abbey who gave generous donations for its repair and upkeep. Even these were later squandered by Abbot Adam of Kendal on lavish entertainments for influential supporters of his pursuit of the Carlisle bishopric. Such antics would normally have rendered the abbey ripe for immediate destruction following the Dissolution, but a petition of parishioners resulted in its retention as a local church and place of refuge.

Travelling eastwards across Wedholme Flow, with the purple hills of Dumfries and Galloway piled against the sky, I found an even more impregnable place of refuge in the thick-walled church at Newton Arlosh, built round a typical borderland pele tower and entered through a midget-size door. From here the landscape stretched out over marshes, over Bowness

Newton Arlosh church

Common and Glasson Moss to the puddled mud flats of the firth. I saw
unusual 'haaf' fishing nets, for trailing the Solway shallows, drying on the
grassy shore.

Bowness-on-Solway is a sleepy wriggle of old farms and cottages on a
slight rise. Nearby the once prosperous community of Port Carlisle remains
with a terrace of cottages and a few wood pilings at the end of an overgrown
canal, once an important eleven-mile link with Carlisle. Behind the houses is
a line of odd turf mounds, the last bumps of Hadrian's Wall running out to
sea. The place is silent. Not far away a sturdy fortified farmhouse keeps
watch over the marshes against raids that will never come – unless the
population of Annan decide to collect their bells from St Michael's at Bowness. The original bells, so the story goes, were once stolen by a Scottish
raiding party from Annan to prevent future alarms being rung. Somehow on
their trek back across the flats they lost them in the mud. So the Bowness
parishioners counter-attacked, stole the Annan bells and hung them at St
Michael's where they remain to this day. Every time a new vicar is installed
here, the Annan Provost formally requests their return. This, in turn, is
politely refused by the English.

'Other than that, things are pretty quiet.' I was chatting with a middle-
aged farmer, watching his cows on the marshy meadows near Burgh-by-
Sands. 'The old dog died a couple of years back.' Long pause. 'Course, she
was going on fifteen years, y'know, so it weren't surprising.' Another long
pause. 'Can't think of much else happening really.' He let out a long contented sigh. 'Never does round here.' We nodded slowly in unison and went
on watching the cows. Rippling wavelets edged up the mud flats. The tide
was coming in.

114.

9. The Wilds of Pendle-Bowland

I was in silver limbo.

Mist smothered the high moor and the sleeves of my anorak were sheened with moisture. The sweet smell of heather hung about me as I groped up the rocky path to the high flat back of Pendle Hill.

'Tha'll happen have a bit of weather.' I should have listened to the warning of the shepherd in Newchurch. The village was a tiny place, a peppering of thick stone cottages along a steep dip in the road below the bulk of Pendle. I almost missed the church, hidden behind hedges. On the west wall of the bell tower was the 'Eye of God', an oval protruding stone with a distinct pupil peering out over the surrounding moors. 'Tha's for witches.' The shepherd's face imploded with wrinkles and he laughed. 'Tha's what they says, anyroad. They says it were a charm agin them witches.' He nodded his

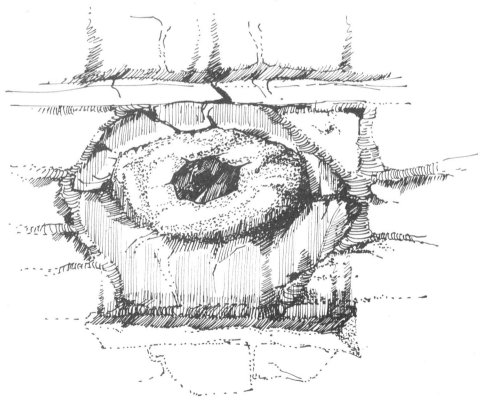

The 'Eye of God' · Newchurch

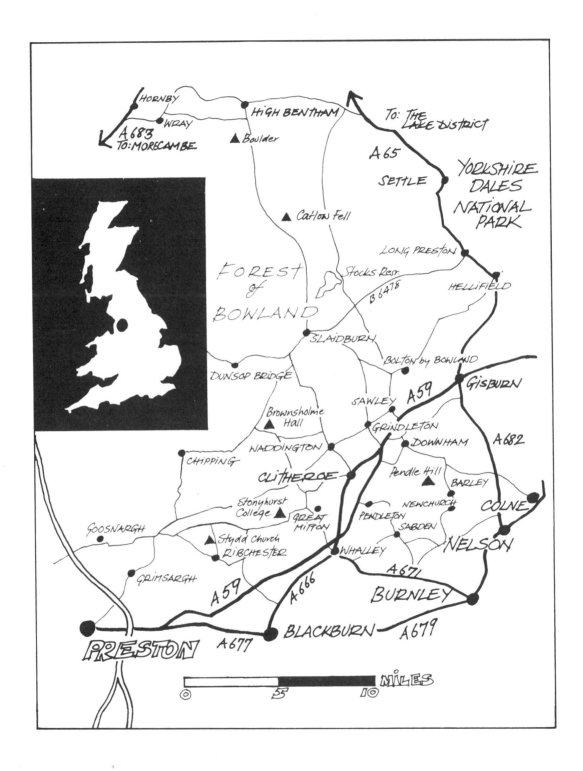

head toward the isolated farms and cottages straggled around the base of the hill as if the infamous Pendle witches were still in residence.

I had heard the tales. For generations Lancashire children trembled in early beds, fearful that their errant mischievousness would bring parental dispatch 'to't Pendle folk' and terrible torment on those misty moors. Today many of the local legends are regarded with disdain, dismissed as the feudings of miscreant families whose hysterical accusations and counter-accusations resulted in their mutual destruction. But that was not the way the superstitious country folk around Pendle interpreted the gory incidents in 1612. Old Chattox ('a very old withered spent and decreped creature'), one of her contemporaries, Mother Demdike ('the rankest hag that ever troubled daylight'), and her wild and 'fearsome ugly' daughter Bessie, had long been regarded with trepidation by the residents of these lonely hills. In March 1612 Mother Demdike's granddaughter Alizon was refused a handful of pins by the pedlar John Law and, being a creature of high passion, hurled a violent curse at the terrified man which instantaneously caused him a stroke. However, he survived the ordeal, 'with his head drawne awrie, his eyes and face deformed, his legges starcke lame', long enough to testify at her trial in Lancaster. His tale and the indictments of a local magistrate, Roger Nowell, led to the imprisonment not only of Alizon Demdike but of eighteen other local witches accused of such scurrilous crimes as communing with imps and the Devil himself (Bessie Demdike was said to possess a third nipple for suckling the Lord of the Underworld), desecrations of graves, at least sixteen murders, and even a plan to destroy Lancaster castle by incantation. Panic gripped the region. One of Nowell's assistants wrote in his journal, 'Is every person a witch in these hills? I have a list in excess of a hundred. Every day I receive more names. Where will these things end?' No one was safe. Alice Nutter, a gentlewoman of fine reputation, whose large house still stands at nearby Roughlee, was somehow assembled with the accused and hanged with eight of the others on 20 August 1612. Mother Demdike escaped by dying of 'natural causes' in her cell.

The executions captured the attention of all Lancastrians. The Clerk of the Court, Thomas Potts, kept meticulous records of the proceedings and published these the following year as *The Wonderful Discoverie of Witches in the County of Lancashire*. Two centuries later the tale was revived in Harrison Ainsworth's book, *The Lancashire Witches*, and became a permanent fixture of Pennine folklore. Ainsworth relied heavily on the seventeenth-century diaries kept by Nicholas Assheton of Downham Manor and made him – and that mysterious, misty mountain – heroes of the piece. Others added to the romanticism. Learned treatises attempted to prove that Pendle was the

Mother Demdike (from an 18 cent. engraving)

setting for Edmund Spenser's *Faerie Queene* (1590). Spencer Hall wrote of the hill as 'more like a living creature stretch'd in sleep, its couch the forest, and its cape the sky'. McKay's *Pendle Hill in History and Literature* (1888) presented an overview of its folkloric importance, and the verses of Henry Houlding created an almost Tolkienesque mythology abounding in mysterious towers, wizards and captured damsels. Robert Neill's *Mist over Pendle* (1951) keeps the legends alive.

'Most of it's rot.' My shepherd-companion was not at all impressed by all the pen-scratching inspired by Pendle. 'It's just a gert bloody hill. My dad wouldn't have none of it. Folk were daft, he said, and he were right. They'd lie brooms across doorways to stop witches gettin' in and throw salt in t' fire when they felt scared. They carved them special witch-posts. And my grandma when she were making her own butter she'd shove a great poker, red hot, into t' cream to burn t' devil out and stop butter being "bynged". I thought it were a bit daft then but I didn't say nowt. She'd clout me.' His face crinkled again. 'She'd have scared all of them witches off, given arf a chance. She were a terror.'

118

But up here in this silver world of moist mists and silence the sceptical shepherd's humour was less reassuring. I remembered Nicholas Assheton's phrase in Ainsworth's book: 'Pendle Forest swarms with witches. They burrow into the hillside like rabbits in a warren.' Before leaving Newchurch I'd browsed through the village shop brimming with witch-lore. A life-size tableau of cauldron-scraping cackling hags was accompanied by a corny taped commentary which no longer seemed quite so corny. 'On wild and stormy nights when the clouds are scurrying across the moon you may hear their fiendish laughter. . . .'

Something grey and huddled moved suddenly in front of me. The mist was thicker now and cloying. I stopped and stood very still. It continued moving and something else, off to my right, began a wraith-like undulating. Then all around me objects I had taken for boulders began rocking violently. My heart was pounding like an overworked piston. A bellowing *baaa*! burst through the greyness. Sheep! I was walking through the middle of a flock. The shepherd would have been amused.

I was lucky. The mist cleared as quickly as it had come and sun filled the hill, the browning bracken and the purple deeps of the heather. Damp stalks gleamed. A curlew whirled against the clouds, hurling its hollow cry at a world invaded by me and my flock of soggy sheep, Roman-noses sniffing warily at the sudden brightness. The wind rattled the sharp-bladed nardus grass and brought the smell of cut hay scooping up the flanks of the hill and across the high summit. I could see the fields below Sabden and Barley bound by a spiderweb of lanes and paths. The chimney-crusted skylines of Nelson and Burnley stretched along the Calder. Invisible from the foothill villages, they seemed over-close from up here. To the north stretched the domed loneliness of Bowland, the empty grey hills of Lee Fell, Calder Fell, Mallowdale Fell and Burn Moor receding into a hazy nothingness. A flash of silver marked Stocks Reservoir and the Hodder Valley near Slaidburn. Scatterings of square woods, the deep green of sitka spruce plantations, seemed out of place in the emptiness.

I walked on to the 'Big End' of Pendle near the gurgling spring where the first Quaker, an impoverished shoemaker, George Fox, refreshed himself in 1652 after his momentous vision of a new faith. As he wrote in his journal, 'We came near a very great and high hill, called Pendle Hill – I was moved of the Lord to go up to the top of it. I saw the sea bordering upon Lancashire; and from the top of this hill the Lord let me see in what places He had a great people to be gathered.' His ideas were greeted with interest in the noncomformist hill-country, but the authorities were distressed and imprisoned him at Lancaster Castle in 1664.

Pendle is the kind of place where one expects to have great thoughts. It was also a place for lighting bonfires either as warning beacons against regular raids from the ancient Viking stronghold on the Isle of Man or as celebrations of coronations and great victories. In a less dramatic context it provided an ideal base for the farmer-sponsored 'flagman' to wave his large black flag during the harvest season at the first sign of inclement weather from the west or noisy little 'chipping duster' storms from the north. Also, according to a farmer-friend, the hill and the loneliness of the surrounding countryside have created a froth of odd customs and eccentricities. Particularly bizarre are the activities of the 'Nick o' Thungs', an all-male club whose activities include annual meetings on the first Sunday of each May in a secluded clough between Barley and Rimington and the regular recitation of such doggerels as: 'Thimbering Thistlethwaite thievishly thought to thrive through thick and thin by throwing his thimbles about, but he was thwarted and thwacked, thumped and thrashed by thirty thousand thistles and thorns for thievishly thinking to thrive through thick and thin by throwing his thimbles about.'

But Pendle possesses more sinister links with a hazy and strange past in the days of the 'old religion'. Its very name, Pen-dle, is said to mean 'Hill of the Idol', reflecting its importance as a centre of pagan worship. The nearby villages of Grindleton and Grimsargh are thought to be named after Fairy Grim, the Devil himself; Goosnargh was a 'place of enchantment and devil sacrifices', the Ribble the sacred river of Baal, and Whalley, gentle Whalley, the centre of Druid worship. Not until St Mungo and other sixth-century saints moved westward from their coastal niches did the town abandon its pagan ways and become 'the Pendle Jerusalem', a base for early Christianity in the region.

It was time to head towards this Whalley. Reluctantly leaving my mountain eyrie for the softer foothills and woods of the Ribble valley, I set off on wriggling roads through Barley and on to Downham, home of the Assheton family. The village nestles with all the mellow charm of a Cotswold community around a grass-bordered stream. Broad sycamores and horse-chestnuts give deep shade along the curving main street. The Assheton house peers over the valley from its vantage-point by the church. The family first arrived here in 1558 and has remained in residence ever since, remodelling its Elizabethan manor in classical mode during the nineteenth century. The pub, appropriately enough, is called the Assheton Arms and twice a year villagers gather here to pay their rents while farmers tuck into a hearty dinner provided by Lord Clitheroe. The church, the old stocks, the greens, the ancient trees, create an atmosphere wholly inconsistent with the popular

Downham

image of smoke-bound Lancastrian cotton towns and Coronation Streets. The same holds true of other delightful villages around the Bowland Moors. Bolton by Bowland slumbers around a large triangular green and cross. The ornate tomb of Sir Ralph Pudsay, who sheltered the unfortunate Henry VI after the battle of Hexham in 1464, rests in the church, just up the hill from the butcher's shop (housed in a very authentic 'Tudor' building dated 1835). The less reputable William Pudsay floundered in financial insolvency during the reign of Elizabeth I and created his own mint using locally mined silver until informers caused him to flee the law and await the Queen's pardon in hiding.

A short distance to the south-west is Waddington, a second refuge of Henry VI in his desperate search for sanctuary which ended with his capture by Yorkists in Clitheroe Wood. Flower-strewn gardens line the stream as it meanders through this tranquil place of stone cottages, almshouses and Old Hall, home of the globe-trotting entrepreneurial Waddington family. The only problem for residents is the angry ghost of Peg O'Nells who haunts the banks of the river Ribble claiming victims every seventh year as retribution for her premature death down a nearby well.

Slaidburn, a few switchback miles to the north, is far too active a place during the summer months to bother about ghosts and the like. Visitors flock here during weekends to enjoy drives over the dramatic Trough of Bowland and backroaders should come out of season or stick to the quieter lanes around Bolton by Bowland and over Catlow Fell to High Bentham. Yet the village possesses great charm with its cobbled courts, tight twisting streets, riverside meadows and the 'Hark to Bounty' Inn where one of the rooms is preserved as an ancient 'forest court'. The church is usually quiet. A sign on the door reads: 'Visitors may photograph any aspect of this ancient church they desire' – a welcome change – and subjects abound, including a pillared Jacobean chancel screen and squire's pew-box, a collection of dog-whips for the farmer's unruly hounds, and a splendid three-decker pulpit with canopy.

'Excuse me.'

I was admiring the fine screen carving and failed to notice a small, elderly lady in a long green coat standing by my side.

'Would you wish a dog?'

She stared at me very intently as I tried to make sense of the question.

'Do you mean do I want a dog?' I asked.

She continued to study me. 'He's only little but he barks too much.'

I made some joking reference to the dog-whips which left her totally unamused. 'Would you wish a dog?' she repeated.

I hardly thought my faithful feline companion Fred would welcome a canine intruder, but was curious and asked her where the creature was. She gave me a puzzled look and pointed over my shoulder to a spot half-way up the nave. 'He's only little but he's harmless.'

I turned and I saw nothing. I thought maybe he'd vanished into one of the pews. The little lady was under no such illusion. 'He always sits there,' she said, quietly, looking at the empty floor.

I mumbled some excuse and moved rather hastily toward the door.

'It's a shame about his ear, isn't it?' she called after me.

When I was half out of the door I heard what sounded like one very shrill bark and stepped back inside. The lady was smiling at the still empty floor. It must have been the door hinges. An odd place, this Pendle country.

Chipping is yet one more hidden Bowland delight, clustered along a narrow road on the edge of the lacework of lanes around Beacon Fell. The church is a jumble of styles and influences, much of it rather mediocre, but the capitals of the north aisle pillars with their grimacing faces, coiled serpents and rich tracery possess all the irreverent vitality of the Romanesque period. Note the one with the four faces in various degrees of inattention and outright boredom during long services. Maybe a more tolerant approach to religious devotions was a characteristic of these outlying communities. Certainly during the long religious feuds of the sixteenth century this secluded part of the country provided a safe haven for Catholics who worshipped in a chapel at nearby Leagram Hall endowed by Richard Sherburne during the reign of James II. The spiritual devotion coupled with the extensive wealth of the Sherburne (Shireburn) family is evidenced by their alabaster and marble memorial chapel at Great Mitton church (designed by Richard himself), and the ambitious Stonyhurst Hall, now a well-known Roman Catholic college.

Regrettably, religious tolerance was not a feature of Henry VIII's reign, and the Dissolution brought a sudden end to the abbeys at Whalley and Sawley. All that remains of the latter is an entrance arch and a few scattered pillar-stumps, but the former was a major thirteenth-century Cistercian centre situated on meadows by a broad bend in the Calder river. Woodlands still frame the remnants of gateways and chapter house from which John Paslew, the last abbot, was dragged off to execution at Lancaster castle in 1537 for his participation in the Pilgrimage of Grace. A short distance away, ancient stone crosses in the churchyard covered in Saxon carvings are reminders of the importance of this site in the very earliest days of Christianity. The church itself is a treasure-house of arcaded pews, fourteenth-century screens, a priest's door and sanctuary knocker, and one of the finest collections of choir stalls with misericord carvings in the north of England. What confidence and humour these early wood-carvers possessed! Examining the intricacy of these tiny masterpieces one can almost hear their guffaws and chortles as the husband-bashing wife armed with a frying pan emerged from the hard oak, and the furies of St George's battle with the dragon were captured in a few artful chisel strokes – possibly even a reverent silence as the 'Face of God' misericord emerged, benign and timeless with thick curling beard and the slightest of smiles.

Unlike many later churches, overbearing and humourless in their religiosity, this place possesses a warmth and humanity essentially rural in character. The villagers enjoyed life and had little time for humbug. When the witch-hunting magistrate Roger Nowell had himself an enormous ornate pew delivered to the church for his own use, reflecting his new-found status in the county, the parishioners refused to admit it and stowed it in a nearby barn for seventy years while they 'deliberated' the matter. They recognised intuitively the fleeting nature of life and all its overblown successes. They knew that outside stood those Saxon crosses more than a thousand years old. They knew too that the north porch contained worked stones of Roman origin brought from nearby Ribchester, the ancient fort of Bremetonacum. Little wonder they gave short shrift to Mr Nowell's grandiose ideas.

Originally built at the junction of two Roman roads during the governorship of Agricola in the first century AD, much of Ribchester's six-acre site has been washed away by course-changes in the river Ribble. The remainder, with the exception of the granaries and the old baths, lies deep under the church and surrounding cottages. A pleasantly cramped museum down the lane from the church contains an array of urn fragments, jewellery, lamps, coins, inscribed stones, a fearsome bevy of primitive carved heads and a replica of Ribchester's most notable discovery, a complete Roman ceremonial helmet discovered by a local youth in 1796. Heavily ornamented with fighting soldiers, the helmet possesses a life-like face-mask and even space for the wearer's curling sideburns.

I strolled over to the bath-house site immediately above the steep river banks to the north of the museum. Young volunteer diggers were toothbrushing their way through muddy patches of rubble in trenches. One young man was working at the low end of the site once used as a Victorian rubbish dump. 'I'm sick of willow-pattern,' he grumbled. So far he'd found nothing recognisably Roman, but was recording every shard meticulously on a scaled plan of the dig. 'Problem is, this place has been gone over so often in the past, there's nothing left.' I reminded him of the helmet-discovery and the dredging up of Roman Doric pillars from the river and their subsequent

Roman Ceremonial Helmet. Ribchester

use as supports for the portico at Ribchester's White Bull pub. 'That was two hundred years ago!' he retorted. 'I'm not that patient.'

About a mile outside the town, on my way to the Bowland Moors, I came across a small, barn-like building complete with Norman doorway and tiny windows – the twelfth-century church of St Saviour's at Stydd, last remnant of a small estate owned by the Knights Hospitallers of St John of Jerusalem. Most of the other buildings in the complex – dormitory, refectory and cloisters – were pulled down centuries ago to clear the land for cultivation. But this miniature church remains with its plain octagonal pulpit and suspended sounding board, and a spirit of austere sincerity which characterised the early crusaders.

I could see the fells looming up ahead but detoured briefly to visit Stonyhurst, the famous Roman Catholic college that emerged bedecked with cupolas, domes and ceremonial entranceways from the rather more modest Elizabethan home of Sir Richard Sherburne. The extensive façade, reflected in two ponds, is balanced by the delicate St Peter's Church, styled after King's College Chapel in Cambridge. Under the beams of the great hall stands the massive oak table on which Cromwell slept heartily before the

Moorland Farm near Slaidburn

battle of Preston. The school museum and library contains a wealth of treasures, including the Book of Hours of Mary Queen of Scots, an embroidered cap of Sir James Moore, a cape of Henry VIII, and the priceless seventh-century copy of St John's Gospel from St Cuthbert's coffin, the oldest English bound book known to exist.

A smaller but equally impressive structure is the nearby Parker family home, Brownsholme Hall, with its ornate columned entrance and a rather erratic series of open days to the public. The Parkers, appropriately enough, were royal park keepers and seem to have amassed a considerable fortune evidenced by the casual expenditure of £104,000 by Thomas Parker in the early seventeenth century on landscaping his extensive grounds prior to a visit by Royalty.

Then comes the moor again – the broad unwalled spaces of Bowland – a scorched scalp of olives, browns and purples. Heavy rains had burst open hillsides and 'water brast' erosion streaked the slopes with peaty earth. I avoided the often-busy Trough, taking instead the old high road, gated until recently, up on to the wind-blasted heights of Catlow Fell. I left the camper and meandered off along sheep paths. The sun was bright, no mists this time. An ocean of heather stretched in all directions. Less than half an hour away were the thick black cities of the Lancashire plain and Blackpool with her gory glories not far beyond. Yet here was a buzzing white silence, bouncy paths, and a sense of infinity rarely found in the little frantic worlds beyond the hills. A thin stream slipped by through the dark earth, chuckling in the shadows. Further down the streams merged and rolled down the dales, Roeburndale, Hindburndale, and Littledale, to the meandering Lune. Scratches of Roman tracks still remain up here. Ancient stones mark the high points, hardly distinguishable in the wave-like undulations of the moor. And the silence seems to go on for ever.

Of course, it's all illusion. The moor has edges, immediately visible as I rolled over the crest and made the long descent down Tatham Fells. Close to the road a huge glacier-stranded boulder rests by itself in the heather. Below, the faintest of evening mists, burnished by a sinking sun, hung over High Bentham. I lost myself once again along serpentine lanes, sometimes across the moor, sometimes bounded by high hedges, and emerged wrist-weary in Wray, one of Jessica Lofthouse's favourite villages. The descriptions in her book, *Lancashire's Fair Face*, of the native crafts still practised in the community less than four decades ago – oak swill and basket making, rabbit snares, clog block-making, nail-making, bobbin-making, wheelwrighting – are a sad indictment of all too rapid change.

Hornby is a second uncharacteristically beautiful village in this part of

oulder · High Bentham

Lancashire whose prominent sixteenth-century castle shares fame with those of Lancaster and Clitheroe and whose founder, Sir Edward Stanley, gained immortality in Scott's *Marmion*. The tales of Scottish wars and the Royalist conflicts in which the castle and its owners played prominent parts would fill a fair-sized book. After those moorland pauses, however, I was merely content to enjoy the ivy-walled mellowness of this delightful place from a grassy knoll by the Wenning, and wait for the pub to open.

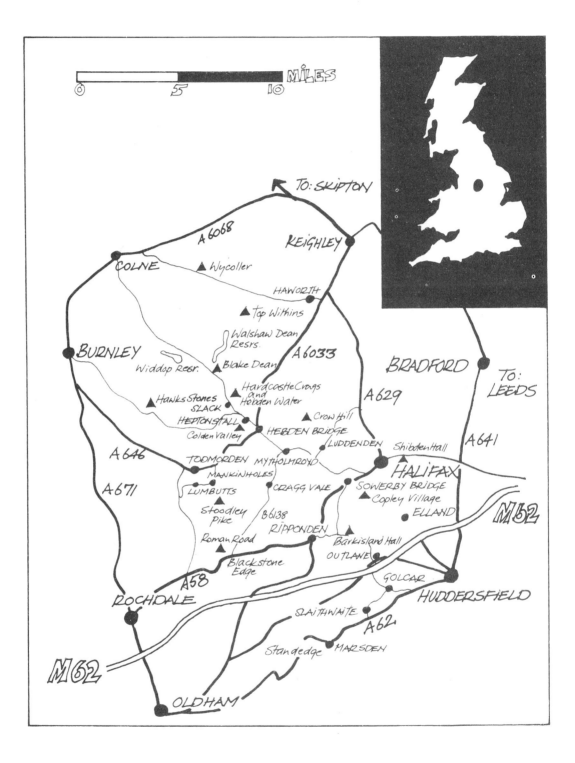

10. The Pennine Mill Towns

Once again I was high on the Pennine moors, this time around the fringe of Brontë country, above the deep valley-clefts of the Calder and the Colne, the Ryburn and the Worth. On the cresting summit the dark heathered curves lay still under a brooding sky, an ancient land, the last somnolent stumps of a great mountain range thrown up by the stirrings of the earth hundreds of millions of years ago. There are no trees and few walls, just the constant rushing of wind across the cotton grass and the occasional cry of a curlew – an abrupt sound, a hollow resonance full of the loneliness of the moors. The poet Ted Hughes understands this region and in his 'Remains of Elmet' describes:

> Where the millstone of sky
> Grinds light and shadow so purple-fine
> And has ground it so long
> Grinding the skin off the earth
> Earth bleeds her raw true darkness
> A land naked now as a wound
> That the sun swabs and dabs . . .

From Blackstone Edge along the Pennine ridge, deep gulleys carry streams down peat hillsides. As the streams descend they merge and cut large swathes out of the earth and, further down, form steep valleys dotted with groups of trees. The first farmhouses appear, low brown chains of buildings held in the earth by the weight of their almost windowless walls. Further down, where the rolling sweep of the hills is broken into fields and lanes, buildings cluster in hollows or, like Italian mountain villages, cling to the sides of steep bluffs around the stubby spikes of parish churches.

There was a break in the clouds overhead and the sun lit the hilltop community of Golcar. Dark stone terraces were bronzed and the washing on scores of clothes-lines fluttered and flickered brilliantly. Then the clouds closed and the village melded again with its hillside.

Long terraces of stone cottages are packed together tightly. The moorlands stretch all around, open and endless, yet the little town huddles itself like a nervous snail in its shell, on the edge of a steep drop into the valley. This seems to be a characteristic of communities in these Pennine foothills, reflecting their origins during the early days of the Industrial Revolution when this sheep country, blessed with clean, bouncing streams, became the birthplace of Britain's vast textile empire. For centuries farmers on the high terraces

131

Golcar

above the valleys produced crude forms of cloth in their isolated homes. The clusterings of hamlets led to a more concentrated form of cottage industry, and tortuous packhorse trails linked these tiny outposts of activity to regional markets, particularly Halifax. Then, in less than fifty years (1790–1840), inventions of spinning and weaving machinery, the introduction of water and steam-power, and the construction of canals, turnpikes and railways, transformed these tranquil valleys into a prime industrial nucleus.

Golcar's museum in a row of hand-loom weavers' cottages below the church presents a picture of life in the early days of home-based industry along with displays of clog-making, a major local activity in the late nineteenth century. Houses were built as close as possible to the mills and, because of the invariable shortage of flat sites, all the other community buildings – the church, the hall, the post office, the pubs, the shops – joined in the scramble for land. The result was a density that would astound the staunchest advocate of compact development – a tightness of form that

provides ample subjects for sketches, and a powerful contrast to the bound-less spaces beyond.

Moorland walkers often experience a sense of unease on the desolate plateaus. Even on a bright summer day when the cotton grass is in full bloom, the hills never take on that brilliant green quality of lowland pastures but retain a brown tinge as if still numbed from winter. I remember one alarming experience when I was hiking on a section of the Pennine Way near Standedge. One moment a watery sun was shining through low clouds, then, without warning, I was enveloped in a cold shroud of fog. Visibility was immediately reduced to a few yards. The path became indistinct, at times disappearing altogether. Underfoot became progressively softer; the peat squelched and gurgled as I felt ahead with my stick. Occasionally the fog would lift a little to reveal an eerie landscape of 'moor hags', strange mounds of peat, shaped by streams and wind to resemble crouched figures or strange crawling creatures that seemed to writhe and struggle in the half-light. Rather than let my imagination play with these shapes, creating dragons and ogres, gnarled witches and groping hunchbacks, I should have taken their warning and retraced my steps. As it was I forgot that moor hags mark Pennine bogs and marshes and, in turning to avoid a particularly menacing creature, found myself knee-deep in a cloying mire. Faint memories of boy scout training came in handy. I remembered not to struggle and eventually, through a process of careful tugging on clumps of marsh grass, managed to extract myself, almost losing my boots in the process.

Looking back at my antics on the moors, I realise I did everything wrong. I forgot my compass, I kept walking in fog after losing the trail, and I failed to look for danger signs. Nevertheless I eventually found my way out, unlike the many less fortunate individuals who, according to local tales, were lost for ever in these treacherous bogs. Tales also tell of horses and even complete packhorse trains engulfed in these upland swamps. Before the valley lands were cleared of forest the old packhorse trails followed the higher open ground linking farms and hamlets on the valley 'shoulders'. According to *The Journal of a Travelling Gentleman* (1798),

> The low places were feared by the sparse population as places of evil . . . They were deeply forested and dark, full of tales and legends. Creatures, the like of which would never be found even on the plains of Africa were said to lurk in the shadows, and hogies of all shapes and sizes made the river marshes their home. When the packhorse trails crossed the valley bottoms they did so with alacrity, plunging down from the open terraces without twist or turn, leaping the river in a single bound and scurrying up the other side.

Whereas most packhorse routes were rough affairs, rarely surfaced except on the long, steep drops into the valleys (the Buttress at Hebden Bridge is a fine example), the Romans thought nothing of building their neat, stone-paved causeway over the Pennines to Manchester in 125 AD. A segment at Blackstone Edge – if it really is Roman – is one of the best-preserved in Britain.

These roads were remarkably durable and used principles of engineering that were largely discarded until the emergence of such eighteenth-century road-builders as John Metcalf, better known as 'Blind Jack of Knaresborough'. This man's ability not only to find his way around without sight but to determine the best routes for major turnpikes, puts my flailing antics in the fog to shame. In 1759 he was awarded the contract to construct a section of the Wakefield to Manchester road across the notorious Standedge Marshes. Ignoring all local advice and proposed routes, Metcalf set off with his great cane, traced his own line out across the bogs and developed an ingenious system of road building on wet land using compressed bundles of

134

Barkisland Hall

heather beneath a stone and gravel surface. Not known for his modesty, he recorded this achievement in his diary: 'It was so particularly fine that any person might have gone over it in winter unshod, without being wet. This piece of road needed no repairs for 12 years afterwards.' Today the graceful curves of the M62 carry long-distance traffic over the bleak Pennine ridges in minutes, reducing their awesome stature to a few glimpses of scraggy heather heights and vistas of cities from the last scarps.

Hidden-corner explorers should avoid the main highways and slip away down the side roads, particularly those that run north and south like switch-backs between the valleys. There's a memorable route northwards from Golcar, just skirting Outlane, that plunges up and down through tiny villages unmarked on most maps. Some parts are so steep that cobbles have been specially set to give a better grip for wheeled vehicles. Be ready to stop at a moment's notice to peer over drystone walls at old manors and ornate 'clothier's' mansions (Barkisland Hall is one of the most notable examples) or pause at moorland pubs and listen to the endless anecdotes of the older regulars. It's one of the best ways to enjoy and appreciate the true flavour of these hills.

135

Other scenic side-road drives include the high road through Heptonstall and alongside the crags at Hawks Stones to Burnley, the narrow road via Blake Dean and the Widdop Reservoir to Colne, and the wind-blasted drive from Haworth to Hebden Bridge via the A6033.

An even better way of exploring the central Pennines is to use leg-transport and lose yourself on the serpentine paths and trails throughout this upland region. With the exception of the Yorkshire Dales and parts of the Peak, there are few areas of walking country in the north to match these moors and valleys. The Pennine Information Centre at Hebden Bridge has enough recommended walks to keep the average hiker active for a year. One of the best-loved (and a little over-crowded on summer weekends) is the stroll along Hebden Water, past the cluster of cottages and tiny tea-room at Midge Hole, into the wooded glen below Hardcastle Crags. The path continues alongside a bounding, pooling stream to Gibson Mill and the remnants of pillars at Blake Dean. These once supported the towering trestle bridge carrying the construction railway and workers from the old shanty town of 'Dawson City' to the emerging moorland reservoirs. Further back, stepping stones at Fowl Hill carry the path up the steep south side of the glen on to the tops again around Slack and across the broken cliffs of Eaves Wood to Heptonstall, nucleus of these ancient moorland trails. Standing on the edge here one peers into the quiet seclusion of the Colden Valley, once home of nine mills.

Lower down, the old towpath alongside the Calder canal leads past barge pools, worn locks and leaning canal cottages on into Todmorden. A loop walk back to Hebden Bridge can be made following the path round the church, up past Far Longfield farm, and the Water Wheel Tower at Lumbutts, through the high hamlet of Mankinholes with its unique packhorse drinking trough and then down the long slope to Burnt Acres Wood and the Calder Valley. Parallel to the path but on higher ground is the Pennine Way itself, swooping round the stone finger of Stoodley Pike and across the Calder, northwards past the string of Walshaw reservoirs, past Top Withins (the alleged setting for *Wuthering Heights*) and on over Ickornshaw Moor, wriggling toward the Yorkshire Dales. A four-mile detour west from Haworth Moor leads to the half-deserted village of Wycoller with its bridge-laced stream (the 'clam bridge' is thought to be of Iron Age origin). Mrs Gaskell and Charlotte Brontë both used this compact cotton-weaving community as a setting in their novels, and the creation of a Country Park here has ensured its preservation.

The current penchant for long-distance footpaths has resulted in the recently-created 'Calderdale Way', a fifty-mile loop from Brighouse to

Packhorse Trough · Mankinholes

Todmorden and back, passing through every variant of the Pennine scene and providing an overview of the region's history and form. Less dramatic but equally informative is the circular Colne Valley walk between Golcar and Marsden passing the colossal Titanic Mills, the deserted hamlet of Nathan's, and the nestled mellowness of Marsden churchyard with its ancient stocks and packhorse bridge.

One of my own favourite walks climbs up the edges of woods on the east side of Hebden Bridge to the pub above High Royd farm, over the heathery bleaks of Crow Hill and the ancient way-stone of Churn Milk Joan, and down past deserted farms and moorside mills into the tight cleft of Luddenden Brook. Luddenden village, packed around the church and the seventeenth-century Lord Nelson Inn, is another upland weaving hamlet laced with narrow alleys. Half a mile south toward the Calder Valley is one of those sturdy Pennine manors, now converted into an inn and locale for 'medieval banquets'.

Heptonstall, situated high above the valley-bound community of Hebden Bridge, is one of the most unusual settlements in the Pennine foothills. Walk up the steep cobbled streets past the stone terraces of old mill cottages. From here the whole history of this compact region can be appreciated at a glance. On the high fells are the old farms, many now abandoned. Lower down, clusters of stone buildings with façades punctuated by long rows of mullioned

Luddenden

windows were once the weavers' cottages – home of the Yorkshire woollen industry. At first the cottages were mere refurbished barns located by the clean Pennine streams, but as the industry began to flourish, groups of specially designed cottages were built lower down the hillside. Ted Hughes once again captures the dense-dour flavour of the place:

> Black village of gravestones.
> A hill's collapsed skull
> Whose dreams die back
> Where they were born.

There are two parish churches here. The first, built between 1256 and 1260 and dedicated to St Thomas à Becket, is now a dramatic remnant set in a cemetery of ponderous millstone grit headstones said to contain the remains of 100,000 bodies. John Wesley was not impressed by the ruins on a visit here in 1772 and described them as 'the ugliest I know'. The 'new' church located only a few yards away was built in the mid 1800s and possesses a recently modernised interior.

Not far away, under the entry arch to the cemetery, across the Weavers Square and along Towngate, is a third church, an austere Methodist chapel. Take a look at the visitors book filled with names from all over the world. This is no ordinary chapel. Not only is it octagonal in design, but also the oldest existing Methodist church continually in use since inauguration (in 1764).

From a distance this tight hilltop village resembles a sturdy fortress and indeed was used as such during the Civil War when Col. Robert Brayshaw garrisoned 800 of his Roundheads here in 1643. He beat back an attack by the Cavalier General Mackworth and 2,000 men before leading a judicious retreat into the Pennine mists, leaving the unfortunate community to the pillaging of a much-reinforced Cavalier army that attacked again a few weeks later.

From Heptonstall the old packhorse lane, the 'Buttress', drops abruptly down into Hebden Bridge across the narrow stone bridge and into the main square. It was here that the third stage of the weaving industry began with the construction of factories during the early nineteenth century. Except for the brief but bloody era of the Luddite revolts, industry in the Pennine valleys flourished. Factories were crammed into every square inch of flat land, streams were diverted, dammed, culverted and bridged; their clear cold water, fresh from the high millstone ridges, was used and re-used in a score of complex cleansing processes.

The stone factories with their tall chimneys often occupied so much of the

Calder Valley near Mytholmroyd

valley floor that little space remained for the workers' cottages, so they were sent scurrying up the steep valley sides at amazing gradients. There's one particular terrace where the 'front side', facing the street, has two storeys and the 'backside' six! If you have difficulty finding this remarkable piece of Pennine architecture, ask any of the local residents.

In the last few years this once-dying village has experienced a cultural renaissance which, while not restoring the mill-economy, has certainly made long-time residents and enthusiastic newcomers far more conscious of valley-heritage. Old, age-stained recipes for Dock Pudding, Trunnel Pie and Havercakes have been dragged out of the drawers, brass bands have been revived, the medieval Pace Egg Play of Good (St George) versus Bad (the Black Prince of Paradine) brings in the Easter crowds. Unusual valley games – Billets and Spur and Knell – are attracting more and more participants, witch-posts have been spotted on old cottages, and the sound of clogs echoes once again on the steep slope of the Buttress.

Ernie Clough of Marsden thinks all the recent attention and activity is a bit odd. 'We've been livin' like this for generations. There's nowt new wi'

pigeon-rearin' and clogs and that. I bin wearin' them for seventy years. Just because some young 'uns 'ave discovered 'em everyone's making a fuss. S'bloody daft.'

One very retired clog-maker I met in a Sowerby Bridge pub was equally sceptical. 'I were a clog maker for thirty years 'till they started bringing in the machines for doin' it. I had my own shop in Mytholmroyd. I've still got my stock knife and hollower for shaping the block. I used alder – they lasted for ever out of alder. Today they use beech and any old stuff. If you get three years use out of them you think yourself lucky. I did everything myself – the shaping, the ironing [shaping the iron sole] the clicking [cutting the leather uppers] and the lasting. Nowadays the craft's gone out of it. There's a few trying to bring it back but the trouble is that people've forgotten what good clogs are really like. I often wonder if I shouldn't start up again and show em!'

Canal lovers will find much of interest in Hebden Bridge. The Calder Canal passes through the town and there's a scenic towpath walk that enthusiasts can take as far as Brighouse or beyond. The path itself is in good condition although somewhat slippery in the short tunnels, and in Sowerby Bridge has been made into an attractive central feature of the town – a highlight of the walk eastwards.

On one of my strolls I chatted with a resident of a canal-side cottage near Mytholmroyd, a middle-aged ruddy-cheeked Yorkshire wit.

'Tha'll not get through, tha' knowas,' he shouted from his doorway.

I asked him why not.

'Was it thee singin' back aways?'

Now I do in fact have a habit of venting my vocal cords a little when walking. I find marching tunes particularly conducive to the maintenance of a steady pace. However, I am usually at my best without an audience and thus save some of my most rousing selections until I'm deep in the country, with only cows and sheep as companions. On this particular occasion I'd been unaware of the cottage and immersed in a rendition of a particularly boisterous Sousa piece when interrupted by the man's enquiry.

'Tunnel's collapsin'. Wi' a voice like that tha'll likely bring t' bloody roof in!'

After more non-too-subtle repartee we adjourned to his tiny house and sat chatting for an hour or more over glasses of beer. He told me that his father was a 'legger' in the three-mile-long Standedge canal tunnel at Marsden that linked Yorkshire with Lancashire, deep under the highest part of the Pennines. 'They built it small and the only way for t' barges to get through were for somebody to lie on his back and walk on t' roof. That's what he did. For twenty years all told. Tunnel were nearly three miles long and on a good day he'd make three trips each way. For a bet he once did it five times an' nearly killed himself.'

He told me many similar stories of the old days and I left awed by the men who built and worked the Pennine Canals – so awed, in fact, that I forgot to sing as I walked through the tunnel and the roof stayed up.

While Heptonstall and Hebden Bridge both have a unique appeal, try to visit as many of these old Pennine towns as possible. Haworth, of course, is perhaps the best known and still possesses a strikingly sombre beauty, even though its steep main street has now become a line of twee shops selling the typical range of tourist goods from overpriced Shetland shawls to 'Souvenir of the Brontë Country' ashtrays (from Hong Kong). At least the Black Bull is still here, Branwell Brontë's favourite watering hole, and for all the hurly-burly of the visitor trade is a remarkably pleasant place for a morning pint before the crowds arrive. However, with the exception of the charming thirteenth-century Bridge Inn at Ripponden (near the Pennine Farm Museum), the best pubs tend to be those higher up on the moors like the

the Bridge Inn · Ripponden

nearby Blue Ball and Beehive, the Scape at Scapegoat Hill above Golcar, the Pack Horse Inn on the High Colne Road, the (lower) George near Slaithwaite, the Sportsman's above Todmorden, and the Hinchcliffe Arms just outside Cragg Vale village.

The latter is a small but attractive hillside community, once headquarters of the counterfeit-coiners in this part of Yorkshire. 'King David' Hartley and his gang were particularly notorious during the 1770s for clipping the edges of golden guineas and re-striking them as Portuguese pieces. Although he was eventually executed at York for high treason (and buried at Heptonstall) the illegal tradition was carried on by others in the Cragg Vale/Mytholmroyd area and at one point the activity was so widespread that regular coiners' feasts were held, much to the embarrassment of local officials.

The valley roads converge on Halifax, the most visually dramatic of all West Yorkshire cities, clustered in a rocky, cliff-edged bowl, with the black grime from long-dead mills still stuck in the pores of its sand-blasted towers. Daniel Defoe was one of the first to discover the place in his early eighteenth-century *Tour through the Whole Island of Great Britain* when most of the 50,000 parishioners were employed in the domestic manufacture of 'kersey' and 'shalloon'. 'I thought it was one of the most agreeable sights I ever saw,' he comments. Then came the Industrial Revolution, brought by the canals and the easy transport of coal from the coalfields of the Yorkshire plains. Cottage industry was abandoned in favour of mills – those enormous overpowering edifices, 'swollen platitudes of stone', towering above tight terraces and pumping out their thick black grime. Opinions of the city changed rapidly to such remarks as 'From Hell, Hull and Halifax, may the good Lord deliver us'. This was known as 'The Beggar's Litany' and expressed the fear of vagrants over the city's strict theft laws whereby anyone stealing cloth valued at more than $13\frac{1}{2}$d was punishable by beheading at the Gibbet. This gruesome implement was last used in 1650 and a replica stands today on Gibbet Street, above the town centre. Then all that too passed. Today we find a city in the process of rediscovering itself. The Victorian town hall now rises golden-glowing like a Malayan temple. Even such structures as the castle-like Dean Clough Mill, epitome of the 'dark satanic mills', has retired with grace, like a monster transformed with a kiss into a (somewhat aged) princess. On the outskirts the fifteenth-century Shibden Hall sits in rolling parkland, a valuable repository of Pennine crafts and industry.

Most notable of all, though, is the rebirth of the famous Piece Hall, once one of Europe's most renowned Cloth Markets. Opened with great ceremony in January 1779, the market consists of a series of balustraded galleries surrounding a large central courtyard. More than 300 salerooms

144

The Halifax Gibbet

provided barter space for buyers from as far afield as London and Belgium. What a turbulent scene this must have presented on market days! The Cloth Halls of Leeds, Bradford and Huddersfield were minuscule by comparison. Today it is a little more serene, full of tiny craft shops and known for its Saturday market which brings visitors from all over western Yorkshire.

Equally renowned is the town's Wainhouse Tower built in the 1870s. Although it was originally conceived as a dyeworks chimney, John Edward Wainhouse converted it into an elaborate tower complete with a 403-step staircase and viewing platform. It is said that he did this to spite his neighbour, Sir Henry Edwards, who built a high wall round his property to restrain the prying eyes of the *nouveau riche* Wainhouse family. The tower, of course, provided Wainhouse not only with a bird's-eye view of all Edwards's land, but with magnificent panoramas of Upper Calderdale. Visitors who make it to the top will notice, just past the valley viaduct, rows of terraced houses around an old mill known as Copley Village, the first of the 'mini-

The Buttress - Hebden Bridge

utopias' constructed by Yorkshire's philanthropic industrialists for their workers. This community was developed by Colonel Akroyd, one of England's wealthiest mill-owners, during the mid-nineteenth century.

Other moorland roads descend into Todmorden, Elland, Sowerby Bridge, and the sedate community of Keighley in the Aire Valley. Although these towns lack some of the intimate charm of the smaller Pennine villages, each has its own distinct flavour, and Todmorden in particular contains numerous fine examples of Victorian civic architecture, strong and sombre stone structures reflecting the one-time prosperity and importance of these upland communities. There's also Todmorden Hall, by far the oldest building in the town and home of the Radcliffe family since 1603.

But always, when wandering the narrow streets of these communities, climbing their steep steps between tight terraces or admiring the work of skilled stonemasons, so evident on the town halls and churches – always there's the moor, the sweeping flanks leading upward to the great, empty, Pennine Plateau, those wastes, browned by sun and storm, ravaged by gales, torn by tumbling streams. It's a part of England that should be explored, but explored with respect and care. There's a power in these hills and these villages that is truly Yorkshire.

146

11. The North Midlands 'Lung'

Surrounded by cities and capped by the Peak District National Park is a tranquil region, a 'natural lung' of rolling meadows, woods and stately homes all within easy reach of more than three million people. While tourists flock along Dove Dale footpaths and crowd the souvenir shops at Matlock and Buxton, only the more discerning travellers wander the deep hedge-rowed lanes south of Ashbourne, descend the dark stairs to the Saxon crypt at Repton, or wander the empty heaths and forest tracks of Cannock Chase. So – here's another hidden corner that could accommodate a few more explorers with no detriment whatsoever and maybe even help reduce some of the pressure on the Peak Park.

I began my ramblings at the timber-framed Old Gingerbread Shop in Ashbourne with a plateful of homemade gingerbread and a pot of tea. This famous product (supplied to Fortnum and Mason in London) was reputedly gleaned from the recipe of a French prisoner held in the town during the Napoleonic Wars. The smell of baking bread and biscuits filled the tiny restaurant next to the sales counter and customers avidly devoured their mid-morning snacks. Outside, the Thursday market crackled along with the cries of the cut-price man and the crush of shoppers among the stalls sloping down to St John's Street. Pink and blue chintz-patterned porcelain plates, seconds from the nearby Stafford potteries, rose in precarious columns next to mounds of cheeses and home-cured purple-fleshed ham. Farm machines, spiky and bright, lined the edge of Union Street, and pork pies filled the windows of butchers' shops along 'The Butchery'. Pubs abounded, most notably the Green Man and Black's Head with its sign suspended from a 'gallows' over St John's Street. James Boswell was enamoured of this civic hostelry in 1777 and particularly touched when the landlady, 'a mighty civil gentlewoman, curtseying very low, presented me with an engraving of the sign of her house'. The sign itself is topped by a carving of a 'blackmoor's head' scowling on one side and beaming with delight on the other, possibly an early 'before and after' advertisement for the delights within.

Once there were even more pubs than today, but round the corner is a gothicised monument to a local millionaire iron-founder, Francis Wright, whose prime aim in life, other than making his next million, seemed to be the eradication of local drinking houses and the abolition of Ashbourne's annual fairs owing to 'their licentious and unseemly influence on the populace of the town'.

Philanthropy abounded here. The Victorian town hall was erected by local

tradesmen in 1861 as a gift to the community, and Church Street, one of Derbyshire's most distinguished thoroughfares, is lined with locally-funded almshouses. On the north side of the street stands the Elizabethan grammar school founded by Queen Elizabeth I in 1585 in response to a petition by the local Cokayne family. Nearby, in a stately line of Georgian and Regency mansions is the house where Dr Samuel Johnson often stayed with his colleague, the Rev. Dr John Taylor, the resident 'squarson' (combined squire and parson). Devotees of Dr Johnson will appreciate the memorial to him at nearby Uttoxeter showing him in an uncharacteristically penitent pose!

Then the tight street opens out and St Oswald's Church, 'the cathedral of the Peak', rises high over a spacious churchyard. This is 'the finest single spire in England', according to George Eliot. Gargoyles peer down from the pink stone tower and similar Romanesque touches continue inside around the pillar capitals. Slumbering on enormous stone and marble tombs are prominent members of the Boothby and Cokayne families, decked out in their finest medieval attire and surrounded by colourful heraldic crests. The most moving work, however, is the simple Penelope Boothby memorial in sparkling white Carrara marble showing the tiny child who died at five years of age, hands curled on her pillow, sleeping on a quilted mattress.

The silence of the chancel softly lit by twelve finely-proportioned lancet windows contrasts sharply with the raucous frenzy of Ashbourne's Shrove Tuesday festival which begins here and becomes a two-day football match between the Up'ards and the Down'ards (residents on opposite sides of the river) in which everyone is expected to join. The aim is to score goals at the mill wheels of Clifton and Sturston, two villages three miles apart, but most of the time the activity is concentrated around the town streets and the river Henmore. Some claim the custom originated as a contest between Ashbourne and the rival community of Compton, then a noisy Irish-flavoured factory village of clockmakers, iron foundries and corset-stay works. Today Compton is little more than a quiet suburb of the town and the real rivalry now exists between local publicans, competing for the lucrative trade of enthusiastic visitors.

Similar annual attention is focused on the nearby Peak village of Tissington where one of the most elaborate of Derbyshire's 'well dressing' ceremonies is held every Ascension Day. There's a scenic walk here from Ashbourne along the old railway line, now a grassy path. The origins of the celebrations are obscure. Some claim they stem from pagan worship of water-nymphs who required annual tributes of flowers to ensure abundant supplies of water. In a region of carboniferous limestone, the regularity of water supply was at best tenuous and on occasion disastrous. The Manifold

The Tissington Well

river, for example, a tributary of the Dove, often vanishes entirely for much of the year and flows through an underground channel, leaving the river bed parched and pebble-dry. So it's hardly surprising that villagers felt the need to ritualise their fears and placate ill-fortune. They were particularly grateful during the Black Death of 1348 when the population of the country was decimated and not one casualty was recorded here. Wily locals did a lucrative trade distributing Tissington well-water to residents of less fortunate areas.

150

Today the celebrations are renowned for their richly decorated floral pictures created from hundreds of tiny natural objects – flower petals, feathers, alder-cones, lichens, pebbles, moss, crystalline rock and wild fruits – all packed into moist clay. Five wells are 'dressed' and the long procession led by the clergy and choir moves from one to the other, blessing the water and leaving behind a different 'picture' at each well. The scene is straight from a calendar of Olde England with cosy stone houses grouped round a triangular green, the Jacobean hall of the FitzHerberts peering over hedges and a Norman church shrouded by trees. Although every year the number of visitors increases one can still sense the authenticity of the celebrations. Similar ceremonies are held on the village saint's day at Barlow and Eyam, Youlgreave, Stoney Middleton and Tideswell, but they are less elaborate than those at Tissington.

The remnants of another pagan ritual can also be found at Abbots Bromley, a long, winding village with a market-place of mellowed brick buildings around a fine buttercross and an atmosphere of untrammelled traditions. The dance or 'running' is held on the Monday after the first Sunday following 4 September to commemorate the granting of hunting rights to the villagers in Needwood Forest, an area near Burton-on-Trent long since ploughed into arable land. Elements of the ritual can be traced to ancient Basque and Soule dancers in the south of France and even to the bushmen of the Kalahari, who still use a similar form of dance to ensure successful hunting forays.

The event begins at dawn as the six Deer-men dressed in Tudor costumes carry their replicas of reindeer heads, three black and three white, on a twenty-mile loop of local farms, bringing good fortune and fertility to the land. Others involved in the strange proceedings include the Hobby Horse, the Fool, Maid Marion (the 'Man-Woman'), and a Bowman, all of whom dance and cavort to the music of a melodeon player and the beat of the Hobby Horse's snapping jaws. The celebrations continue all day, culminating in the main street of Abbots Bromley with the Deer-men acting out the battle of the black and white antlers – an eternal conflict of God and Devil, night and day, life and death. There are symbols heaped on symbols in the intricacies of the ritual and it's an anthropologist's delight as well as a fascinating day out for the casual spectator.

Many such customs have been discouraged by a strict clergy or integrated so completely as to lose significance. Yet at nearby Repton, deep in the ground below St Wystan's church, one is transported back to the earliest days of Christianity in Britain, long before the church gained its stranglehold on the culture. Here, down a flight of narrow steps, I found a tenth-century

Anglo-Saxon crypt, a tiny cruciform chapel supported by simple vaulting on four free-standing pillars. Decoration was minimal. There was little to suggest that this was once the capital city of Mercia, an important seventh-century monastic centre, a burial place of kings and bishops, and the repository of the body of St Wystan. The saint was greatly venerated in the Middle Ages and the tale of his murder became a celebrated legend. 'A column of light', so it goes, 'shot to heaven from the place where he was murdered and remained visible for thirty days.' King Canute (Knut) was so impressed by the significance of his relics that he had them moved for safe-keeping in the eleventh century. A portion was later returned to the sanctity and quietude of this tiny subterranean chapel.

Across from the church are the remains of a twelfth-century priory incorporated into one of England's oldest public schools, founded by Sir John Port in 1557. Segments of the foundations stretch out into the cricket field with its billiard-table grass and thatched pavilion. A couple of miles to the east, deep in the woods, proudly domed and columned Foremark Hall is today used as an associated preparatory school.

Tutbury, known for its hand-cut crystal glass and the ruins of an imposing castle, also has a notable early church, an eleventh-century Norman structure with seven-tier doorway and imposing nave framed by bold pillars. The tympanum over the north doorway is thought to be Anglo-Saxon.

The finest specimen of Norman architecture in the region, however, is Melbourne's St Michael with St Mary Church, a massive, fortress-like edifice on the outside, a graceful harmony of round arches and light within. Pevsner, in an unusually effusive mood, describes it as 'one of the most ambitious Norman parish churches in England'. The large size of what would normally be a modest village church is explained by its role as a secondary diocesan centre for the Bishop of Carlisle who frequently had to flee here from Scot raiders in the north. The plan has a basilican flavour with a tower raised on four broad arches over the transept. Entering through the ornate five-tier west door one moves past a hefty tub font perched on four stubby pillars, out into a soaring nave lined by five bays of rotund columns. The capitals are simply decorated and the arches incised with chevron patterns. The design is bold but not cumbersome. Light flows in through round-arched clerestory windows illuminating the cream stone and remnants of early wall painting, and filling the narrow side aisles with soft shadows. One can sense the remarkable confidence of its builders and masons even in the Romanesque doodles on the chancel arch capitals, teeming with saints, devils, a cat and fox, all intermingled with exotic vegetation and abstract patternings. Here the stone-carvers gave free rein to

Cruck House · Melbourne

their volatile imaginations – a wonderful release in an otherwise restrained masterpiece.

But there's more to Melbourne than just an impressive church. According to seventeenth-century illustrations, the adjoining Melbourne castle was an exotic fantasy of towers and crenellations of which nothing remains today. However, the stone was used in the creation of much of the village and Melbourne Hall, home of Queen Victoria's famous Prime Minister, Lord Melbourne, after whom the Australian city was named. This is a comfortable Palladian structure by a large lake set in formal grounds, slightly Versailles-flavoured, but far more intimate. A wrought-iron pergola known as The Birdcage is the finest work of Derby's Robert Bakewell and sits, dainty as lark-song, among the estate trees. A yew tunnel, reputedly Europe's largest, provides a sombre contrast to broad vistas and sweeping lawns. Podgy cherubs kiss (and shake hands?) on a stone plinth and Van Nost's 'Four Seasons' monument in lead is a technically brilliant but unduly heavy rendering of a romantic subject.

Beyond, in the town itself, the architectural riches continue with the large tithe barn by the church, an authentic cruck house in High Street, and recently restored thatched Tudor cottages. An old forge near the church is still active and the Cook almshouses on High Street memorialise the birth-town of Thomas Cook whose worldwide travel and holiday empire began when he organised his first excursion from Loughborough to Leicester in 1841 for 570 teetotallers attending a Temperance Rally. Ten years later he was arranging trips for 165,000 passengers to the Great Exhibition and promoting his popular idea of 'personally conducted tours'. Other unusual ventures included the transport of an expedition to relieve General Gordon at Khartoum involving 18,000 soldiers, 130,000 tons of food and 70,000 tons of coal on 800 whaling boats. Such ingenuity deserved success!

On the fringe of Melbourne is the old-fashioned hamlet of King's Newton with a coaching-days flavour, and Staunton Harold reservoir, a rural picnic area for visitors exploring the remarkable range of country estates open to the public in this region. A country walk leads past the lake at Melbourne Hall (The Pool) across Home Park and through woods to Staunton Harold Hall, a Cheshire Home, and the chapel, now National Trust property. Over the west door are the bold words of Sir Robert Shirley, owner of the estate and distinctly anti-Cromwell:

When all things Sacred were throughout ye nation Either demolisht or profaned Sir Robert Shirley, Barronet, Founded this church.

The date was 1653. Shortly afterwards he was sent to the Tower and died at the age of twenty-seven. Cromwell resented his impudence and thought his money would have been better spent raising a regiment.

Sudbury is another Royalist creation, a perfect 'model' estate village, an all-brick seventeenth-century gem whose cottages with their high-pitched roofs and tall chimneys frame a lavish hall. Completed in the late seventeenth century, it is the Restoration style at its most flamboyant, rejoicing in the end of Cromwellian dourness. George Vernon, the squire, regarded himself as something of an architect and revelled in detailing the façade complete with cross-hatch brickwork, stone cupola and massive columned entranceway. Inside is even more extravagent with a 138 ft Long Gallery, Grinling Gibbons's carved woodwork in the drawing room, rich Bradbury and Pettifer plaster ceilings and Louis Laquerre's Baroque murals in the salon. As a slight diversion an odd turreted brick structure was built close to the house, and is known appropriately as 'The Eye Catcher'.

What an ordered, organised world these wealthy men must have enjoyed! One wonders how they would have reacted to the popular 'medieval banquets' currently held at Hoar Cross Hall to the south and the fact that a total of seven palatial homes in the region have all opened their doors to the public. The Curzon family home, Kedleston Hall, is probably the finest Robert Adam house in the country and famed throughout Europe for its great marble hall supported by twenty Corinthian columns of pink alabaster. Statues and monochrome panels of Homeric tales grace the walls, and the floor is a bold design of Derbyshire stone and Italian marble. Elsewhere the works of Van Dyck and Reynolds adorn ornate walls and visitors are led open-mouthed under the vast rotunda dome, through the state dining room, past the gilded organ in the music room, to the Indian Museum with its collection of ivories, silver and examples of Lord Curzon's artistic endeavours. The estate church, needless to say, is a repository of Curzon monuments.

Ednaston Manor, further to the west, only opens nine acres of gardens and woodlands to visitors, but Blithfield Hall, sprawled across the hilltop above a broad boating reservoir, offers extensive Stuart era collections in a setting of finely carved woodwork and a magnificent oak staircase. The wild Bagot goats with prominent horns and black faces are not, I am told, half so fierce as they look. I didn't check.

Alton Towers, one of Staffordshire's rural playgrounds, hardly needs mention in a book of this kind. Nevertheless, much as I avoid crowds, I found the exotic gardens sprinkled with fountains, a Chinese pagoda, a Roman bath, a Swiss cottage and oceans of rhododendrons, one of the most diverting experiences of the journey. Much of it grew out of the creative genius of Charles, 15th Earl of Shrewsbury, and his nephew John who lived here from 1831 and designed the turreted and galleried fantasy-mansion while completing the Dutch, Terraced, and 'Her Ladyship's' Gardens.

I left from the southern entrance by a startlingly pink gatehouse with an odd tower. An elderly man was weeding the garden and I asked him about this additional Alton idiosyncracy. 'It was red once, Venetian red, very classy, but it all fell off and they painted it this pansy-pink.' He pointed to the high walk on top of the gatehouse. 'There was always somebody supposed to be up there watching out for the Earl. He moved about fast and you had to be quick. When you saw him charging down this way you had to rush out and get the gates open before he arrived, otherwise he'd give you a right bawling out. Moved like the bloody crackers he did!'

The village of Alton is a cosy cluster of streets on the edge of a precipice overlooking the Churnet valley. Past the White Hart and Bull's Head, a beehive-shaped lock-up stands by the roadside, a sturdy stone edifice built in 1819 to house local ne'er-do-wells. Near the church a preparatory school and Victorian-Gothic convent with an ornately tiled roof form a quiet enclosure around the stubby remnants of a medieval castle.

The remains of Croxden Abbey, a couple of miles further south, are a little more substantial, although the construction of a road through the middle of the complex seems insensitive, to say the least. The legend that King John's heart is buried here is erroneous. Apparently the miserable monarch's organ ended up at the similar-sounding Croxton Abbey in Leicestershire.

A final climax to this array of stately homes is the Anson family estate of Shugborough, created largely from Admiral George Anson's lucrative spoils following daring naval escapades which included the capture of a Spanish galleon with a £400,000 cargo of gold. The admiral's love of China led to the creation of the Chinese House in the grounds, and the 'Cat Monument' was once thought to immortalise his faithful travelling companion. Other notable works include a Doric Temple, one of the first examples of the Greek Revival style in England, two other Greek reproductions, and an enormous replica of Hadrian's Triumphal Arch in Athens – yet one more memorial to the affluent admiral.

All this hall-hopping may be a little too culturally exhausting for most travellers. After two days I'd had enough and drove up onto the wild forest-and-heath landscape of Cannock Chase, a favourite hunting ground of the Plantagenet kings. Here the wind smelled of pines and I could see for scores of miles in every direction. Forestry paths led me through the newer plantations to the ancient oaks at Brocton Coppice and the peace of the Sherbrook valley. I found a few of those peculiar fly-catching sundew plants

The Alton Lock-up

among the marshy patches and wandered westward across the heather and gorse hillsides. Tracks are well-marked and the silence blanket-thick. Only twelve miles away is the edge of the Birmingham–Walsall–Wolverhampton conurbation. But here, lolling among bracken, you could easily think yourself in the highlands of Scotland or some remote Welsh wilderness, sharing the solitude with curlews and the occasional frenzied lark.

Further to the east I followed the footpath from Cannock Wood to the extensive Castle Ring earthworks, a five-sided bank constructed by the Britons way back in misty prehistory. Sitting on the crest of a nearby hill, I looked over the Trent valley across toward Derby. I could see the glittering Blithfield reservoir, specked with sails. Even the power stations near Rugeley had a certain simple majesty from this vantage-point. Strips of dark green woods marked the lordly estates, small and insignificant in the broad sweep of landscape, rolling away to the limestone crags of the Peak: On the far horizons large cities glowered, hectic and dark. But below was all lane-laced greenness under a bowed blue sky, a lovely breathing-space for their frazzled residents – and me.

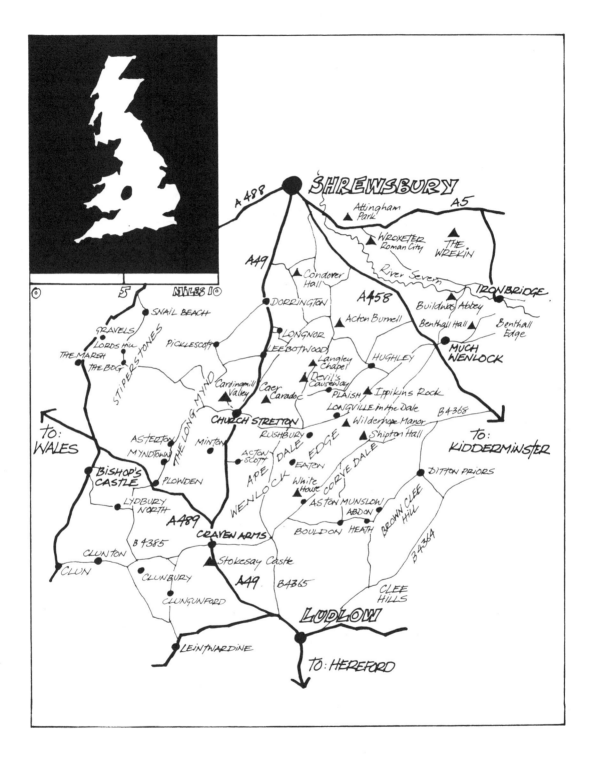

12. The Shropshire Hills

A land of cosy, dozing vales below the bare rounded tops of ancient Silurian hills – the last ripplings of the Welsh massif and the first pastoral undulations of England. This is old Shropshire, A. E. Housman country, full of his rotund images (not always geographically accurate but immediately recognisable):

> Wenlock Edge was embered
> And bright was Abdon Burf
> And warm beneath them slumbered
> The smooth green miles of turf.

And the thick, warm silences where

> Clunton and Clunbury,
> Clungunford and Clun,
> Are the quietest places
> Under the sun.

So the mood rolls on in 'The Shropshire Lad' and others of his poems, steeped in the flavour of deepest England. I could, I suppose, leave this chapter entirely to Mr Housman and get on with the next, but there are surprises and delights here he missed – enough to make it a tantalising place for hidden-corner explorers crossing the brooding heights of Stiperstones Ridge, Wenlock Edge, Brown Clee Hill, the Long Mynd, and the Wrekin's lonely peak.

Other writers found their muse in these hills and vales, most notably Mary Webb, author of such romantic novels as *The Golden Arrow* and *Gone to Earth*. Hardy-like, she steeped herself in local folklore, basing her tales in such easily recognisable places as 'Shepwardine' (Church Stretton) and relishing legends teeming with devils and witches. She saw Much Wenlock as 'very Rip Van Winkle . . . somewhere in the Middle Ages it had fallen asleep and if you should wonder at the fashion of its garments you must remember that it had not, since the day it fell asleep, changed its coat, its hosen or its hat'.

Way up on the Stiperstones she sensed the wild spirit of the 'Devil's Chair', a fantasy of shattered rock:

bleak, massive, untenanted, yet with a well-worn air. It had the look of a chair from which the occupant has just risen, to which he will shortly return. It was understood that only when vacant could the throne be seen. Whenever rain, sleet or mist made a grey shechinah there people said, 'There's harm brewing.' 'He's in his chair.' Not that they talked of it much; they simply felt it, as sheep feel the coming of snow.

Old Lead Mines · Stiperstones

This is desolate country. The broken remnants of lead mines litter the northern slopes. Odd-named hamlets, Snail Beach, Gravels, The Marsh and The Bog, are scattered empty-eyed among mounds of weed-grown slag. At Lords Hill cottages cower in the scrub and the immense stone bulk of an engine shed collapses below the smelting chimney. Rusty narrow-gauge tracks lead nowhere and a black tunnel pierces the hillside behind scribbled 'Danger' signs. The Romans were the first to dig the mines. Spasmodic revivals were always half-hearted. The redoubtable walker-writer Walter White passed this way in 1860 and was not impressed by the activities which 'hardly compared with those of Durham and Northumberland, either in their mechanical appliances or in the energy of the labour . . . They seemed to be playing at mining; they were two boys breaking the ore and one man washing it with a sieve in a tub of water.'

Over the moorland crest of Stiperstones lanes wriggle off into isolated valleys with stringing hamlets, unsigned and unannounced. This is still wild country relished by writers and other eccentrics, notably Shropshire's most

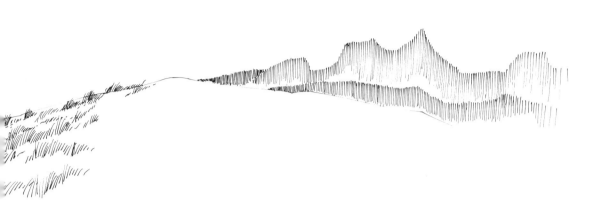

famous rake, Squire 'Mad Jack' Mytton. He inherited an immense fortune in 1798 at the age of two and died in a debtors' prison thirty-six years later after a raucous, brawling life of hunting, gambling, drinking (rationed to six bottles of port per day and a bottle of brandy for breakfast) and generally creating havoc in these quiet hills. He managed to 'destroy a time-honoured family and a noble estate, the inheritance of five hundred years', and yet is remembered with far more affection than the most generous mild-mannered philanthropist.

Somehow (I've never been quite sure how) I reached the A49 at Dorrington and drove south, detouring to admire Longnor's two halls and the delightful Early English church. An unusual stone stairway leads up the outside wall to the interior gallery, peering down over the box pews.

Past Leebotwood with its sprawling thatch pub I entered prim, chintzy Church Stretton. Along the main street box-frame timbering, for which Shropshire is noted, begins to emerge, soaring to a creative peak, as we shall see later, in the hill town of Ludlow. The church is bold Norman with blind-arching on the exterior walls, a pure nave and a tiny stone fertility figure, a Sheila-na-gig, on the outside wall above the north door. The flavour of the village is slightly French. A dainty square clusters below the sweep of the Long Mynd, which rises abruptly behind the church to bare moorland tops. Tight valleys known locally as 'batches' slice into the whale-backed hill. One of the most noted (and over-popular) is the Cardingmill valley. Others like Ashes Hollow and Callow Hollow to the south are quieter places, and the tiny hamlet of Minton with its cottages, green and manor house by an ancient mound has all the silent fullness of a Housman scene.

I climbed narrow Burway Hill up on to the dome of the Long Mynd. Sheets of heather, bracken and whinberries spread in all directions, and hillsides dipped away steeply to tiny sparkling streams. Paths and tracks invited lonely rambles across its ten-mile length and a sign marked the route of the ancient Port Way trail. Broad vales, fresh as the air and clear as glass, stretched eastwards around Caer Caradoc over toward the sharp escarpment of Wenlock Edge and the prominent outline of the Wrekin. A buzzard hung, wings quivering, waiting for movement among the heather roots. In moist places where waters gathered to move off down the long slopes, patches of bog moss held the pink, bell-shaped flowers of the bog pimpernel. Sundew and butterwort waited, like the buzzard, for their next meals. These innocent-looking plants are insect eaters. A raven, alone and very black, flew slowly across the tops releasing one grating rasp before disappearing over the far edge of the Mynd. Two gliders from the club on the west scarp curled upwards in the warm-air spirals.

After a quiet stroll by the solitary pine plantation on the summit I followed the very narrow and steep Port Way road off the Mynd into the little basking hamlets of Asterton and Myndtown. At Plowden the long hill sinks to earth suddenly. The nearby picturesque Elizabethan hall was home of the Plowden family whose gloomy chapel forms part of the multi-buttressed Norman church at Lydbury North. The south transept chapel here, bright and beautifully crafted, is dedicated to a second great local family, the Walcots, whose large red-brick mansion was the home of Robert Clive, father of Britain's Indian empire.

Another most notable home is the old Roberts family pub, the Three Tuns Inn at Bishop's Castle, famous for a century of home-brewed ales. In the early nineteenth century there were more than 23,000 pubs in Britain brewing their own beer. By 1880 the number was down to 12,000 and by the outbreak of the First World War, 1,500. Today there are about 20! Fortunately the resurgence of interest in real beer is promoting a significant trend toward pub-brew beers. Peter Milner, who took over the Three Tuns from the

162

Roberts family, has already added a stout to his regular production of two bitters and a mild. Whereas most home-brew installations tend to be haphazard affairs, the Three Tuns boasts a Victorian tower brew-house with the beer flowing by gravity-feed from one floor to the next, mash at the top, boiling and fermenting in the middle and casking at the bottom. Production ranges from around ten barrels per week in winter months to more than forty in summer when the modest little pub experiences weekend deluges of enthusiasts. This is a most difficult time, though, to produce consistently good beer. In August particularly there's a constant danger of 'wild' yeast drifting in the air and causing fermentation to go awry. March is the ideal brewing month but not a particularly popular time for hefty drinking. 'There are dozens of pitfalls with your own brews. If I'd known them all I perhaps would have stuck to my old job,' Peter Milner told me as I sampled his strongest bitter. He was once an engineer and worked in South America and Africa before deciding to take on the pub with his wife Janet. 'I was lucky. John Roberts helped me a lot to keep things going. I think I've just about got it right.' I didn't hear any complaints from the customers.

Above the pub is the Bishop's Castle town hall with its octagonal clock tower, peering down the long, steep hill lined with pubs, antique shops and stores selling crafts and home-produced jams. The unusual timber-framed building up the cobbled ginnel alongside the town hall is aptly named 'The House on Crutches'.

Housman's Clunton, Clunbury and Clungunford are all appropriately peaceful places nestling in a quiet valley alongside the B4368. Clun itself is larger and, as a crossroads town, has a rather noisy and dusty charm. A ruined Norman keep on the edge of a great earth mound peers down at the small market square and tiny court house museum. The river is crossed by a picturesque saddle-backed bridge with five thick arches. Behind the main street are the 1614 almshouses founded by Henry Howard, Earl of Northampton, as a 'refuge for decayed tradesmen'. Like other such institutions explored on these journeys, the warden and 'twelve poor men' were once provided with gowns displaying the founder's heraldic device. They were required to leave their tiny homes round the quadrangle to attend services in the adjoining chapel at regular intervals and to 'wholly give themselves to the service of God, and to pray for the Peace, Tranquillity and Concord of all Christendom'. Nowadays the regimen is a little less severe and on the evening I visited the town, a group of elderly residents was marching off to the new village hall to watch a play by a travelling troupe of actors and artists. I had no particular plans so tagged along and enjoyed *The Last Cottage*, a rather melodramatic portrayal of declining village life. Tea was

The House on Crutches. Bishop's Castle

served in the interval by a flushed group of ladies ('no one told us about making tea') and the play romped on to its fiery conclusion followed by a rather half-hearted discussion on the relevance of its 'message'. A squirely figure with tweed jacket and bristling moustache seemed to be the only enthusiastic participant, boring everyone with name-droppings about 'Harry – Harold Pinter y'know' and 'Old Tom – Tom Stoppard y'know', what marvellous fellows they really were 'once you got to know them, y'know'. The audience finally tumbled out into the night and the young actors packed the scenery into their travelling bus and vanished off down the lanes to their next venue. The pensioners from the almshouses thought it had been 'just marvellous', although three of them had slept through the second half.

I was fortunate that evening and had one more surprise awaiting me as I drove south to the hillside village of Leintwardine, pub-pretty by the river Clun. The Lion Hotel near the bridge looked a little too country-chintz for my tastes that evening and I went seeking an alternative place of refreshment. I found it at the Sun, one of the most unusual pubs in Shropshire situated in the front parlour of a terraced stone cottage. I entered through a creaky green

164

door and found myself in a hall with a large round table. A lace cloth covered most of its highly polished surface and a bowl with three roses stood in the centre. It was a most un-pub-like pub. An elderly lady peered round a door on my left leading into a kitchen. I thought I'd trespassed into someone's house and was about to leave when she told me the parlour was on my right. I pushed open an unmarked door and entered a small, smoky room with five old men sitting on benches facing one another on either side of a cast-iron fireplace. The conversation paused and they all looked up. We exchanged greetings and I took a seat behind them against the wall. A copious refectory-type table took up most of the room, standing on a polished red-brick floor. A dartboard hung from the wall in the corner along with a Queen Victoria's Jubilee poster in a frame, a series of blotchy photographs of rugby teams, and a stirringly dramatic painting entitled *An Awful Apparition*. There was no bar. One of the men, presumably the landlord, rose from the huddle of heads and shoulders and asked if I cared for a drink. I ordered a pint of bitter. 'Mild's better,' he told me sleepily. So I had mild – an excellent velvety pint. The old men resumed their slow conversation full of long pauses and puffs on ancient pipes, and the late evening ticked on to closing time the way it must have done for decades.

There's a saying thought to have originated at Leintwardine:

> God bless the squire and his relations
> And keep us in our proper stations.

It couldn't have come from anywhere more appropriate!

And Ludlow couldn't be anywhere else but on its high hill, castle-proud, towered and bowed above the river Terne. What a delight this place is, inviting long, leisurely explorations (preferably out of season to avoid the occasional summer crowds). Artists particularly will relish the box-frame timberwork of the Feathers Hotel somehow holding itself together in lop-sided disarray since the early seventeenth century. Gourmands also relish the rich English fare 'served by comelye and complyante wenches'. Across the street by Jones's pork shop, laden with home-cured hams and sides of bacon, is the reconstructed Bull Hotel containing remnants of the fourteenth-century 'Peter the Proctor's House'. Just around the corner, in a courtyard off Church Street, is the Rose and Crown, first licensed in the sixteenth century. Then comes famous Broad Street described by the normally restrained Nikolaus Pevsner as 'one of the most memorable streets in England'.

From the high end by the porticoed Butter Cross, the wide street tumbles downhill edged by cobbled 'banks' under the narrow ginnel of crenellated Broad Gate, one of the seven original gates in the town walls, and out to the

The Feathers Hotel · Ludlow

hump-backed Lulford Bridge over the river. The upper northern end is a
continuous array of fifteenth-century timber-framed structures above a
colonnaded arcade – a Hollywood film-set for a Dickensian tale, except that
it's all real. The elegant Angel Hotel has been on the site in one guise or
another since 1555. Parallel Mill Street is a similarly broad but more
restrained enclave of Georgian and Regency frontages spoilt only by the
profusion of parked cars.

Tight alleys lead back behind the Butter Cross to the museum and St
Laurence's Church, one of the largest parish churches in the country. The
tower rises 135 ft, higher than the castle, and one enters a space of cathedral-
like dimensions, soaring Gothic arches, splendidly ornate screens and a
large reredos teeming with carved saints. Angels peer down from the
painted beams above the high altar and the choir misericords are decorated
with satirical carvings depicting 'The successful Townsman' with his cured
hams, 'The Drunkard' sleepily caressing his flagon, a sly fox-like Bishop
preaching to a congregation of geese, a caricature of the exotic forms of
female headress popular at the time, and, best of all, an ale-wife guilty of
short-measuring her ale being carried off by the Devil.

166

The equally satirical antics of St Laurence are told in gory detail in the chancel and depicted in brilliant colour on the east window. Apparently when the pagan hoards dominated Rome in the third century AD they murdered the Pope and instructed Laurence to bring them the church treasure. The young man agreed and brought all the poor and sick of the city, declaring, 'Here is the Church's treasure'. The pagans were not amused and roasted the saint over a gridiron while he taunted them with his famous, 'Your meat is done enough: you may eat your dish.'

The churchyard is a welcome swathe of grass and trees in this compact little town. A. E. Housman's ashes rest behind a plaque on the north wall. At the far side is yet another of Ludlow's surprises, the medieval Reader's House, adorned with floral plaster ceilings and a three-storey Jacobean porch in elegant timberwork.

Beyond the Butter Cross, smart ladies in furs take coffee at the Castle Lodge. The drive leads past cannons, through towering walls, into the broad courtyard of the castle, a favourite of Edward IV and still actively used for Shakespearean dramas during the town's two-week summer festival. Here the two ill-fated 'princes in the tower' lived before Edward V's succession to the throne, when they were hastily dispatched to London and cruelly murdered along with many other members of the royal family. The remains of the Norman inner bailey are well-preserved. Most notable are the Council Hall where Milton's *Masque of Comus* was first performed in 1634, and the unusual circular Norman chapel. This is one of five such churches built in England inspired by the ideas of the Knights Templars.

Just down the hill outside the walls are the simple remains of another twelfth-century chapel, a single vaulted cell open at one end. Nearby a stately Regency mansion, owned by Lord Clive and residence of Lucien Bonaparte (Napoleon's brother) in 1810, is now used as the Ludlow Craft Studios and Gallery.

For those unfamiliar with this region, Ludlow is a most delightful surprise. I left and drove along the three Clee Hills topped by 1,790 ft Brown Clee. Ancient earthworks litter this wild area, most notably the Nordy bank fort and the double earth banks of Caynham Camp. Folklore abounds with tales of witches and devils on the high places, and local superstitions are still regarded seriously by older residents. Any pregnant woman, for example, seeing a hare on the Clees is advised to make a small tear in her dress to prevent her offspring being born hare-lipped. Similarly an anxious spinster desirous of marriage should place a ladybird on her first finger and carefully watch the direction in which it flies away while singing:

Wenlock Edge

> Ladybird, ladybird, fly away, flee,
> Tell me which way my wedding's to be,
> Uphill or downhill or toward Brown Lee.

The most striking views over this restless country of hills and edges are gained from the Ditton Priors–Abdon road along the northern flanks of Brown Clee. The road continues round the western slope and turns off to Bouldon, passing the little Norman Church at Heath, and on into the gentle sweep of Corve Dale.

Wenlock Edge rises undramatically from this side, a fifteen-mile ridge of Silurian Limestone stretching from Benthall Edge above the Severn Gorge to the village of Craven Arms. The B4368 along the southern flanks avoids the spectacular views but offers three notable diversions. The first is Aston Munslow's 'White House', home of the Stedman family for over 600 years and displaying a remarkable range of building techniques from the thirteenth-century rock-hewn undercroft and the fourteenth-century Cruck Hall, to a Tudor cross-wing and an eighteenth-century Georgian extension –

all in the one building. There's also a thirteenth-century dovecote, a cider house, and a country life museum of ancient agricultural implements, kitchen equipment, stables, granary and dairies.

A few miles further on is Shipton Hall, an Elizabethan masterwork of golden stone with large square windows set beside an enormous stable complex reminiscent of Inigo Jones. But most impressive of all on this southern fringe is Stokesay Castle at Craven Arms, a magical fantasy of lopsided timber-frame gatehouse, beautifully carved with monsters and biblical scenes, and a well-preserved thirteenth-century manor house surrounded by a deep moat. At the southern end of the massively buttressed main hall rises the Great Tower, 66 ft high and almost 40 ft across and also buttressed. The opposite end overlooking the church is a warped timber-framed extension, projecting from the thick stone shell of the manor. Inside one explores richly panelled rooms set with enormous fireplaces – a perfect setting for the ghosts of knights, squires and courtly ladies to come prancing out of the walls in a gay gavotte. The inhabitants here were an unwarlike lot, and for all the aggressive arrow slits and thick walls, surrendered immediately

169

Stokesay Castle

to Cromwell's forces in 1645 even before a warning shot was fired. Possibly grateful for time and effort saved, the Roundheads left the place intact for our delight today. Unfortunately they vented their rage on the church when a Royalist party sought refuge here in 1646, blasting the nave with cannon shot and destroying the chancel. Again, however, we benefit, as the church was rebuilt ten years later and is one of the few examples of Puritan-era architecture complete with box pews, stone floor and a partial three-decker pulpit.

Immediately to the north of Wenlock Edge in the delicate undulations of Ape Dale is the Acton Scott Working Farm Museum, a centre for craft-demonstrations and an example of a Shire-horse-powered farm. Further east is Wilderhope Manor, an Elizabethan house with towering chimneys and extraordinarily ornate plaster ceilings. Mary Webb used it as Jack Reddin's home in her best-selling *Gone to Earth.* Although owned by the National Trust, its role as a Youth Hostel limits public admittance to Wednesday afternoons.

Ape Dale is yet another evocative Housman scene graced with soft slumbering hamlets where 'peace comes dropping slow'. Rushbury nestles in meadows with its timber-frame manor and Early English church. Eaton is submerged in trees, a few scattered houses and a church containing one of those rare medieval wooden effigies. Then:

> The vane on Hughley steeple
> Veers bright, a far-known sign . . .

except that as far as anyone can remember Hughley never had a steeple and Housman was merely exercising a little artistic licence.

Wander at will among country lanes here and begin the steep climb up from Longville in the Dale on to the watershed of Wenlock Edge, peering down off precipices over Ape Dale and the slow rollings to Shrewsbury. Remnants of limestone quarries can be found around Ippikin's Rock, a steep cliff named after a robber who hid all his treasure in a cave here only to have it blocked in by a landslide. The irate fellow still haunts his hideout and one has merely to stand alone on his rock and whisper:

> Ippikin! Ippikin!
> Keep away with your long chin

to conjure up his spirit complete with gold chain and terrible grin. Alas, we have no confirmation of the effectiveness of this rhyme as Ippikin invariably pushes the speaker over the cliffs.

172

Washing-place. Much Wenlock Priory

Ideally one should walk the Edge. Paths leave conveniently from two pubs, the Plough in the south and the Horse and Jockey near Much Wenlock in the north. A short detour leads to the legendary Major's Leap, another craggy precipice, where the Royalist Major Thomas Smallwood of Wilderhope Hall leapt with his horse to keep secret despatches from his Roundhead pursuers. The horse met an unfortunate end but Major Smallwood somehow managed a Tarzan-type descent through tree branches and continued on foot to make his delivery.

At Much Wenlock the Edge slides to earth and we descend into a town of limestone, brick and timber-frame buildings unspoilt by modern intrusions with a sturdy plaster-and-beam Guildhall and the remnants of an eleventh- and thirteenth-century priory. Stately trees frame the site, originally used as a convent by St Mildburga in the seventh century. The Danes destroyed most of the buildings in the late ninth century. Encouraged by Lady Godiva, it was rebuilt in the following century only to be destroyed once again, this time by the Normans. Roger de Montgomery then founded the Cluniac monastery in 1080 and these are the elegant ruins here today. Most notable are the carved panels on the monks' octagonal washing-place, the vaulting of the library and the graceful three-tiered blind arching of the chapter house. There's a pleasant cosiness about the place, surrounded by large Elizabethan houses and parkland.

Much Wenlock is an excellent base for more countryside sorties. Nearby is sixteenth-century Benthall Hall, a romantic stone-built structure containing exquisite plaster ceilings and an intricately carved oak staircase. Like other houses in this once-Catholic part of the country there are hiding places and priest-holes – even in the entrance porch!

Just beyond the hall one abruptly leaves the gentle Shropshire meadows and tumbles through the nature-trailed Benthall Edge Woods into the steep Severn Gorge, brimming with power stations, pylon lines and all the famous industrial remnants of Coalbrookdale – culminating in Telford's world-renowned bridge at Ironbridge. This popular area is well worth a day's exploration (preferably out of season).

Buildwas Abbey is a chunky remnant of the Transitional era between Norman and Early English. Most of the nave columns remain, thick, cream-stoned with barely pointed arches. It seems to have enjoyed a relatively uneventful history as a Cistercian house except for occasional bouts with 'the levity of the Welsh' who destroyed crops and carried off the abbot in 1350. Most notable is the chapter house, entered through a plain three-order door and down five steps, now used as a repository of grave slabs and carved stone fragments beneath a delicately vaulted roof.

From here it's only a short drive to the majestic Wrekin, created by mythical spade-wielding giants and used often as a beacon in times of conflict. Oddly named features on its flanks suggest heavy folkloric associations – Hell's Gate (a gap in a prehistoric earthwork), Heaven's Gate, Needle's Eye, Bladder Stone and Raven's Bowl. Walks up to the summit are pleasantly untaxing and rewarded once again with views across the hill-pimpled Shropshire countryside.

A loop drive from here north-west along the B4380 passes the broken remnants of the Roman city of Wroxeter (Viroconium). This outpost during the long conflicts with the British Prince Caradoc (Caratacus) was later an administrative capital for the borderlands complete with forum, market, temples, courts and baths. A few miles beyond is Attingham Park, Lord Berwick's eighteenth-century home, sitting golden-proud in Repton's landscaped park, graced by an enormous columned portico and Nash-designed picture gallery.

Then curling south again on country lanes we return to Mary Webb country and the eminent sixteenth-century hall at Condover, all gables and chimneys at the end of a short yew drive (open August). The unremarkable church here contains a collection of charming monuments, notably the sculpture of Alice Cholmondeley and her baby (sad story) carved by her husband Reginald.

Acton Burnell boasts a tall, four-towered, fortified manor set in a wooden valley. Like Stokesay this is largely a thirteenth-century creation but less well maintained, in quiet, cedar-shaded grounds. Nearby are the remnants of a castle barn 150 ft long, thought to have been the site of England's first parliament assembled during a year-long visit of Edward I. The unusually large church contains more prominent monuments.

Two miles south on a side road to Cardington is a far more modest church, the tiny Langley Chapel built in the early seventeenth century and hardly changed since. Elegant box pews for the locally affluent, rough benches for the labourers, and a simple (movable?) pulpit all reflect a stern faith and the steady certainty of 'proper stations'.

Further along the Cardington Road is an odd stretch of cobbled road, possibly a Roman road but known locally as the 'Devil's Causeway'. Laid in one night by a creature with horns and hoofs, it remains the Evil One's territory and woebetide any godless human who passes along it at midnight. Good men are spared but sinners have to run a fiery gauntlet.

Near Plaish and the exotic Tudor chimneys of Plaish Hall (not open to the public) we enter Housman territory once again, a tree-crowded country with bosky bushes and pretty, damp lanes, mossily green as holy wells. Deep hedgerows glisten with meadowsweet, honeysuckle and harebells. Ploughed fields sparkle, stiff seas of clods glinting in the wind. Blackberries, bursting with juices, cluster against the sky, dark as thunderbolts.

There's a bitter-sweetness here in Housman-land, a sense of beauty too fine to endure and memories of a fleeting euphoria. The last lines, appropriately, are left to him:

> Into my heart an air that kills
>   From yon far country blows:
> What are those blue remembered hills,
>   What spires, what farms are those?
>
> That is the land of lost content,
>   I see it shining plain,
> The happy highways where I went
>   And cannot come again.

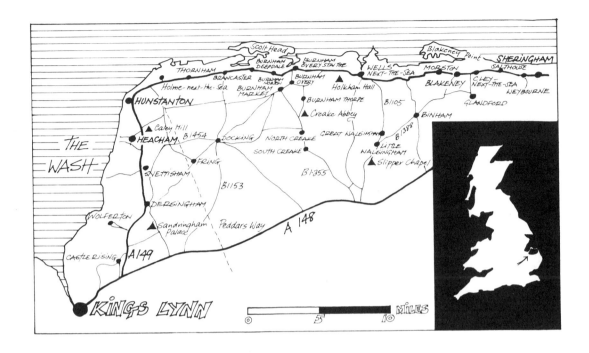

13. The Norfolk Coast

Surf prattled over the shingle ridges of Scolt Head Island – an effervescent hiss, a pause, then a long grinding of pebbles as the sea pulled in on itself for the next wave. Further down the beach, patches of marram grass flexed stiffly in breezes and warm air skimmed up the dunes, smoothing their sides. Across the water, hillocks and copses floated above a shimmering heat-haze.

It seemed I had the island all to myself, four and a half miles of sands and saltings, a favourite nesting ground of terns, occasional resting place for seals, and quiet as the galaxy. A ferry boat had carried a dozen passengers over from the tidal flats at Brancaster and most had disappeared into the dunes within minutes of our arrival. I had two hours before the next boat and lots of nothing to do in the salt-stung nowhereness.

I travelled north from King's Lynn to explore this curious stretch of coastline and at Castle Rising made one of many impromptu stops along the way. Remnants of a sturdy, blind-arcaded keep built by the Earl of Arundel in the late twelfth century stood proud above a deep moat. Adversaries, possibly disheartened by walls 9 ft thick, avoided the place and its history seems to have been uneventful except for the confinement here of Queen Isabella, accused of conspiracy in the death of her husband, Edward II. She is said to have gone insane and villagers claim that her screams and howls can still be heard on quiet nights. The elderly 'sister' who showed me round the nearby Trinity Hospital Almshouses told me that none of her eleven resident companions had heard anything, but admitted 'We're all a bit deaf.'

Founded by the Earl of Northampton in 1615, the Hospital established strict criteria for eligibility including the willingness of each inmate to attend church three times a day in special cloak and hat uniform, to say set prayers in her room at allotted intervals and to be 'of honest life and conversation, religious, grave and discreet, able to read (if such a one be had), a single woman, no common beggar, harlot, scold, drunkard haunter of taverns, inns and alehouses'. I was shown the Founder's Room facing onto the grassy quadrangle around which the small terraced cottages were grouped. 'Queen Mary used to come a lot when she was in residence at Sandringham. She enjoyed the company,' my guide told me as we climbed the stairs above the entrance arch to the treasury room still clad in Jacobean panelling and containing an ancient chest. 'The rules are not so strict nowadays but most of us still go to church on Sundays in the scarlet cloaks with the Northampton crest.' I was curious about the tall witch-like hats that were once part of the standard dress. 'Oh, we wear those only on special occasions, Founder's Day and such. Matron has the nicest hat, it's got three corners and a lovely black ostrich feather.' I visited the church, a most impressive restored Norman creation with fine blind arching at the west end and a riotous Romanesque font, full of leering faces.

Whereas nearby Sandringham, the most informal of all royal palaces, has its normal curious crowds, the Victorian–Gothic Wolferton Station Museum at the end of a rhododendron-lined lane often has none. Here Eric and Helda Walker have managed, in spite of 'stroppy villagers and unhelpful Sandringham officials', to preserve the retiring rooms created here by the Great Eastern Railway in 1898 at the cost of £8,000 for King Edward VII and Queen Alexandra. This was the royal station, last used as such by Queen Elizabeth II in 1965, and among hundreds of items the collection includes chairs and furnishings from the GNR Royal Saloon, original gold-plated door fittings and Queen Victoria's portable bed, which, she wrote in her diary, 'always travels with me'.

Beyond the lacework of Snettisham church's west window, a masterpiece of the Decorated style, is tranquil Heacham, nestling away from the main road. A large, triangular green is edged by cottages with steeply pitched roofs and a most unusual eclectic house seemingly made up of bits and

Norfolk Coastal Scene near Blakeney

pieces of old churches and country mansions. St Mary the Virgin church contains numerous monuments to the Rolfe family whose most notable member, John Rolfe, married the Indian princess, Pocahontas. They returned to live here prior to her death in 1617 at the age of twenty-two.

On the edge of the village is the popular Caley Mill, centre of the local lavender-growing industry founded by Linnaeus (Linn) Chilvers in 1932, and expanding every year. I wandered the narrow lanes to the distillery at Fring. The two larger stills here can take up to a quarter of a ton of blooms at one time, and steam is passed through to vaporise the oil in the purple flowers. This is then condensed, the residual oil and water separate naturally and the oil is drawn off to be used for perfumes – or even for medicinal purposes, according to Nicholas Culpeper, the revered seventeenth-century physician-astrologer, who recommended: 'Two spoonfuls help them that has lost their voice, the tremblings and passions of the heart, the faintings and swoonings, when applied to the temples or nostrils; but it is not safe to use it where the body is replete with blood and humours, because of the hot and subtle spirit wherewith it is possessed.'

I continued along the quiet byways around Fring, crossing and recrossing the faint outlines of Peddars Way, a remarkably straight ancient road linking Holme-near-the-Sea with the Breckland wilderness to the south (Chapter 14). The rolling fields, an occasional windmill and large flint farms give the area a gentle mellowness. The earth bursts with fertile juices. Streams trickle below rampant hedgerows and everything moves at a snail's pace in this little hidden world, fat with time.

Hunstanton to the west, Sheringham and Cromer to the east are the resort towns, not without charm but ballooned with bingo-addicts and disco-dancers during the summer. The rest of the coast offers the silted remnants of old seaports, churches both quaint and grandiose, old bowed pubs, windmills, and unfamiliar tales of Horatio Nelson. Occasional flurries of tourists can soon be escaped in the tranquil isolation of marsh flats, dunes and empty strands. Mussel-rakers move slowly through the shallows. More tiny ferries run from Morston and Blakeney to the six-mile shingle beach and nesting grounds at Blakeney Point. Pony trekkers and horse-drawn caravans wander the backroads in the lazy rolling hills behind the coast, and salivating whelk-lovers watch their favourite delicacies being boiled by the thousand in copper cauldrons at Wells-next-the-Sea.

'They're best soft and hot,' I was told by the burly man hauling straw baskets full of steaming whelks in the sheds at the far end of the quay. 'When they're cold they go rubbery and tough. That's the way most people eat 'em – cold with vinegar. Me, I like them cooked up with onions and potatoes, maybe a bit of bacon.' I asked him why I hadn't seen whelks for sale away from the coast. 'They all go to France. Have a look at the packing plant next to the church. They'll show you.' Here a cluster of ladies in bright blue overalls sat round a table manipulating wooden-handled pins like surgeons as they extracted whelks from their shells with a single wrist-flick. Two men packed them into boxes ready for freezing and dispatch to the Continent. I wondered why they all went to France. 'It's a delicacy to them – they pay much better prices than over here. Stands to reason.'

A Wells Whelkman

Season Font - Burnham Deepdale

The coastal villages are cosy huddles of flint, carr stone, clunch (chalk) and brick, thickly shrouded in trees and flowering bushes. Beyond the perfumed lanes are vistas of endless marsh and dune, cut by creeks. Fishing boats and yachts move cautiously in the chocolate-mud estuaries and gulls skim the riggings ever hopeful of a free meal. Holme-next-the-Sea and Thornham doze quietly above the saltings. Brancaster attracts energetic outsiders to its golf course, sailing club and Jolly Sailor pub, and St Mary's church at Burnham Deepdale boasts an Anglo-Saxon round tower and one of the finest Norman 'season' fonts in the country.

It stands just inside the door, a modest square structure supported by four corner columns and a central shaft. Along the top is a frieze of lions and leaves, and below, on three sides, delicate bas-reliefs depict the activities associated with each of the months. The winter season appears a leisurely period of Christmas feasting, drinking (January) and keeping warm by the fire (February). Later come the digging, pruning, Rogationtide processions, weeding and mowing of March to July followed by sheaf binding (August), threshing (September), corn-grinding (October) and pig-killing (November) in time, once again, for the long winter rest. The whole creation is utterly charming and almost identical to fonts found in northern France except that the farmers there prune trees in April, not March. The only one in Britain to compare with St Mary's is the larger lead font at Brookland in Romney Marsh (see Chapter 20).

An ancient rhyme sings of

> London, York and Coventry
> and the Seven Burnhams by the Sea

and tells of the latter's famed medieval prosperity. Burnham Deepdale is merely one of the five remaining Burnhams clustered like hazelnuts along the coast and the Burn river. Just down the road is St Margaret's Church at Burnham Norton, also with a Norman font and remnants of a Carmelite Friary founded in 1241. Burnham Overy Staithe has a small marina and was built as a granary and maltings port when the sea receded, leaving the older village of Burnham Overy stranded inland with only its windmill, watermill and rather confused Norman church as evidence of a substantial past. Burnham Market, on the other hand, is a prosperous community of colourful houses with steep-pitched roofs edging neatly trimmed greens. Across from a peculiar bank building, all wrought iron and pebbles in effusive Victorian style, is a wine shop with a range of vintages more appropriate to Hampstead than hidden Norfolk.

Burnham Thorpe is exclusively Nelson-country with its mecca, the Lord Nelson Inn, set back from the road beside the great flint barn claimed as one of little Horatio's birthplaces. Others insist it was the Parsonage, now demolished, where his father held the living. A few hold it was a humble shooting box. But these are minor debates compared to far grander assessments of Nelson's character and achievements that keep Les Winter trapping the pints from gravity barrels in the back room and serving them by tray in his tiny pub-parlour crammed with Nelsonia. For here is the official gathering place of Nelson-lovers from all over the world. The day I visited, an American and his very blonde wife were claiming to possess 'the biggest goddamned collection of Nelsonia, bar none, our side of the Irish Sea'. A fish and chip shop owner from Hythe was most put out because no one seemed interested in the display in his restaurant – 'It's only small, mind you, at the side of the frying shop; seats about twelve but all the walls, everything is

Les Winter and friends

covered with. . . .' Les Winter has seen and heard it all. He's probably a world authority on Nelson. He's written books, been featured on TV and radio documentaries, and possesses one of the largest accumulations of memorabilia in Britain. He can spot the fakes as soon as they open their mouths. Only an honoured few ever get to see his 'study' on the other side of the passage from the high back pews in the parlour. Sometimes he joins in the discussions, but mostly he seems content to carry the beer and smile the smile of a tolerant professor. I asked him why he thought so much of the famous admiral. 'Well, he was a little man wasn't he? Short and thin. And he had a lot of things wrong with him. His health was poor and he was vain, very vain. But he was a brave man, and more important, he was a just man, just in everything he did. People loved him for that.'

Les came to Burnham Thorpe in 1966 and decided to restore the pub as far as possible to its original 1650 state, 'the way Nelson would have known it when he had his celebration dinners here'. Although the place is tucked away, unsigned, in the secluded Norfolk countryside, those intent on finding it always do and follow with a stroll across fields to the church, burial-place of the Nelson family. The lectern here is constructed from *Victory* timbers and the Rev. Hibberd's guidebook, gushing with effusive prose, contains a useful history of the parish. Les's book, *Hero's Country*, is a more straightforward and richly illustrated description of Nelson and the Norfolk he knew.

A few miles further south are the remnants of the thirteenth-century Augustinian Creake Abbey set in meadows by the river Burn. Nearby are the two impressive St Mary's churches at North and South Creake. I found the latter brimming with 'Visitor's Day' celebrants filling all the pews below the magnificent carved angels on the hammer-beam roof. The vicarage lawn was laid for tea. Four long trestle tables were covered in crisp cloths and scores of cups and saucers. Sandwiches and cream buns were piled under polythene wraps and the ladies of the town were butterflying around, all a-dither at the unexpected popularity of the event. 'The weather,' bubbled one of them. 'It's never been so lovely.' I was curious about all the people. 'Yesterday it was Walsingham's Assumption Day so a lot have come from the shrine.' Along the lane past the vicarage came a procession of wheelchairs and individuals with various afflictions walking slowly up the hill past the pond and into the church. A very tall lady in thick spectacles nodded. 'They come here for the blessing, then they all walk around the church singing hymns. It's wonderful.'

At Houghton St Giles is the much-restored fourteenth-century Slipper Chapel where pilgrims left their shoes and walked the rest of the way to the Shrine of Our Lady in Little Walsingham. A revival in the importance of the Catholic chapel has led to the construction of an enormous bentwood canopy for outdoor services and a flourishing shop full of religious artifacts and ornate descriptions of the vision of Lady Richeld in 1061. She was the wife of Walsingham's lord of the manor and claimed to be instructed in a dream to build a replica of the Nazareth house in which Gabriel appeared to the Virgin Mary. This was done and 'England's Nazareth' became a focus for thousands of pilgrims including monarchs, noblemen and even Roman patriarchs who pronounced a visit here to be the equivalent of a journey to the real Nazareth. A huge Augustinian priory was built in the twelfth century and a fourteenth-century parish church dedicated to St Mary. For a while the tiny town relished a greater reputation than Canterbury. Even Henry VIII made a barefoot pilgrimage here before confiscating its enormous wealth during the Dissolution and burning the statue of Mary in Thomas Cromwell's Chelsea house 'so that the people should use no more idolatrye unto it'.

Today Little Walsingham is a charming community of timber-frame buildings along narrow streets and alleys splayed out from an irregular 'Common Place', complete with octagonal pump and Shire Hall museum. The Anglican shrine is a disappointing piece of Italianate architecture externally, but inside one wanders through a Byzantine gloom glinting with gold, icons, candled-chapels and richly adorned statues of the Virgin. The infirm pray at the Holy Well and drink the waters. The smell of incense is everywhere. Upstairs is a tiny Byzantine chapel missed by most visitors. Then it's out again into the brightness with strolls to the adjoining college, the abbey ruins, into the Methodist centre and the refurbished parish church with its enormous seven-sacrament font (sadly disfigured) and the odd little Russian Orthodox church in the old railway station. There's only one problem. Three times I was approached by newly-arrived pilgrims pleading: 'Is there anywhere we can get a cup of tea?' Somehow the village has resisted overt commercialism and teashops are scarce.

A few miles up the road, though, at Holkham Hall, one of the purest eighteenth-century Palladian mansions in the country, there's tea galore, along with a garden centre, a pottery shop, picnic grounds, lakes, and strolls through lavish pink halls and state rooms to view paintings by Rubens, Van Dyck, Gainsborough and a statue gallery of priceless Greek, Roman and Renaissance works. Unfortunately the place has become over-popular in recent years and hidden-corner explorers may prefer to visit instead the cathedral-like churches along the coast from Blakeney to Weybourne. Pausing first, of course, for some of those whelks at Wells-next-the-Sea, one of the unusual mini-resorts on this strange coastline. Ponderous warehouses line the waterfront above a silted estuary, ignoring the pathetic gilding of bingo parlours and fish restaurants. Tiny streets of 'continuous architecture', strings of flinty cottages, walls and outbuildings, climb slowly from the quay toward the church and the Buttlands, a broad green edged by Georgian houses. The fishermen live here, the 'spratters' with their 'pair-nets' (a single net dragged between two boats), the 'Wells-whelkers' and their 'shanks' of whelk-pots, the 'butt-draggers' and their cruel bars of iron hooks dragged along the muddy bottoms to catch dabs, and a handful of old 'eelers' proud of their now little-used barbed tridents or 'pritches'.

Once these tiny coastal communities were wealthy ports, centres of a flourishing fish and wool economy. Their churches, like the wool churches of Suffolk, reflect this long period of affluence. Blakeney is a beautiful non-bingoed coastal village of thatch and flint cottages preserved intact by 'new-affluents' from the Midlands. Exclusive hotels with manicured grounds line the waterfront and a fifteenth-century Guildhall undercroft is a

185

Cley-next-the-Sea

reminder of its past importance as a trading centre. A Carmelite friary was founded here in the late thirteenth century and the port's long prosperity was supplemented by lusty periods of piracy and smuggling by locals, constantly irritated at excessive customs duties and the frequent requisitionings of fish by monarchs. Decline came gradually as coastal embanking and draining, inspired by Cornelius Vermuyden's success in the Fens, altered tidal patterns and currents and brought silting to the harbour channel. Blakeney church, dedicated to St Nicholas, patron saint of fishermen, stands on a hill overlooking the saltings and wild dunes of Blakeney Point. The main Perpendicular tower, 120 ft high with soaring buttresses, is echoed by a smaller 'beacon' tower at the east end. Inside the spacious interior many of the medieval furnishings have been lost, although a few worthy misericords can be found in the choir.

Inland a little way is the model village of Glandford, a flint-and-brick creation of Sir Alfred Jodrell with a Perpendicular restoration of an earlier church, and Sir Alfred's most unusual Shell Museum. Binham is an even more flinty community of large farms around the remnants of a twelfth-century Benedictine priory and St Mary's church, an impressive display of Early English and Norman styles. Weybourne, back on the coast again, also

had an extensive priory, a thirteenth-century Augustinian creation whose ruins overshadow today's modest parish church.

Cley-next-the-Sea, with its old windmill and sense of tight-knit timelessness, is a favourite subject of itinerant artists. The broad curve of beach is almost a mile out now across the marshes. Yet the large eighteenth-century Customs House is evidence of a once-flourishing wool trade with the Continent. So is the imposing church of St Margaret's, noted for the unusual clerestory of alternating arched and circular windows along its vast nave, and the fifteenth-century Perpendicular porch. A rather more poignant memorial to the source of Cley's wealth is the post office, decorated with the bones of sheep.

Salthouse possesses another of these imposing coastal churches on a prominent bluff above the often-flooded coastal strip. I arrived here at lunchtime. A small cottage by the side of the road was selling bunches of that succulent seaweed, samphire, and brown shrimps, sweet, crisp and tiny enough to be eaten whole. I bought far too much of both, drove along a marsh track to the edge of a shingle ridge by the beach and cooked lunch while Fred stalked the shallows in search of his own delectables.

Once again, I had the place all to myself.

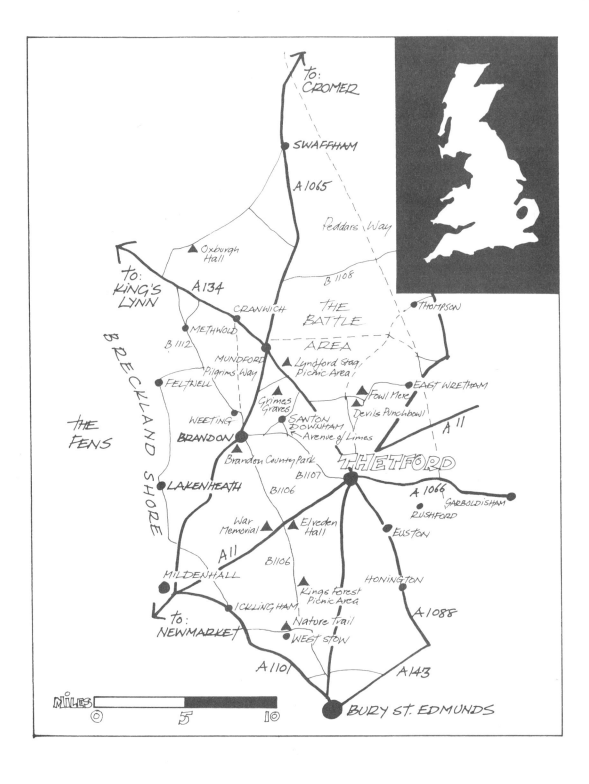

14. The Brecklands

I arrived in the middle of a storm. The day had been heavy with growlings and a jaundice-yellow light sheened the pines at the edge of the heath. It was warm – that sticky, sickly heat of stagnant air, the sweat of autumn's moisting rot. Birds silhouetted against the clouds flew erratically without their normal grace toward the horizon. The sky darkened. A wind buffeted my camper on the narrow road and I pulled to the side, sheltered by the forest. Expectancy hung over the warren. And then it came, a whirling banshee of winds tearing at the trees, sending the gorse into seething furies and screaming as it snapped branches, brittle as bones. Bits of bark flew past like sawdust from a power saw. The smooth surface of a forest lake, one of the Breckland meres, smashed in a million pieces sending frothy wavelets among the reeds. Rain followed wind. Fat globules of water hit the earth like exploding eggs. Lightning flashes illuminated the night-black grass. Rocking trees became lines of ghostly soldiers advancing across the open plateau. A terrified rabbit, a young one, lost its way and ran this way and that, its cotton-ball tail a white beacon of despair. A tiny white flower, roots and all, landed on the windscreen and remained stuck in the wiper as its petals were ripped out and scattered. The storm was a rampaging creature, gorging and tearing at everything in its path. The primitive spirit of the Brecks was out and howling that evening, and I was very impressed.

They call it 'the great East Anglian desert'. The area is certainly empty of both people and communities and is among the most sparsely populated in England. Once it was largely smothered in wind-blown dunes. A seventeenth-century diarist likened it to 'the Sands in the deserts of Lybia'. Whole estates were submerged beneath those inland-moving waves, destroying the very sheep pastures that had caused the damage in the first place. As occurred in so many other parts of Britain, nibbling sheep left nothing but stunted grass behind them in their constant search for nourishment. Saplings, bushes, shrubs, anything that could tame the gales and storms roaring across this flat land were pulverised in the never-closing jaws of those deceptively modest creatures. The sands moved in and the sheep moved on. The landowners contributed in other ways to the emergence of wasteland by discouraging the ambitions of tenant farmers in order to improve the pheasant-rearing capacity of their estates. Rare birds also breed here, the great bustard, the stone curlew and the exquisite golden pheasant. Among the gorse and bracken wilds one can still find little-seen plant species – the field gentian, the Spanish catchfly and maiden pink. It is, like other hidden corners, a land apart.

189

'The Great East Anglia Desert'

But definitely nothing like a desert today. The Forestry Commission has seen to that. Now more than eighty square miles are planted with Scots and Corsican pine in addition to more sensitive deciduous woodlands, beech, birch, sycamores, oaks and even a magnificent avenue of limes (created in 1880) near Santon Downham. Only one segment of the Brecklands maintains the old infinities of sandy gorseland rolling off to hazy horizons. Known menacingly as the 'Battle Area', it is, as its name implies, empty unforested land set aside for official armed exercises. Red flags are raised to indicate tank and shooting activity. The rest of the time the gates are usually open and unmanned although 'no entry' notices are clearly posted. I was lucky enough to find a local resident with a permit who knew his way around the unmapped roads and tracks. We entered the area somewhere north of East Wretham. Regimented lines of pines fell back and the road emerged onto a high plateau, empty except for occasional shell-torn copses and abandoned farmhouses. The view from horizon to horizon was of a primordial emptiness, a space uncluttered by man-made intrusions. Half a mile across a heath

scattered with gorse bushes, a family of deer stood against pines watching us. A mere sparkled between trees and the cries of coot and grebe chattered across the summer-burnt grasses. A heron waited patiently in the shallows and a bird called from the forest, its song a musical release, a long liquid trill. Butterflies – clouded yellows, camberwell beauties and white admirals – frittered over patches of golden ragwort. And above was the great bowl of sky, so close you felt you could reach up and touch it. Clouds sailed across trailing long tongues of shadows in their wake and the air was crisp as an apple, snap-fresh from the branch. It was a slice of ancient England, the kind of place in which one could imagine hunting parties of skin-clad tribesmen pursuing bear and deer across pathless wastes, armed only with flint-head spears and heavy-browed instincts.

The famous Grimes Graves lie on the western edge of the Battle Area. In a large clearing surrounded by more pine forests are literally hundreds (estimated 370) of circular hollows resembling bomb-craters. These are the collapsed remnants of mine shafts thought to be more than 4,000 years old, first excavated in 1869 by the Rev. Greenwell, and varying in depth between 25 and 40 feet, down to the 'floor stone' layer of flints in the chalk bedrock. Interconnecting galleries had been carved out and crude pillars left to prevent collapse. Scattered everywhere were antlers, sharpened as picks and flint-gouging tools. A bulbous fertility goddess crudely carved in chalk was one of many objects unearthed here. Others included the skeleton of a miner, crushed in a roof-collapse thousands of years ago. One wonders at the determination of these early men, scrabbling with their antler-picks in a dusty gloom, illuminated by tiny chalk lamps of animal fat. But at that time flint was gold – the mainstay of those tiny societies – essential for defence, the capture of meat, the carving of domestic implements, and the scraping of skins for clothing.

Even today the craft of flint-knapping is still practised in nearby Brandon, a flint-built market town on the edge of Thetford Forest. Recently demand for top-quality 'black flints' by more than 2,000 flintlock gun clubs in the USA led to the removal of the workshop from the rear yard of the Flint Knapper's

Fertility Goddess - Grimes Graves

Arms in main street to larger premises on the Bury St Edmunds Road. But the process remains strictly traditional. For more than 300 years the Edwards family have been knapping flint, and the pub sign shows one of the Edwards at work with his pad and hammer.

Much of the work is done on the thigh, as one of the assistants explained to me. He carefully examined the shape and structure of a large nodule, about a foot across and resembling a miniature Henry Moore sculpture, then placed it on a leather pad on his left knee. 'It's got to have the "give". If you "quartered" a piece like this on a bench it'd likely break into six, m'be eight pieces. I need four, all about the same size.' He slowly turned the nodule until it was in precisely the right position and brought a hammer down sharply, breaking it into four clean-edged pieces. The black-purple flesh glinted like glass within its chalk shell. 'Now this is the hard bit, what they call flaking.' It didn't look hard at all. He rested one of the quarters on his knee pad and proceeded to chip off equal-sized flakes of flint, curved on one side, straight on the other, with quick sharp flicks of a pointed hammer. 'It's a bit like cutting diamonds, you've got to know your stone or you end up with a useless pile of chips.' At a nearby bench a second assistant was 'knapping' each of the flakes on a small anvil by tapping it with a flat-bladed knapping hammer until it was reduced to the appropriate size and shape. This varied between half an inch and an inch square, depending on the type of gun for which it was intended. 'We supplied most of the flints during the Napoleonic wars,' the assistant boasted. 'Brandon was pretty important in those days. Good place to have an arsenal, too, hidden away in the wilds.'

You could hide a city in that forest today, although local authorities and the Forestry Commission have done their best to make it accessible and attractive to visitors. Picnic sites have been provided at King's Forest and Lynford Stag the latter a pleasant stroll from Lynford Lakes and the Arboretum at Lynford Hall Forester Training School. At West Stow the two-mile King's Forest nature trail passes through a reserve for fallow deer and badgers. And at Brandon a thirty-acre county park surrounds a mansion off the Bury St Edmunds road.

But best of all are the quiet woodland walks from Santon Downham approached along that famous avenue of limes on the Thetford road. According to parish records, this modest little community of modern timber houses (imported from Scandinavia!) was once almost entirely submerged beneath blowing sand in the seventeenth century. The renaissance came with the development of the forest in the 1930s and the establishment of a nucleus for Commission employees and a visitors' information centre. The basic two-mile walk loops round a portion of the forest near the Little Ouse river, through groves of Scots and Corsican pine interspersed with birch, beech and oak. Other less-travelled paths lead off into the still gloom of mature woods and along open river meadows sprinkled with musk mallow, mouse-ear chickweed, moonwort fern and grape hyacinth. I spotted a coypu, a beaver-like creature, scurrying alongside a stream. A few miles to the east I spent a couple of snoozy hours by a tiny pond at the Devil's Punchbowl and, as evening crept over the heath, listened to the chatter of mallard and gadwall on nearby Fowl Mere.

For the more ambitious there are longer walks such as the towpath from Brandon to Thetford along the Little Ouse, segments of the ancient Peddars Way near East Wretham, and the somewhat overgrown and very lonely Pilgrim's Way from Weeting Castle (weathered white stumps surrounded by a dry moat) to Cranwich.

Alternatively one can seek relief from nature's solitude in the pleasant heart of Thetford. Large inns and a watermill grace the riverside walkways and sensitive precincting encourages visitors to enjoy the old curling streets at a leisurely pace. On the southern edge of the town is an abrupt mound like an overgrown sandcastle close to the point at which the Icknield Way crossed the Little Ouse. Its origins are obscured by Thetford's long and vigorous history which includes frequent attacks and sackings by the Danes and its role as King Canute's capital during the more peaceful eleventh century. At various times over twenty churches, four hospitals, three priories and even an official mint flourished here, although little remains today except the few flinty stumps of the great priory of Our Lady to the north of the town centre. Fortunately there's an excellent museum under ornate carved-beam ceilings at The Ancient House, a timber-frame structure round the corner near the Bell Hotel. From the exhibits here one can well believe the strange legends which abound in Thetford. The Bell itself, a rambling, sixteenth-century structure, is reputedly haunted by Betty Radcliffe, a notorious landlady murdered by her jealous lover, the hotel stableman. Under the castle mound is said to be an ancient palace, still intact and filled with treasure. Others claim the mound was a centre of a local sun-worshipping cult. Out on Brandon road, Warren House was once a leper colony and the country round about is said to be plagued by the ghost of a former inmate complete with hideous white face and burning eyes.

Visitors, though, tend to be more interested in the tangible apparition of Thomas Paine near the Bell, one of the instigators of America's War of Independence against Britain and, by all accounts, an irascible, arrogant little corset-maker who claimed to be 'the author of the most useful and benevolent book ever offered to mankind'. He was referring to his famous treatise,

194

The Rights of Man, which sold over 50,000 copies in the first week of publication in England, but, under threat of sedition-action, sent him scurrying off to France. A previous pamphlet, *Common Sense*, printed in 1775, had advocated the immediate independence of the American colonies and was revered by the revolutionary regime in France who instantly made him a citizen of the Republic and were duly influenced by his third work, *The Age of Reason*. He later settled in the newly declared 'United States' and died in 1809 on a farm granted to him by the government. His remains were transferred (against considerable opposition) to the town of his birth by William Cobbett, celebrated author of *Rural Rides*, and he was later commemorated by the golden statue here, commissioned by the Thomas Paine Society of the United States. Although said to have no sense of humour whatsoever, even he must enjoy a chuckle now and then at the ironies of history!

From Thetford I detoured east to the charming village of Garboldisham and the 'clay lump' cottages constructed of that most primitive of materials, large blocks of sun-dried clay. So long as the structures have 'a wide hat and a good pair of boots' (overhanging eaves and solid foundations to keep the moisture out of the clay), the material is almost as durable as brick and can be found, in various forms, in all parts of the world. In South Africa they call it 'Kimberley Brick' and in Mexico 'adobe'.

To the south, woodlands and heath give way to broad sweeps of arable land and one moves gradually from flinty Norfolk to the bowed thatch villages of Suffolk. Rushford slumbers beside the Little Ouse in dappled glades of ash and yews. A three-arch medieval bridge eases itself across the river and calendar-cottages peer doe-eyed over reeds and water-lilies. A long, tree-lined avenue leads on to Euston, a village with all the ambience of the deep south. An enormous cedar bent in its own majesty shades the estate cottages, rebuilt here in the seventeenth century to improve vistas from the Hall. The church is reminiscent of Wren's later designs; golden-stoned in a gold-green field, it sits by itself like a haughty damsel awaiting admirers. The Last Supper altarpiece and the pulpit, laced with angels, cherubs, flowers and fruits, are thought to be the work of Grinling Gibbons. In contrast, the hall is a more eclectic creation with Regency overtones, bright red brick against green lawns, and adorned with window awnings and all the flavour of a Wodehouse tea party. The only distracting elements here are a prominent pillbox in the grounds and the foreign language spoken by estate workers. I asked one man working in the garden for directions to a nearby village and he launched into the most convoluted dialect I have ever heard in England. I asked him to repeat his instructions, but to no avail. All I could make out, with difficulty, was the final 'haav ya gottimm naaa'. I nodded, smiled, and lost my way.

Robert Bloomfield, the eighteenth-century 'Suffolk Poet', lived at nearby Honington and, supported financially by local landowners, spent much of his time wandering 'Euston's watered vale and sloping plains' collecting material for numerous works. Best remembered is *The Farmer's Boy*, full of the Suffolk countryside and the juicy rotundity of its landscape.

Possibly inspired by Bloomfield, the Iveagh family of Elveden Hall determined to make better use of their Breckland estate and reclaimed thousands of acres for cattle, sugar beet and lucerne production. To date, however, they have been reluctant to open their remarkable Taj Mahal-styled residence to the public. The austere external façade hides an exotic fantasy of domes, ornately carved arches, mountains of sculptured Carrara marble, mosaics, and teeming oriental extravagances which required more than 300 men and six years of labour to complete. The work began with a previous owner, the deposed King of the Sikhs, Maharajah Duleep Singh, and was completed by the Guinness Brewery family under Lord Iveagh. The nearby parish church was also the brain-child of this unlikely and involuntary partnership – a Victorian-Gothic fantasy of immaculate flint flush-work, brimming with statues, angels and enough ornate extravaganza for three cathedrals.

Among the old port-towns of the 'Breckland Shore', that ancient line between the once-marshy fens and the heaths, I discovered more evidence of abundant wealth. In a contemporary context one can find it in the American airbase estates, particularly in Lakenheath where a peanut-butter-and-jelly culture imbues local stores, and streets lined with Corvettes, Cadillacs and air-conditioned Winnebago motor homes are the epitome of a petrol-guzzling affluence. But, more significantly, I found it in the churches, many of them masterpieces of the Decorated style and obvious expressions of gratitude to a generous God who served the region well. These were the early 'wool churches' created at a time when King's Lynn was one of England's prime ports, exporting wool from the great Breckland flocks.

At Lakenheath sixty wooden angels peer down on the odd bench ends, a superb thirteenth-century font, and kneeling hassocks made from squares of fen marsh grass. At Mildenhall they cluster even more intensely a fluttering of faces and wings high above the nave with ornately carved spandrels supporting the aisle roofs. But best of all is the enormous double hammer-beam roof of the St Peter and St Paul church at Swaffham where more than 200 of these carved creatures, open-winged and bearing shields, hover above their gaping admirers.

Two detours are recommended from Swaffham. Oxburgh Hall, a four-

Oxburgh Hall

Castle Acre

square brick masterpiece surrounded by a moat and with a gate tower 80 ft high, is one of the finest medieval buildings in East Anglia. It is still occupied by descendants of the Bedingfeld family who began construction here five centuries ago. Many modifications were made subsequently, including the replacement of the drawbridge by a more permanent three-arched affair, but the most notable rooms, the tapestry-hung King's and Queen's Chambers in the gatehouse, are preserved intact along with the cut-brick spiral staircase. Many of the needlework panels in the King's Chamber were the work of Mary Queen of Scots, and indicate a powerful artistic vision of nature and living creatures – made more poignant by her fear of impending death.

While Oxburgh retains its hall, Castle Acre has long been without its castle. The earthworks of William the Conqueror's son-in-law, William de Warenne, are still intact close to the ancient Peddar's Way, that ruler-straight track linking the Roman garrison at Colchester to diminutive Holme-next-the-Sea on the north Norfolk coast. The French-flavoured hilltop village, entered through the remnants of a bailey gate, clusters around a green shaded by lime trees. Beyond, the chalk uplands stretch out empty and desolate, belly-buttoned by ancient marlpits. The village faces inward and the odd-named Albert Victor and Ostrich pubs provide solace from the alien

198

terrain. A lane wanders past the church downhill to the remains of the eleventh-century Cluniac Priory by the river Nar, one of the finest examples of bold Norman architecture in Britain. The west front, richly tiered with blind-arcading, rises high above the meadows, gloriously aloof. The adjoining Prior's House is, by contrast, a comfortable Tudor enclave of large fireplaces and bowed beams. Sunlight shafts through leaded lights, gilding the whitewashed walls and casting long shadows across the lawns. From the hilltop long dark lines on the horizon mark the fringes of the Breckland forests.

I headed south again for one more journey through that pineland wilderness. This time there was no storm. After a long day of lowering greys, the sky snapped open at dusk and the brilliant red eye of the sun peered out across the heaths. The black-grained bark of trees turned crimson, and patches of crystallised resin sparkled brilliantly. A nineteenth-century writer referred to the Brecks as 'an inhospitable land, an empty quarter to be hurried though by all who value their safety and their sanity'. That evening they showed another face, a gentle profile, blushing with quiet modesty. I sat on the edge of the heath waiting for that magical silence just before night. The forest vibrated in rosy shadows and waited with me.

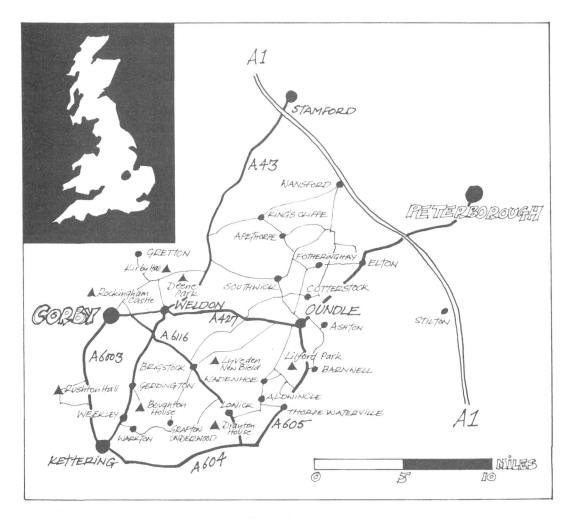

15. Oundle and the 'Eastern Cotswolds'

At first I didn't believe it. True, the landscape was a little less rolling than the hills around Broadway and Chipping Campden, the vegetation perhaps a trifle more sparse. But the Cotswold feel was here, the golden-stoned intimacy of the villages, the steep gables, the clustered chimneys, the woodlands and broad horse-chestnuts shading old inns.

I was actually in Northamptonshire just west of Peterborough, where segments of ancient Rockingham Forest still remain, at least in name, and

200

river meadows follow the meanderings of the Nene. They call it 'the county of squires and spires' and it possesses both in abundance. At times one feels an intruder on a vast private estate. It also boasts long and intimate links with the royalty of Britain. Richard III was born in the shadow of that most magnificent of rural churches at Fotheringhay, its arching buttresses and octagonal lantern tower reflected in the placid river Nene. Henry VIII's last wife retired to the seclusion of a small manor close to Oundle's St Peter's church. More recently, in 1938, the Duke of Gloucester made Barnwell Castle his home and spent 'ripping days' here with his cronies (who apparently all addressed him as 'Gloggins').

Other regal personages paused for briefer intervals. Queen Elizabeth I was entertained by the Brudenells of Deene Park in 1566 and remarked on the excellence of the banquet. (It was a later descendant of the Brudenells, the 7th Earl of Cardigan, who led the Charge of the Light Brigade.) Edward I's wife, Eleanor of Castile, passed through the tranquil village of Geddington in 1290 and her visit was commemorated with a richly decorated cross. Unfortunately she was deceased at the time and in her coffin on the way to London from Harby in Nottinghamshire. Twelve similar crosses marked her route, of which three remain today. Geddington's is undoubtedly the finest. Queen Victoria slept overnight once at the rambling Haycock Inn at Wansford near the A1, still a popular hostelry. It would be interesting to know whether she brought her own bed with her which, according to Eric Walker, owner of the Station Museum at Wolferton in Norfolk, she invariably did (see Chapter 13).

But the most notable regal resident of all was Mary Queen of Scots who lost her head in the great banquet hall of Fotheringhay Castle in 1587 after sixteen months of imprisonment there. Alive she had attracted a wide range of descriptions, from –

'A famous queen,
And a great lover! When you hear her name,
Your heart will leap. Her beauty passed the bounds of modesty . . .'

to the less complimentary –

'The witch from over the water,
The fay from over the foam . . .'

Dead, she brought an embarrassed peace and today attracts informed visitors to the unassuming grassy hump, the only remnant of the castle, and the famous Talbot Inn in Oundle, a splendid grey-gold edifice in a grey-gold market town brimming with towers, turrets and ball-finials. The Inn is

Geddington Cross

thought to originate from a seventh-century pilgrim's hostelry and was substantially rebuilt in 1626 with stone brought from Fotheringhay Castle. The large oak staircase leading to Mary's imprisonment rooms came too. A small gate dividing the stairway marked her outer prison confines and the imprint of a tiny crown on the balustrade is claimed to have been made by her ring as she gripped the rail on her way to the block. The management delights in tales of this kind and has found evidence to suggest that her appointed executioner lodged at the Talbot the night before the event and 'partook of pigeon pie, drank a quart of the best ale and made a merry discourse with a serving girl 'till an early hour of the morning'. Not surprisingly, 'Executioner's Pie' is featured prominently on the hotel menu along with the rather tasteless (ethically at least) 'Filet Mary Stuart'. More susceptible residents are constantly on the look-out for Mary's ghost, said to haunt the area by the staircase window, peering out defiantly at the courtyard below.

Tom Laycock calls himself 'a passable know-all' and thinks of the Mary-enthusiasts as 'ghoullies'. The very epitome of a Northumberland squire, Tom has only lived in the area since his early retirement five years ago but is already regarded as something of an expert by those who meet him at the King's Head in Wadenhoe or the Montagu Arms in Barnwell, two of his most favoured niches. 'The trouble is, most of them miss the best places. They scootle for an old one-two around Oundle, then off to Fotheringhay, a peep at a couple of the halls and that's it, very nice, toodle-oo, must come back sometime and ta-ta. Very unfortunate. Miss the best. Great shame.' I had met an alter-ego and very pleasant it was too. 'Take our church tombs,' he began. 'I'd say we've got some of the finest in the country – bar one or two in London, of course – splendid things, hardly visited at all. Don't mean the gravestones. I'm talking about the memorials inside the churches. Can't see them from the road, y'know. Got to get out of the car and do a bit of walking. Some of 'em don't like that!' He paused and enveloped half a sandwich in his extraordinarily broad mouth, shrouded by a silver moustache. 'Listen, if you've got a bit of time there's a couple of places I'd advise you to see. . . .' And so began an exhaustive description of his discoveries interspersed with anecdotes and experiences (many suggesting remarkable imagination and virility on the part of the local populace and totally unprintable) – all of which makes the job of hidden-corner exploring totally absorbing, even if one does spend a disproportionate amount of time in pubs.

The countryside around Oundle is littered with squirely estates and grand mansions. A few are well-known and open to the public on a regular basis – Boughton House, Lilford Hall, Deene Park, Rockingham Castle, Rushton

Hall – but the remainder are quietly hidden away in woods or down long, unmarked drives. In this distinguished landscape, church and gentry lived harmoniously for most of the time, reinforcing one another's ambitions and needs. The church welcomed the financial assistance of the wealthy landowners, who in turn expected places to be set aside for distinguished memorials reflecting their standing and generosity, and ultimately, special consideration from God and his advisers in the afterlife. Thus we often find humble village churches filled with those richly adorned memorials so much admired by Tom, enthusiastically extolling the virtues of their occupants. In the church at Apethorpe, a beautiful mellow village of thatch and stone-roofed cottages around Willow Brook, I found the towering tomb of Sir Anthony Mildmay complete with swathes of alabaster curtains and grecian-goddess females, firm-breasted (boldly exposed too), representing Justice, Pride and other lofty principles. His immodest epitaph begins: 'Here sleepeth in the Lord with certain hope of resurrection, Sir Anthony Mildmay, eldest son to Sir Walter Mildmay, Knight Chancellor of the Exchequer and Privy Counsellor to Queen Elizabeth . . .'

Sir Anthony lay in typical devout fashion with praying hands beside his wife Grace on an immense square base. An expression of devout anticipation filled his marble face. Nearby, in surprising contrast to his extravagances, was a tiny floor-level tomb on which rested the perfectly-carved figure of a young child, hands clasped and asleep, with a bonnet tied round its head. I couldn't make out the dedication which was refreshingly short and simple.

At Southwick Church, the epitaph to the local landowner George Lynn who died in 1758 suggests a tranquil pastoral life spent adding bits and pieces to his adjoining manor house. Apparently he intended to undertake a career in law, then, as the words suggest, changed his mind:

> But early quitting these severer Studies,
> For the calm Pleasures of a rural Life,
> He greatly improved by a most elegant Taste
> This his parental seat of Southwick.

A famous French sculptor of the period, Roubiliac, designed the life-size three-dimensional tableau in white alabaster on the north wall of the chancel which has Lynn's distressed wife languorously strewn around the urn containing his remains. A large medallion above shows Mr Lynn's profile peering into the far distance. The whole creation might have become banal had it not been for the human touch of his wife's left shoe gently loosening itself from her foot and her apparent dozing. One wonders what the other

Fotheringhay Church

Lynns, memorialised in plain black stones on the chancel floor, would have thought of all this rococo.

At Lowick Church the Greene, Mordaunt and Sackville families, who successively owned nearby Drayton Hall, all decided they wanted pride of place in the church and full recognition of their status. So here they all are crammed together in regal splendour – Sir Ralph Greene holding hands with his wife (a most unusual posture in such memorials), the relaxed figures of Sir John Germaine and Lady Mary Mordaunt, the elephantine tomb in white marble of the Sackvilles, and the tomb-chest of an intruder, Edward Lord Stafford. One might conclude that there can be no monuments more imposing than these in the region.

One would, however, be mistaken.

Take a short journey to Warkton, another delightful village on a steep hill below the Boughton House estate. The church sits partly in fields below a silhouetted line of elms, an eighteenth-century Palladian chancel extruding from its Perpendicular nave. Here in white alabaster and grey marble are four huge tableau-memorials to the Montagu family, without doubt the finest collection in the county. An elderly lady in a pink hat frittered among flowers by the pulpit. 'Come in, come in. It's only me.' Her face had a sparkle one normally associates with fairy godmothers. 'My turn for flowers,' she explained and shook two glove-covered hands at me. 'Roses – they're so prickly this year, have you noticed? My hands get so sore if I don't wear these.' She giggled and put down a pair of scissors on the lectern. 'Is it the monuments?' she chirped. I nodded. 'Well, you must have this.' She picked up an information board and handed it to me. 'It tells you all about them – the Montagus you know – "our" Montagus we call them. I think the best . . .' A sonorous voice, presumably the vicar's, rumbled away in the vestry somewhere. The little lady paused in what I imagine was about to be a lengthy description and scurried off through a door. I carried on without her.

Roubiliac was again responsible for the most powerful groupings of John, the 2nd Duke, and his wife Mary. In similar style to the Lynn memorial, he introduces the medallion motif for John, and has Mary gazing griefstricken at its outline, surrounded by weeping damsels – all life-size and meticulously detailed. Across the aisle is Mary's own tomb with an urn being draped in flowers by children above figures of the three fates. Finally (four tableaux exist here, but the one for Elizabeth, Duchess of Buccleuch, is distinctly inferior to the others), there is a combined Robert Adam and Van Gelder creation for a second Duchess Mary, full of drama and highlighted by a sinister shrouded woman and an angel, vigorously pointing to yet another urn. And all this in one tiny country church!

Regrettably, the fairy-godmother lady never reappeared and I continued on to Barnwell and the last of the major monuments. Actually there are two, one of which I wouldn't have found without the help of a retired gamekeeper whom I met by chance outside the Montagu Arms. I was sitting on the bank of a stream that wriggled down the length of the village, wondering how it was I'd never ventured through this idyllic part of Britain before. Round a curve in the stream I could see a high single-arched bridge and the craggy outlines of the castle, owned by the Duke of Gloucester. The ruins of a thirteenth century fortress rose up behind a sixteenth-century manor house built by the Montagus, and the whole complex sat in simply landscaped grounds. 'Not a bad-looking place, then, is it?' The retired gamekeeper in breeches and high-laced boots stood beside me and we chatted about the village. I told him of Tom Lacock's insistence that I visit the little chapel at the top end of the stream. All the Earls of Sandwich ('bar one and another half – they lost bits of him in a battle') were buried here, and a huge floor-to-ceiling tomb, studded with shields, stands at the east end in memory of the boy-earl drowned in the castle moat ('a witty and hopeful child', according to his inscription). 'You won't get in,' he told me. 'They're making new keys and the vicar's away.' I was disappointed. 'Go look at old Latham's memorial, in the church.' He pointed at the steeple of St Andrew's on a rise above the stream. 'He weren't royalty or nothing, just vicar here. More'n fifty years. A good man. N'ont so fancy as others, but it don't need to be, does it? He chatted wi' God, every day, so he'd be all right, I reckon.'

A testament to such charitable efforts as hospital and school building, the providing of pensions and 'the yearly clothing for 43 poor children all of which do amount of £300 by the year', is detailed on a wall plaque outside his 'hospital', opposite the church. Inside St Andrew's on the south wall of the chancel is Latham's restrained memorial depicting a modest and obviously devout man contemplating a bible. A great stillness, a sense of other-worldliness, pervades the work. 'Nice-looking fellow, in't he?' the gamekeeper called out as I emerged. 'Only an ordinary chap, too.'

'Ordinary' is hardly the word for the Rothschild family, a branch of which occupies a large estate just north of Barnwell. Charles Rothschild, a distin-guished lepidopterist, first became enamoured of this secluded corner of England eighty-five years ago when he discovered it to be a haunt of a very rare species of butterfly. He, like Latham, was a philanthropist and helped design a village of gold-stoned thatched cottages (semi-detached!) for his employees, complete with green, church, and an old-world pub named after his beloved butterfly. Today Ashton is known for its extraordinary 'model' character, occasional summer festivities, Morris dancing, and its annual

Wadenhoe

World Conker Championship. Charles's daughter, a world authority on fleas, continues to live in the Rothschild mansion (not normally open to the public).

While not all villages in the region can match the conscious ambience of Ashton, most possess distinct charm and a physical unity characterised by honey-coloured stone, sturdy grouped chimneys, thatch or mossy stone tile, and a spirit of docile timelessness. All the flavour of Cotswold villages is indeed here, but the tourists are not. Most pubs cater to local trade and have avoided the plastic-palace/instant-medieval impositions of brewery designers. Even the more popular places such as the King's Head by the river Nene at Wadenhoe have maintained much of their original character. This is one of my favourite Northamptonshire villages, graced by a sixteenth-century dovecote near the manor house, an old toll-house, and a long tumbling street to the river, all overlooked by the church with an unusual 'gable' tower, set on a steep grassy hill.

Elton off the A605 is another attractive village typical of this undiscovered

region. There are many more – Apethorpe, King's Cliffe, Weekley with its ornate seventeenth-century almshouses, the slow curl of Grafton Underwood's main street beside an overgrown stream, John Dryden's birthplace in the Old Rectory at Aldwincle, the broad vistas from mansions lined along the escarpment-edge at Gretton, the restored manor and barn at Thorpe Waterville, and the refined Georgian house imperiously watching over river marshes at Cotterstock. A great cosiness characterises these places, a rotund rurality – bowed roofs of thick thatch, brambled lanes leading nowhere, the feathery tips of silver birches fringing the last remnants of Rockingham Forest and clustered copses on the edge of ploughed fields.

One can smell old wealth everywhere, the measured dignity of tradition and ancient authority. Halls and stately houses open to the public have long tales to tell of England's most powerful families. The riches displayed – the tapestries, the paintings, the porcelain and the armour – are merely glimpses of the once overwhelming opulence of life in these rolling uplands.

The grandiose shell of Kirby Hall, an unusual mixture of Elizabethan and Italianate influences, is as impressive as the others even without its roof. James I adored the place and successive members of the Hatton family maintained a stately formal garden, portions of which still remain today. A second shell, the never-completed Lyveden New Bield near Brigstock, built in the shape of a cross by the eccentric mystic Sir Thomas Tresham, is a less grandiose edifice but equally indicative of inherited wealth. Sir Thomas lost his great house at Rushton, confiscated by the state for his involvement in the Gunpowder Plot, yet went on to build his New Bield project, 'a summer retreat', with all the fervour of a journeyman mason.

The 220-acre Lilford Park, now one of the most popular estates around Oundle, only narrowly avoided decimation through neglect, and much of the straggling nine-bay Jacobean hall is still unoccupied. It became famous towards the end of the last century for elaborate gardens and aviaries designed by another creative genius, Baron Lilford, author of *Coloured Figures of Birds in the British Isles*, and today attracts hundreds of summer visitors. In contrast, Deene Park, a sixteenth-century house with a full history, set in extensive grounds, seems to hide away from the outside world, screened by woods. There's an intimacy possibly reinforced by the presence of the Brudenell family here for over four centuries. Like most large houses, it experienced a fluctuating fate. The generous, pleasure-loving Lady Adeline, wife of the 7th Earl of Cardigan (leader of the Charge of the Light Brigade), frittered away a fortune, reduced the family to near-poverty and is reputed to have sold her jewellery and even her underwear in a sale at the hall.

The Dukes of Buccleuch, ensconsced in their vast Boughton House brimming with fine works of art – El Grecos, Murillos and forty Van Dyck sketches – seem to have experienced more stable fortunes. The present Duke is said to own almost 12,000 acres, half a dozen villages, and the rights to large segments of ironworkings east of Corby. Immense 'diggers,' two with beams over 350 ft long, can be seen peering over mini-alpine ranges of opencast spoil-heaps near Gretton and Weldon. It is the seventeenth-century Sir Ralph Montagu, however, who looms large over the family history. Described once by Dean Swift as 'as arrant a knave as any in his time', he was appointed ambassador to France by Charles II and became deeply enamoured of the French way of life and courtly distractions. He remodelled Boughton House in a mansarded style and imported the French artist, Chéron, to design his ceilings. After various close political shaves with the British monarchy, he was finally granted his prime ambition and made a duke of the realm.

Such tales and trappings of power link all these great houses around

Triangular Tower. Rushton Hall

Rockingham Forest. Rockingham Castle and Rushton Hall also have their stories to tell and are well worth a visit. The architectural fantasies of Sir Thomas Tresham, creator of Lyveden New Bield, appear once more in the grounds of the latter where a strange, three-storey triangular tower symbolises the Trinity complete with three trefoil windows on each side, three gables topping each wall, and three chimney smokeholes. Not surprisingly, each side measures 33 feet 4 inches long – precisely a third of a hundred.

But enough of all this extravagance! I wandered again to one of my favourite English market towns, Oundle, and braving the traffic along its narrow main street (surely there must be a by-pass soon?) sought the sanctuary of the churchyard surrounded by ancient mellowed buildings, part of Sir William Laxton's famous school. Town and gown merge most successfully here in grey-gold alleys, courts and quadrangles. Only occasionally in the early evening after classes does it become apparent that 700 boys are being educated here. The town swarms with uniformed look-alikes for a while and then gradually calms itself.

Oundle

The thin spire of St Peter's matches in beauty those other notable creations at nearby Titchmarsh, Lowick and Fotheringhay. Inside the church is spacious and controlled, a neutral setting for the rich south aisle windows in the Decorated style and the brilliantly-coloured, single-legged pulpit. With the exception of the large Gothic tomb of the Rev. John Shillibeer, the walls and aisles are uncluttered. I was curious, though, about the display of rather worn muskets on the left side of the south door. I wondered why guns would be hung in a church.

Tom Laycock wasn't sure either. 'To be honest,' he confessed, 'I hadn't noticed them. But next time I think about it I'll ask.' We were strolling by the Oundle marina watching ducks ripple the pink-purple waters. It was deep evening. 'Happens all the time round here. Think I'm getting to know all about everything – and then find I've missed something obvious – something everyone knows except me.' He paused and made duck sounds which failed to convince the ducks. 'Wouldn't do to know everything, though, would it? Be damned boring. But listen – before I forget – if you've got a bit more time there's a place not too far from here. . . .'

Hidden-cornering never ends.

212

16. The Suffolk Coast

Seven o'clock in the morning may seem an odd time to begin explorations, but in the case of Woodbridge it's the best time. During the peak weeks of summer this charming lopsided town of timber-framed and Georgian houses, sinewed on a steep hill above tide marshes, is rapidly inundated with camera-clicking tourists and the yelpings of impatient children. In the early morning, though, mists slink up Brook Street and Station Road from the river Deben, wrapping the town in a glowing haze. No one was about as I rambled past the old Tide Mill and the copses of boat masts by the quay, up the slope of New Street by the Olde Bell and Steelyard Inn (purveyor of those wonderful Adnam's Ales), into a perfect market-place. Off to the side was the parish church, faced with meticulous flint and stone flushwork. Inside I found an ancient octagonal font with recessed bas-relief panels, a design popular in East Anglia and possessed by almost every church I visited in the old silted villages and ports of this quiet coastal region.

The town's most notable building stands in the market-place by the old town pump – a prim Elizabethan Shire Hall built by the local Seckford family with a Dutch-style gable-end and a double staircase curling to a high door. During the elegant nineteenth century, the great artists and men of letters, Tennyson, Constable and Carlyle, strolled these streets. Edward Fitzgerald, born at nearby Bredfield House, loved everything about this secluded backwater, writing such obscure treatises as *Suffolk Sea Phrases* after years of association with old salts by the quay. A clique of admirers, the 'Woodbridge Wits', gathered about him as his fame spread following the publication of his translated *Rubaiyat of Omar Khayyám*. Todays devotees make pilgrimages to his grave in Boulge, two miles or so north of the town.

By nine, as the town primped and polished itself for the daily onslaught, I was off down country lanes to the south. The mists had slid back to the river and the morning was summer-plump under a broadening sun. Larks rose from cornfields, their songs trailing back like kite-tails. I could smell the coming heat of the day in the sweaty grass, and whiffs of ozone nipped the nostrils as I approached the coast.

Sutton Common, a pocket of heath, bracken and pines in sugar-beet fields, marks the edge of the once vast Suffolk saltings. Before reclamation, a woody wilderness six miles wide in places stretched in an unbroken band between Southwold and the Deben river. Like the Brecklands of Norfolk (Chapter 14) this was valuable sheep-grazing land until the pheasant-breeding mania of the late eighteenth century led to the removal of animals

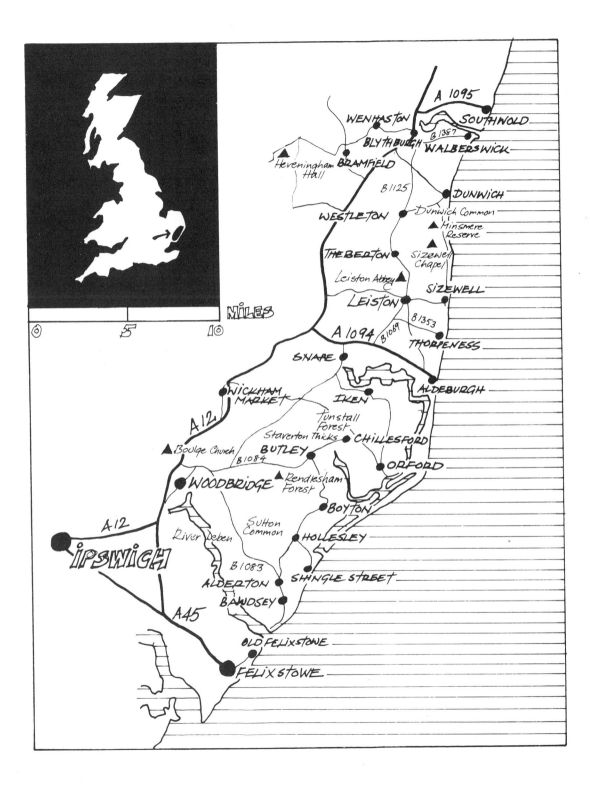

MILES

0   5   10

A 1095

WENHASTON
BLYTHBURGH   B 1387   SOUTHWOLD
                        WALBERSWICK
BRAMFIELD
Heveningham
Hall
                B 1125   DUNWICH
WESTLETON   Dunwich Common
                        Minsmere
                        Reserve
THEBERTON   Sizewell
            Chapel
Leiston Abbey
            SIZEWELL
    LEISTON
    A 1094   B 1353
        B 1069   THORPENESS
SNAPE
WICKHAM   IKEN   ALDEBURGH
MARKET
A 12   Tunstall
            Forest
    Staverton Thicks   CHILLESFORD
Boulge Church   BUTLEY
        B 1084   ORFORD
        Rendlesham
WOODBRIDGE   Forest
                    BOYTON
A 12   Sutton
River Deben   Common
            HOLLESLEY
        B 1083
IPSWICH   ALDERTON   SHINGLE STREET
        BAWDSEY
A 45
        OLD FELIXSTOWE
    FELIXSTOWE

and inhabitants by wealthy estate-owners. Segments still remain, most notably Tunstall Forest, the Staverton Thicks near Butley, Dunwich Common, Minsmere and Rendlesham Forest, a path-laced pine forest, home of red squirrels and fallow deer.

Fringing the saltings are the curving beaches and shingle ridges of a silted shore where rivers meander hopelessly seeking the sea, and explorers lose themselves in pebble-strewn emptiness. Beyond Bawdsey's fortress-like church, a path skirting Ministry of Defence land leads onto empty strands by the river Deben and a ferry makes the occasional crossing to Old Felixstowe.

To the north, Shingle Street is a wind-blasted line of white cottages and martello towers (built to discourage Napoleonic invasion) on the edge of an area frequented by ornithologists. Among the smooth cool pebbles are clusters of yellow horned poppy and sea bindweed sheltering in the lee of the ridge away from sea winds. Enthusiasts can walk beside the river Ore and up the river wall to Chillesford, seven of the loneliest miles in Suffolk.

Tiny villages fringe the marshy flats. At Boyton, in the middle of fields by the church, I discovered the 1736 Mary Warner Almshouses, a three-sided court round the old water pump. An elderly lady sat sunning herself outside her cottage, sewing an intricate quilt of tiny hexagonal scraps of material. 'This is only my fourth one,' she told me. 'It's for my youngest daughter. All the others have one now.' I mentioned the demand for handsewn quilts with traditional patterns, the 'wedding ring' particularly, and wondered if she'd ever thought of selling her work. 'Oh, Lord no. It would spoil it, wouldn't it? I like to make them for people I know – family mainly. I couldn't make them for just anybody. Each of these little patches are from their old frocks and nighties. They remember them from when they were tiny.' We sat together in the bright sun. It seemed a tranquil place, maybe a little too tranquil all by itself in a field, away from shops and people. 'It's the winter that's worst, we never see anybody, not even a black cat. And I'm very annoyed with this new rector.' She nodded at the adjoining flint church. 'He never comes round. I can't go to church as often as I'd like now and he's always buzzing off here and there. Can't think what he does. The old one always seemed to have lots of time.'

At Butley the minimal remains of a fourteenth-century abbey, and an immaculate flushwork gatehouse, stand in the private grounds of a farm. Nearby is the village's thatched church and two men, an elderly thatcher and his young assistant, were resurfacing the long nave ridge with wheatstraw. 'S'best for the tops there, it bends nicely, do y'see,' the older man told me as he carefully selected the wheat, straw by straw. 'I used reed, best Norfolk, for the roof 'bout twenty years ago. It'll last 'nother twenty years, too, I shouldn't wonder. That was when a cottage thatching cost 'round about £30 if that – now s'more like £3,000.' Around his feet were dozens of split-wood pegs or 'spars' used for securing the ridge thatch. 'I use willow spars mostly. Others like hazel and some of the young lads, the fly-by-nights, they use the steel ones.' He pointed at his assistant perched on the ridge of the church. 'He's startin' with a reed roll, 'bout four inches thick. Then the tops of the course oversailin' the ridge are twisted in knuckles and held down usin' a sway sparred into the roll. Then he puts straw wadds down and spars them, then two more rolls covered with pattern courses and all tied down with side ligger-strips and spars lengthwise 'long the ridge. You put in your cross liggers, like a criss-cross, and cut your pattern in the ends. It'll be plain-ish on this one. Then you give it a final beating up with a leggatt and trim it off nice with a shearing hook. And thats what it all amounts to,' he said, grinning at my confusion. 'Hope you got all that on your little tape recorder.' I wondered how long the job would take. ''Bout two weeks or so. We go nice'n steady, 'specially with this sun.' He adjusted the leather pad over the palm of his right hand, gave me another broad grin and carried the wheat straw bundles back along the path to the church. His assistant waved a good-day from the ridge and I left them to their task.

The irascible Aldeburgh poet, George Crabbe, whose work, *The Borough*, inspired Benjamin Britten's opera, *Peter Grimes*, had a rather dour opinion of the local populace, describing them as a

> . . . wild amphibious race,
> With sullen woe displayed in every face;
> Who far from civil arts and social fly,
> And scowl at strangers with suspicious eye.

I saw little woe or suspicion as I roamed the Suffolk saltings, except perhaps in the eyes of nervous sheep peering at me across the nibbled-smooth grass at Orford Castle. This grand, eighteen-sided edifice is the last remnant of a much larger twelfth-century complex built for Henry II. For a while it was home to the Wild Man of Orford. According to legend, a bald, bearded creature resembling a man was dragged up by local fishermen in their nets and handed over to the castle governor for safekeeping. He was fed on a diet of raw fish and taken, quite happily, for daily swims in the sea. This went on for months until, presumably tired of always being on display, the creature escaped and vanished back into the ocean, never to be seen again.

The castle's large circular rooms (exquisite seventeenth-century graffiti on the stair walls) and cramped guardrooms, well-equipped with primitive toilet facilities, are a vantage-point for views across the saltings and shingles fading into sea-hazes beyond Aldeburgh. Wimar the Champlain was responsible for supervising construction. He was so impressed by the skill of his Norman masons that he decided to build a church at the same time, declaring to the citizenry of the little port that 'no longer shall it be required of the pious in Orford to tread the sandy road for pious purposes to distant Sudborne; they have a castle for their defence; they shall have a church, and a noble one at that'. And if the ornately decorated remnants of pillars in the chancel ruins are any indication, it must have been the most noble Norman creation in Suffolk. Unfortunately, only the choir was incorporated into the new fourteenth-century structure. Other features of interest include the floor brasses (gradually disappearing), the old stocks, a painting of the Holy Family by a pupil of Raphael over the Lady Chapel altar – and the delectable aroma from a smokehouse curling in round the open door.

Across the street stands Orford's main claim to fame today, the Butley-Orford Oysterage, renowned for its smoked eel, smoked salmon, smoked mackerel, smoked bloaters and even smoked cod roe plus unusual restaurant offerings of stewed eel, pork and clam stew, salmon steak in oyster sauce, oyster stew and 'angels on horseback' (oysters wrapped in grilled bacon on toast). I passed a succulent lunch hour sampling the wares and moved on along the Alde meadows to the hamlet of Iken. An abandoned church stood on a grassy mound above a tidal lake. Summer buzzed softly in the shallows and reeds rattled in buffets of wind. A sign described this as the assumed site of St Botolph's seventh-century monastery, destroyed by the Danes in 870 AD. Shards of Ipswich-ware dating from that period have been discovered in the excavations, but so far the foundations of the actual buildings have proved rather more elusive. Meanwhile the burnt-out church stands roofless and forlorn near the water's edge.

More recently (in 1969) a similar fate struck the famous Aldeburgh Music and Arts Festival concert hall at the Snape Maltings. After long months of construction, it was gutted by fire on the first night of the 1969 season and had to be entirely rebuilt. Today it stands behind the picturesque nineteenth-century maltings, still used as grain warehouses, along with the Britten-Pears School of Advanced Musical Studies. An adjoining tow path offers a lovely three-mile link with Iken Church.

Aldeburgh, another silted fishing port, is a cosy, rather eccentric resort of sundials and quaint little squares behind a long beach-walk. At the Cross Keys pub, dried sprats are nailed to the beams in the public bar to commemorate the first seasonal catch of the town's famous delicacy. Two

Moot Hall. Aldeburgh

odd towered buildings face across the sands. Apparently these were the headquarters of competing lifeboat companies and the towers were used as lookouts. Further down stands another martello tower and at the southern edge of the town, before the windy strand, is a most unusual eclectic Victorian-Tudor extravaganza with gables, bows, balconies and slit windows all jumbled around a lighthouse. Architecturally dominant, however, is the extensively restored sixteenth-century Moot Hall, a wonderful harmony of stone, flint, brick, timber-framing, carved beams, herringbone panels and leaded lights, topped by two enormous chimneys and decorated with the inevitable sundial. One wonders if the people of Aldeburgh are unusually time-conscious or merely watchless. I counted three sundials within fifty yards of the Hall and I'm told there are more. The Council still meets at the Moot Hall and a museum occupies the ground floor. It's an eminently sketchable subject.

As are the even more eccentric creations at nearby Thorpeness, a twentieth-century Tudor-style resort village with a 'Merrie England' flavour, planned by Stuart Ogilvie and architect Forbes Glennie. A 65-acre lake, The Mere, a golf course and a country club provided the nucleus for twee scatterings of country cottages, a rambling inn, olde-worlde shops, (a hideous concrete church?), all laced with prim hedges, flowered gardens, elegant bird-boxes and even a willow-shrouded duck pond. Although the creation was never completed, it exists as a delightful 'garden-city' fantasy with a windmill imported from nearby Aldringham, and two disguised water towers. One is designed as an imposing towered gateway and the other as 'The House in the Clouds', a brightly painted sham 'house' on top of a tall black tower (the actual house). I chatted with a very colonel-like resident trimming his already trim hedge. 'Lovely place. Bit hectic in the summer, y'know, people renting houses and all that, but gen'rally splendid place to live.' He told me most residents had been able to purchase their homes from the development company. 'Far better. Gives you a stake in the place. Know what I mean? Make sure we keep it the way we want it.' A local shopkeeper was less enamoured. 'Winters are deadly. A hundred people here at the outside. We're leaving after this one.' His wife nodded dejectedly.

Beyond Theberton and Westleton, two attractive villages with thatched churches and greens, I emerged once again on the saltings. The heathland wilderness of Dunwich Common, purple-brown and flecked with heather-blossoms, ends at a vantage-point by the coastguard cottages. Here one can peer out over Minsmere Nature Reserve, home of bitterns, nightjars, marsh harriers and Savi's warblers. A lagoon dotted with islets also provides a haven for the rare avocet and attracts such unusual migratory birds as the

219

Thorpeness

white-rumped and Terek sandpipers. Although access to the reserve is restricted, a six-mile loop walk starts by the cottages, down a steep gulley to the beach below the high Minsmere cliffs, and continues round the southern fringe by Sizewell Chapel (a remnant of the original Leiston Abbey), returning through woods to the common. There's also a short clifftop walk northwards to Dunwich, a scattering of cottages, fish shacks and the nautical-flavoured Ship Inn above another long arc of shingle beach. It's hard to believe that this modest coastal hamlet was, at the time of the Domesday survey, one of the largest and most prosperous towns in East Anglia. During its heyday in King John's reign the town boasted a priory, nine churches, a hospital and a major port of '80 great ships'. Southwold residents were jealous of Dunwich's success and frequent attacks and sinkings characterised the relationship between the two towns. Then the great storm of 1326 began the creeping erosion of the cliffs and the silting of the harbour. Houses, public buildings and churches slid into the waves. All Saints was the last to go, with the nave tumbling over in 1904 and the tower in 1918.

220

Ghosts abound here. Residents claim to have heard the bells of submerged churches peeling out warnings of approaching storms. Shadowy strings of monks walk the clifftops and the restless spirits of long-dead citizens haunt the shingle ridges in forlorn groups, seeking their lost homes. All I saw were pin-pricks of lights along the beach, the tiny beacons of the night-fishermen casting in the surf.

A narrow road passing across more wild heathland, or a lonely three-mile beach-walk, lead to the green-laced village of Walberswick. This too was once a prosperous port which, after silting, retired gracefully around a proud, partially ruined church. Today it slumbers beside meandering creeks wrapped in the soft beiges and muted greens of Tinker's Covert and Angel's Marsh. Even gulls call softly here. Only the men were noisy. Known as the 'Walberswick Whisperers', their bawling voices, so it is said, could be heard plainly in Southwold's main street far on the other side of the river Blyth. I spent a whole day here among the dunes, with a book, a bottle of wine and two excellent cigars – and heard no one at all. In the early evening I was

221

rowed across the river in an impromptu ferry and wandered among the tar-coated fish shacks on Blackshore Quay before a night of revelries and folk-singing at the Harbour Inn.

Southwold is a mellow, old-fashioned resort with broad greens (actually fire breaks created after the disastrous 1659 fire), steeped in the sweet aromas of the Adnam's brewery, home of some of Britain's finest beers. Broadside pale ale has a local reputation for its punch and is named in honour of the great battle of Sole Bay fought just offshore in 1672 between the British and Dutch fleets. Other 'knee-shake strength' brews are specially prepared to honour local events. The famous Rail Ale, for example, commemorated the centenary of Southwold's railway. Local beer deliveries are made by the brewery's horse-drawn drays which clatter round the compact streets of the town, pausing at the Lord Nelson, an old smugglers' inn, the picturesque Sole Bay Inn below the white lighthouse, and the Harbour Inn which has survived centuries of floods.

Southwold is a town for slow walking along the windy clifftops, across the greens edged with Georgian homes, through Market Place framed by the ivy clad Swan Hotel, past Miss Phillips's charming Amber Shop (Scandinavian amber can often be found on local beaches) and on to the town's most unusual delight, the Sailors' Reading Room. Sheltered from the sea breezes, old salts while away the days in this pipe-smoke and pool-playing haven, reading the daily papers in squashy armchairs or immersed in cards at the worn refectory table. The walls are crammed with photographs of wrecks, lifeboats (a lifeboat museum is located in the lighthouse out on the common), and wrinkled sailors. There are prints and paintings of famous ships, models, an ancient octant and all the jumbled paraphernalia of nautical life. Anyone is welcome here. Some of the sailors prefer their own company and retire to the rear pool room while others will regale strangers with tales of dramatic lifeboat rescues in the old 'beach yawl' boats, and descriptions of the intricacies of sea-weir fishing techniques.

I stood by the window with one elderly sailor, his wind-browned face wrinkled as rhino-hide, and wondered at the attraction of the rather pebbly beach, far below at the base of the cliffs. 'Ah, that changes fast as a wink. This time it's a scouring tide, brings nothin' but pebbles. When the making tide comes, your pebbles have gone and its sand 'far as you can see.'

Way out at the north end of the beach was a small amusement pier, Southwold's token acceptance of summertime diversions. 'Much more fun in here,' said the sailor, nodding at his cosy reading room. It's a unique institution and should not be missed.

Neither should St Edmund's Church, the 'epitome of Suffolk flushwork'

Southwold

Sailor's Reading Room. Southwold

according to Pevsner, just past the town museum and the odd St Edmund's Terrace adorned with the painted faces of kings, smugglers and judges. Bartholomew Green provides an appropriate setting for the 100 ft Perpendicular tower. Inside one enters a soaring, cathedral-like space under a majestic hammer-beam roof. Some of the best wood carving in East Anglia can be found here. The fifteenth-century pulpit rises on its delicate single leg, brightly coloured, as are the lectern and the spindle-thin 15 ft high font cover. The lacy sixteenth-century screen stretches the width of the three aisles, each of its thirty-six panels adorned with golden images of saints and angels. Behind are the misericords and the choirstalls with grotesquely carved armrests of griffins and freakish faces. And impishly peeping over all is a Jack o' the Clock, an oak-carved figure of a man-at-arms who rings the bell with his broad sword at the commencement of services.

A similar character perches high on a wall in the Holy Trinity Church at Blythburgh, yet another of the once-proud coastal towns. The voluminous structure, 130 ft in length, sails galleon-like across a hillock above the flat marshlands, with all the fine proportions and lightness of the famous wool churches to the west. The stone floor is open, unlittered with pews, and high above float carved angels, pock-marked with bullets fired by Cromwellian soldiers in 1644. As was often their custom, they removed the brasses and disfigured any 'terrible and blasphemous images' they could find. For some reason they left the remarkable bench-ends intact, displaying powerful interpretations of the seven deadly sins (actually six at last count – Fornication seems to have been obliterated). Slander possesses an enormous and protruding tongue, Greed a bulbous stomach, Drunkenness sits in the stocks, Avarice on his money chest, Sloth lolls in bed, and old Hypocrisy offers up prayers with his mind on other things and his eyes wide open. The antics of Cromwell's soldiers, however, were mere scratchings compared to the celebrated onslaught of the Devil himself. He came, according to the legend, in the form of Black Shuck, the demon-dog, disrupting a church service here on Sunday, 4 August 1577, and causing 'a strange and terrible tempest' to bring down the spire on the congregation, killing at least three of them 'starke dead' and shattering the octagonal font. Others were badly scorched – a sure sign of Devil-involvement. Then, tearing his way past the door with red-hot claws, he chased off to Bungay church wreaking more havoc, leaving two worshippers strangled at their prayers, and another 'shrunken as a piece of leather scorched in a hot fire'. Altogether, not a very pleasant day for the two communities.

Further inland we enter a pastoral region rich in ecclesiastical gems. Tiny St Peter's at Wenhaston also suffered at the hands of Cromwellian

225

sympathisers who smashed the stained glass, destroyed the altar, defaced the pulpit and removed the organ and the carved roof angels. Fortunately, they missed the church's most notable treasure, the enormous painted 'Doom' which was whitewashed in 1545 and only uncovered in 1892. It was removed from the chancel arch to the north wall and can be seen today, as stirring as ever, teeming with sinister grey demons.

In nearby Bramfield's thatched church (across from the curling 'crinkle-crankle' wall of Bramfield Hall) one discovers another fantasy-like feature in the epitaph of mayhem and misery carved on the black tombstone of Bridget Applewhaite:

> After the Fatigues of a married Life
> Borne by Her with Incredible Patience
> For four years and three quarters, baring three weeks
> And after the enjoyment of the Glorious Freedom
> Of an Easy and unblemisht Widowhood
> For four years and Upwards
> She resolved to run the Risk of a Second Marriage
>   Bed
> But DEATH forbad the Banns
> And having with an Apoplectick Dart
> (The same instrument with which he had formerly
>   dispatcht her Mother)
> Toucht the most vital part of her Brain
> She must have fallen directly to the ground
> (As one Thunder strook)
> If she had not been catcht and supported
> By her intended Husband
> Of which invisible bruise
> After a struggle for above sixty Hours
> With that grand Enemy to Life
> (But the Certain and Merciful Friend
> To Helpless Old Age)
> In terrible Convulsions, Plaintive groans or Stupefying
>   Sleep
> Without recovery of Speech or Senses
> She dyed on the 12th day of Sept.
> In ye year $\left\{ \begin{array}{l} \text{of Our Lord 1737} \\ \text{of her own age 44} \end{array} \right.$

Before leaving, take time to examine the delicate intricacies of the chancel screen curving out with finely-ribbed vaulting over the nave. Note the tiny painted flowers and the intensity of the saints on the panels – another medieval masterpiece.

I had originally planned to continue inland, exploring the rolling country-side around Heveningham Hall, Framlingham Castle and the famous wind-mill at Saxstead Green. But it was a warm, rosy evening and there were to be more local folk songs at one of the Southwold pubs. So, putting off those perambulations for another time and another book, I wandered slowly back to the coastal saltings. Gulls were silhouetted against golden wisps of cloud and the marshes eased away to a purpling horizon. Pausing by a still pool, I could see silky mists forming in the reeds. The silence hummed. It was that magical limbo between evening and night and I had it all to myself – once again.

Choirstall carving. Southwold

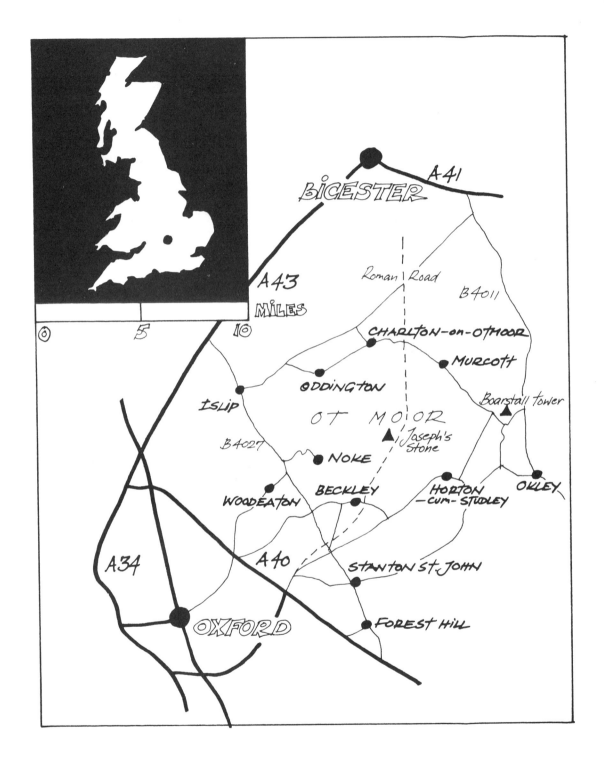

17. Ot Moor

Oxford, honeycombed with quadrangles and cloisters, graced by its golden domes and dreaming spires, is a mere fifteen minutes away by car – even allowing for all those narrow streets clotted by cyclists. Yet perched on the edge of a cliff-like escarpment near Horton-cum-Studley on an early morning steaming with mists, I looked out over an empty land, cut by windbreaks, flat, marshy and mysterious – a sliver of Fen country in the heart of rolling Oxfordshire. They call it Ot Moor although it has little of the traditional moorland character. They also call it 'bewitched', or more evocatively 'sleeping Ot Moor cast under a spell of ancient magic'.

It is certainly one of Britain's few secret places and for centuries was a great swathe of common land used by the seven villages rosaried around its marshy heart – Beckley, Horton, Noke, Oddington, Charlton, Fencott and Murcott (for some odd reason Islip was excluded). The common-land regulations were strict, permitting only two geese and one gander per tenant, requiring the ringing of all their hogs and sheep, and ordering among other things that 'none shall put any Mangy or other infectious diseased horse in the More, sub poena 6s 8d'. That, of course, was before the Enclosure Acts and the ambitious drainage schemes conceived by the always land-hungry landowners. The Duke of Marlborough, who regarded the area as 'a dreary waste and coarse aquatic sward', petitioned Parliament for drainage and allotment rights in 1801. The villagers reacted violently, tearing down official notices and threatening the safety of anyone molesting their ancient rights.

The same happened again in 1814 when they were told they could keep some commonage 'priviledges' if they contributed to the costs of drainage and enclosure. 'With what?' came the outcry, followed by riots and conflicts against armed troops dispatched to quell the disturbances. Odd ditties were sung, expressing the disquiet of the villagers:

> I went to Noke
> But nobody spoke,
> I went to Beckley
> They spoke directly,
> At Boarstall and Brill
> They're talking still.

Or more directly:

> The fault is great in Man or Woman
> Who steals the Goose from off the Common;
> But who can plead that man's excuse
> Who steals the Common from the Goose?

The power of civil authority eventually proved too much for them. A large proportion of the land was drained and commonage rights removed. But even today there are parts of Ot Moor that still retain their rather sinister character – a character well expressed in Thomas Tryte's famous 'Oxfordshire Legend' (condensed):

> A traveller belated sped
>   Athwart the dreary plain,
> And scared with his uncertain tread
>   The waterfowl amain.
>
> He vainly strove, through the dark night,
>   To reach again the way;
> The more he tried to journey right,
>   The more he got astray.
>
> 'Lost Lost', he cried, 'Upon the moor!
>   Lord help me, or I die!'
> The waterfowl screamed as before,
>   But no one heard the cry.
>
> Despair's dark horrors on him fell,
>   He knew nor place nor hour,
> When, welcome sound, the curfew bell,
>   Rang out from Charlton Tower.

He reached home safely and his gratitude was such that he gave a larger bell to the church:

> A bell of weight whose metal tongue
>   Shall speak across the plain,
> To men benighted, loud and long,
>   And bring them home again.

Until recently the Charlton curfew bell was rung every evening between 18 October and 15 March as a guide to 'benighted' walkers.

The traveller in the poem was following the faint lines of the old Roman road between Beckley and Charlton, still the only safe route across the moor. About half-way along is 'Joseph's stone', a large slab near the track thought by some to be a Roman milestone and by others to be a mounting block because of its inscription: 'to help me up when I am down, on my way to the seven towns'.

'They were proper towns, once, too,' I was told by a broad-moustached publican at Stanton St John. 'Leastways, a couple of them were. Noke was quite a place, much bigger than it is today. Fencott's gone altogether, nothing left really. Charlton was where they built the real Oxfordshire waggon – massive wooden machines they were. Islip made the osier cages, "weels" they called them, for catching eels in the Ray.' He pointed out of the window at the flat meadows of the moor, dotted with sheep and bright under a blue sky. 'Not much mystery left now, is there? Just a bit of flat farmland, really. There was talk a while back about putting a storage reservoir in the middle, but everyone got so mad at the idea, they seem to have dropped it. The army does some shooting on a range down there somewhere. That's about all that ever happens.'

'So what about Henry Turgin, then?' An elderly gentleman by the window looked stormily at the landlord from under a wind-wrinkled brow, 'and a few others you know about.'

'Superstition and fancy fairytales,' replied the grinning landlord. 'You'd believe anything about that place.'

This was obviously an old argument. The two antagonists prepared for battle, but the landlord was called away to pull pints for a thirsty lunchtime clientele. 'Take anything he tells you with a barrow of salt,' was his parting shot.

The old man waved his hand in exasperation. 'He's a comer-in. He thinks he knows everything,' he grumbled. 'He's never been across the moor and he thinks he knows it all.'

It turned out that my informant was the sixth generation of an Ot Moor family and was then steeped in knowledge of the area. 'Some folks have a bit of a chuckle when I tell 'em about the "moor-evil", they think I'm having them on or something.' So I asked him about this 'moor-evil' and a score of other things as he regaled me with tales of Henry Turgin and a few more characters lost in the 'pills' (bogs), the haunted blackberry bushes at Beckley, the eel-catchers of Murcott, the 'blackmen' of the moor, and strange shrieks from its centre near Joseph's Stone, during the dark winter months. The sceptical landlord returned near closing time. 'What did I warn you? You'll have got the lot – all the fairytales, all that stuff about people vanishing and screaming stones in the marsh. It's obvious to anyone it's the birds – we get all kinds down there – swans, ruffs, corncrakes, grey shrike, hen harriers – you name them, we'll get 'em. That's your screaming, not his ghosties!'

I left them to their wrangling and set off to explore for myself the ring of villages round the moor, beginning at Islip, home of Anglo-Saxon kings, birthplace of Edward the Confessor in 1004, and totally charming with its golden-stone cottages cascading downhill from the church. 'Here,' I was told by one villager desperately trying to think of some more recent claim to fame,

Otmoor Cottage near Islip

'was where the first English aeronaut landed – crashlanded actually – in 1784. His name was Sadler, James Sadler. He was a pastry cook in Oxford, at one of the inns and he made his own balloon, more than 60 yards round, and flew it from Oxford to Islip on October 4th 1784 – about a five-mile flight altogether. That's about all I can think of really. It's always been a very quiet place!'

The sturdy Oddington church, perched on a rise above the hazy moor, contains a truly gruesome brass of a sixteenth-century decomposing vicar and an unusual coloured *pietà* commemorating Maori soldiers who died in the First World War. It was given to the church by Maggie Papakura, a Maori

princess who married an Englishman and came to live here until her death in 1930. She is buried in the graveyard. Nearby is the site of the twelfth-century Abbey of Ottelei described by Britain's first official travel-writer, John Leland, in 1553 as 'a site upon the moor more fitted for an ark than a monastery'. The unusual crop-blessing ceremonies held in the village on Rogation Sunday are thought to date from that time.

Charlton-on-Otmoor is a cosy village of pubs and thatched cottages, again on higher ground, and grouped around a striking Perpendicular church, with an Early English tower. The only discordant element here is an ugly coach garage on the main street. Inside the church a delicate canopied

Charlton - on - Otmoor

screen, bright with scarlets, blues and golds, divides the chancel from the nave. There are traces of thirteenth-century decorative work, particularly on the pillars and arches of the north nave, and fragments of more complex subjects elsewhere reflecting a regional tendency for painted churches. Even the carved faces on the sedilia corbels are painted. But the most unusual element in the church is the large cross mounted over the screen and always garlanded with branches of box leaves. Some historians claim that this local custom is linked to ancient pagan worship of the goddess Flora, and the village May Day ceremonies in which the 'garland cross' plays a prominent part have a distinctly pre-Christian flavour. In 1857 an observer recorded the carrying of the cross through the village by 'four strong young women with six morris dancers, a clown with his bladder and money box, and a man playing a pipe'. After making a circuit the odd band then continued with the cross over the moor to Beckley and Horton where they were received by the abbey prioress. Today the ceremonies are mainly confined to the village but have change little in the last century.

234

One of the residents overheard me discussing some of the moor tales with the landlord of the George and Dragon pub, two tiny rooms at the end of the village, and took me off to see the remains of the 'blackwater wells' nearby. These peaty springs apparently are no good for making tea ('it all froths up when you boil it') but excellent for curing eye complaints and the notorious moor-evil, a sort of ague that seems to affect cattle and humans in various debilitating ways. 'There's a couple of wells at Oddington, too,' he told me. 'They're even better for the "evil".' John Buchan reinforced this belief in his *Midwinter* when he wrote, 'Moor-evil is ill to cure save by drinking of the Oddington Well'.

Beyond Murcott where the Nut Tree pub dozes beside a duck pond, the road abruptly leaves the moor and leaps up a wriggle of hills with broad vistas back over the hazy flatness. Nearby is Boarstall Tower (only open Wednesday afternoon during the summer), a bold four-square edifice with hexagonal towers at each corner and Elizabethan windows. It was originally built in 1312 as a moated defence tower and substantially renovated in the seventeenth century complete with single-handed clock made by a Woodstock bellfounder, Richard Keene. The garden is a delightfully romantic enclave, home of two tail-proud peacocks, and the work of a twentieth-century Italian gardener, Antonio Pinzani. The loss of the great elms and a beech a few years ago has changed its character, but it's still a pleasant place for a summer stroll.

After a detour to Stanton St John, birthplace of John White, founder of Massachusetts, I paused to sketch the street at Beckley by the side of the church. The locals claim that Lewis Carroll, a frequent visitor to Beckley, got his idea for the great chessboard of *Alice through the Looking Glass* from views here across the meadows below. Thick thatch and cream-stoned cottages, bent and bowed, tumbled downhill to the old Roman road leading out across the moor. The sunlight gleamed like metal on newly-turned furrows of thick black earth. Round the corner on the slope of the escarpment were the haunted blackberry bushes. Fruit is picked for a local dye-making factory, but never eaten by the villagers. 'We're a superstitious lot,' one of them told me, and showed me the remnants of thirteenth-century wall paintings in the church teeming with devils and grotesque creatures. 'Some of us even believe about Benedict Winchcombe – that old Noke tale.' I nodded and waited patiently for one more story of moorland happenings. 'He was lord of the manor, died sometime around 1620, marvellous huntsman he was, famous round all Oxfordshire. They say his soul never rested – he told them in heaven he found it a bit dull so they sent him back to get on with his hunting. Every so often you hear him riding around, mostly in Noke itself,

Beckley

with all the hunt horses, the dogs, the lot. I'm serious now. I've never heard them but I know three Noke people – three that wouldn't lie to save their own mothers – and they've heard the racket more than once. They say there's no doubt, it's a heck of a lot of horses and hunting horns too. Strange i'nt it?'

The village has a long history. On the outskirts are minimal remains of a Roman villa and the church is thought to have once been the repository for the relics of the eighth-century St Donanverdh. An ancient palace was also situated in fields north of the vicarage near the thirteenth-century well and more odd tales are told about Beckley Park, a dignified triple-moated manor on the outskirts of the community.

I moved on to nearby Noke and the old rhyme proved true. 'Nobody spoke' as I explored the scattered remnants of a once-large community situated, for a change, on the moor itself, at the base of the escarpment. In fact no one even appeared.

It was hard to believe this was a centre of learning – albeit a temporary one – when the scholars from Oxford University congregated here in refuge from the ravages of the fifteenth-century plague. Scores of farmers worked the odd-named fields on the fringe of the marsh – Pigstee Ground, Bushy Standard, Big Wadly, Fern Ground, Indigo Meade, Big and Little Cossiter and Judy's Meadow. Even as far back as the Domesday era, Noke was very much a place to be reckoned with. The font in the rather nondescript church is said to have been a gift from no one else but Gundrada, William the Conqueror's daughter. Yet I found the place had an abandoned feel. I could hear what sounded like geese way out beyond the windbreaks, a hollow echoing sound in the stillness of the evening. The earlier sunshine had gone. The colours of the moor were muted, faint greys and beiges receding once more behind a misty gauze. Sheep in nearby fields stood picture-still, their heads lifted as if listening to something only they could hear. A damp chill crept in from the flat fields.

Not wishing to be inflicted by the ague, I scampered back uphill and into the pastoral village of Woodeaton, cosy among its woods and greens, and found comfort in its Early English church. For standing tall over the worn pews, the ancient font and the heraldic shields black with time, was an enormous wall painting of St Christopher carrying the child Christ across a stream teeming with aggressive fish and coiling octopi. A scroll from his mouth contained a faded Norman-French message 'Look upon this image and verily upon this day thou shalt not die an evil death.' After my rambles through this odd little corner of Oxfordshire I found the words pleasantly reassuring.

238

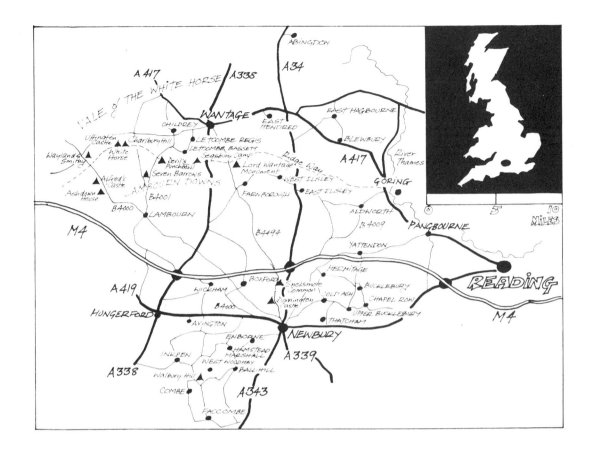

18. The Berkshire Downs

Away to the east, deep in the Goring gorge, the Thames meanders towards London, 'its dikes golden with marsh-marigolds and all the meadows scattered with oases of cowslips; the mornings full of larks and the evenings of the chime of village bells'. Arthur Mee likened the Berkshire landscape to 'a Sullivan overture, pretty and with hints of grander things to come'. There are heaths, pinewoods, cosy vales, and broad green valleys. To the east the burgeoning commuter tide tumbles over Windsor, lapping out along the Thames to Reading. To the north are the rolling fields of Oxfordshire and the secretive Chilterns. And in the west and south are the big bold hills of the downs, dune-smooth, topped by caps of wind-shaped copses and crossed by the ancient Ridge Way.

239

Bucklebury Common

This was the Berkshire I came to explore. I had read Mais's *England's Pleasaunce* – 'There is no way I know of regaining happiness more surely than of wandering along the Berkshire Downs.' Ideally I should have done it on horseback over the cresting chalk ridges from Uffington's famous white horse and Alfred's Castle to the Thames. In fact I remained loyal to my home on wheels with foot-forays whenever the mood was right.

The only problems occurred in the great heathlands and forests around the Buckleburys where I began. A mere hundred yards from the road, one can become lost in a maze of paths through seething clusters of birch and oak. The silence is trapped under canopies of branches. Tracks pass across scrubby areas of gorse and bracken, then submerge again into the gloom. Ancient oaks leer out suddenly, reminding me of the Rev. R. F. Kilvert's enthusiastic description 'grey, gnarled, low-browed, knock-kneed, bowed, bent, huge, strange, long-armed, deformed, hunchbacked, misshapen oak men . . . looking as if they had been at the beginning and making of the world'. He forgot 'mossy'. These tend to be mossy as well.

240

Views out are rare and invariably consist of mere ripplings of wooded hills under an empty sky. They say the common is only five square miles, but if you're lost it feels more like five hundred. They also claim that there are up to 300 footpaths in the parish – all apparently joined in conspiracy to confuse the newcomer. Twenty thousand Parliamentarian troops camped here in 1644, prior to the second battle of Newbury, and were hardly noticed. Scores of squatters, 'broom-squires,' also made their homes on the common, hidden from the casual traveller. Today the villages are more formalised affairs, bent beam and thatch cottages clustered round crisp greens. A long avenue of ancient trees leads into the heart of Chapel Row. There's another mile-long avenue of oaks between Wood Gate and the Blade Bone Inn. Horses trot along the fringes of the forest and walkers slide away down sun-dappled paths.

At Bucklebury a comfortable flint church hides behind plump trees in a graveyard of unusual altar tombs and cast-iron memorial plates. A Norman doorway (*c.* 1150) is topped by a primitive face and maltese cross, possibly a representation of the Knights Hospitallers whose preceptory was located near Brimpton and who, it is said, constructed the north aisle of the church. An eagle's claw in bas-relief and the model of a temple above the blocked north door are assumed to be the personal arms of the Master. A third carving on the south wall of the tower contains a crude crucifixion and a figure in a tall hat working a wheel. Inside is dark. Two odd dormer windows cut into the roof do little to relieve the severity of box pews, heavy minstrel's gallery, black coats of arms, and a ponderous pulpit topped by a sounding board. Swords, tilting helmets (one with the local Winchcombe family crest) and gauntlets adorn the south walls, and a massive oak chest, carved from a single piece of wood, huddles in the corner near the vestry.

Outside again, in a bevy of birdsong, I climbed the steep hillside to Upper Bucklebury and on, across yet more oak, birch and gorse common, to Cold Ash and the tiny village of Hermitage. A brief pause in the pub brought tales of the 'wishing well' water here said to be suitable for curing eye diseases. I also learned about the Old Rectory at Yattendon, once haunted by a most helpful female ghost, always smartly dressed in silk, whose favourite pastime was showing successive rectors' wives where to find undiscovered hens' nests in the hedgerows and ditches along the winding lanes (a pleasant change from most ghost tales).

At Newbury the tales became more gruesome and older residents refer to witches as if they still congregated at nearby Cottington's Hill where, according to a seventeenth-century diarist, 'there's enough witches and wizards living here to drag a ton load o' stones up it'. An investigation carried out in 1912 revealed residents who could actually remember when three local witches were buried alive with only their heads above ground and left to die. Records from Cromwell's time also record the grisly demise of a woman seized by his soldiers and condemned for witchcraft. They tried to shoot her with muskets, but 'with a deriding and loud laughter at them, she caught their bullets in her hands and chewed them up'. So, using an apparently guaranteed witch-execution method, one of the soldiers cut her forehead and shot her under the ear, 'at which she straight sank down and died'.

Of greater renown, though, is 'Jack [Winchcombe] of Newbury', a famous cloth-manufacturing entrepreneur and working-man's hero all in one. Newbury's fame as a cloth centre was largely due to his inventiveness and ingenuity. His rise to riches from humble origins, his popularity with royalty and his refusal of a knighthood after participation in the battle of Flodden ('I intend to remain the equal of my workers and nothing more I ask') impressed the locals beyond measure. The museum concentrates on this era of the town's history, the remains of his home can still be seen in

Donnington Castle

Northbrook Street, and a brass in the church commemorates his death in 1519.

The town has a pleasant market flavour and is famed for its ancient almshouses, the racecourse and the tall ruins of the fourteenth-century Donnington Castle on the northern outskirts, largely destroyed after a twenty-month siege during the Civil War. Nearby is silent Snelsmore Common, yet one more heathland area full of foxes and folklore.

Equally loved by the local populace is the country south of the Kennet, the drives along winding, high-hedged lanes to the villages around Inkpen and the crest of Walbury Hill, terminus of the Wansdyke Saxon earthwork. The unfenced road leaves the rolling fields behind and climbs the steep flank of the hill to Combe Gibbet, a reminder of the region's rigorous past. From here one peers out across a broad chequerboard of meadows, downlands and vales to the north, almost as far as Oxford. To the south the bare-topped hills ease into Hampshire and the emptiness of Salisbury Plain. A. G. Street wrote: 'south of that gibbet post lies a country of poverty and desolation, a country of juniper bushes and rabbits, a land of steep, barren slopes . . . But

Combe Gibbet

looking northward, miles below me, lay the Kennet Vale, a land of rich farms, prosperous villages, snug churches and kindly meadows'. Even on a summer weekend, sharing the view with others, one cannot fail to sense the solitude of these uplands, a no-man's-land between the two landscapes. A path wanders off along the sweeping crest. A narrow road tumbles down to Combe and on round the bow of the hill, past large old barns, to sleepy Faccombe with its flinty church and proud country houses.

Off the crest again, I lost myself in a lacework of lanes and tiny hamlets – Ball Hill, Hamstead Marshall, West Woodhay and enticing Enborne. I emerged somewhere near Avington and discovered a perfectly-preserved Norman church close to the tumult of the Bath road, yet a thousand years removed and tingling with Romanesque decoration. The south door was shrouded in chevron and leaf carvings; the corbels and capitals writhed with grotesque creatures. Best of all was the font, intricately decorated with thirteen figures – politicians, bishops, priests and a pompous chancellor complete with wig.

244

I mentioned the church to a group of locals in the Bear at nearby Hungerford, a pleasant market town on either side of a steep winding street. Once again (so typically) only one was aware of its existence but had 'never had a chance to nip down and take a peep'. The others seemed surprised that anything of that age should have remained untouched ('Thought Cromwell had pretty well got rid of all that kind of thing'). Doubtless it was the old adage about knowing your own backyard least of all. The conversation became more encouraging as they told me of the town's links with John of Gaunt and explained the famous Hocktide ceremony held every Easter Week Tuesday to mark his granting of fishing rights to the townspeople in the fourteenth century. Tutti-men parade with staves and nosegays, claiming kisses from any girl they happen to meet and summoning the tenants of the 'ninety-nine houses' with fishing rights to elect their constable and partake of loyal 'Plantagenet Punch' toasts to John of Gaunt. Most of the town's affairs are still administered by the elected constable, portreeve, bailiff, feoffee and tutti-men, and the Easter formalities include a riotous 'Macaroni Supper', the distribution of scores of oranges and 'hot pennies', and long hectic hours for the poor barmen at the Bear and Three Swans. In fact it was a casual reference to pink elephants that made one of my informants insist on a visit to Wickham. 'Got to show you at least one of us knows a bit about where we live,' he chortled as we drove on country roads north-east from Hungerford.

He stopped outside a large rectory, borrowed the key from the vicar and led me across the road to a crisply flinted Victorian church with an ancient tower, shaded by huge cedars on the crest of the hill. Inside an enormous organ filled much of the north aisle with ugly boxed-pipes painted a peculiar shade of lime-yellow. My informant flicked on the lights with a flourish and a booming 'Tra-la! The elephants!' Following the direction of his pointing finger I peered up and saw the almost-lifesize heads of eight golden elephants complete with tusks and rich adornments peering solemnly down from the rafters. 'Papier mâche,' he explained. 'All from the Paris Exhibition of 1862. They rebuilt most of the churches a few years earlier and brought in these and the angels in the nave.' I looked up again and saw ten enormous angels projecting outwards from the base of the nave beams and resembling the magnificent angel-ceilings of the Breckland shore churches (Chapter 14). 'They're papier mâché, too,' he continued, then pointed to the font. 'This cover is from the Crystal Palace Exhibition, done by New Zealand Maoris.' A much more ancient font, probably Saxon, hid away in the corner. 'And Gilbert Scott carved these himself.' He pointed to the rear pew ends adorned with a bishop and an angel. 'There's a bit of everything in here.' Outside, he

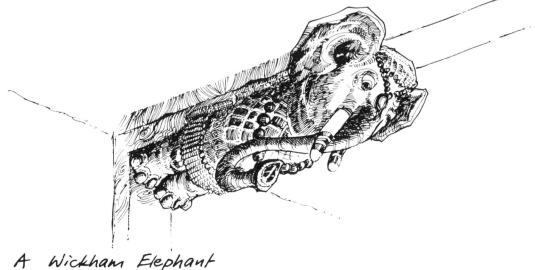

A Wickham Elephant

showed me the stately Wickham House behind the church, its gargoyles grimacing from gutters. 'The old Rectory. It's owned by some Arab now.'

We parted the best of friends and I continued north-west on country roads, along the fringe of the downs to the village of Lambourn. Charles Kingsley loved this place and used it as a model for Whitbury in his *Two Years Ago*, describing the churchyard 'where the dead lie looking up to the bright southern sun among huge black yews upon their knoll of white chalk above the ancient stream'. The church (more hideous gargoyles) and its brasses are worth a pause, but I was ready now for the open spaces and the strange secrets of the Ridge Way.

As its name suggests, the Ridge Way is part of an ancient high-road and trade route once linking the Devon coast with the North Sea. The Ridge Way Path is an 85-mile segment of the original way running north-east across the Marlborough and Berkshire Downs to the Thames and onwards along the northern scarp of the Chilterns to Ivinghoe Beacon. The segment between the Iron Age hillfort of Uffiington Castle and Segsbury Camp is the most dramatic.

They call the Lambourn Downs the 'Desert of England'. As one climbs upwards from the combes, the woods and windbreaks give way to broad chalky-green sweeps of empty hills. There are sprinklings of tiny flowers – cowslip, saintfoin, harebell – on the upland meadows, maybe a few sheep too, and little else. Larks, their trills shimmering down like ribbons, flutter ever-upward. The buzzing jungles of summery banks are left below in the valleys. Up here the hiss of a hill-skimming wind rustles the grass and sends the clouds scudding over the tops of lonely copses.

On my way north from Lambourn across the racehorse country of

Lambourn Downs I paused briefly at the Seven Barrows (actually twenty or more), a mixture of Neolithic and Bronze Age burial mounds heavily excavated and fading into the fields. A couple of miles on I found the Ridge Way, a broad earth track along the crest of the downs, sinuous as a serpent. Although there are alternatives for ardent car-lovers, I left the faithful machine behind and headed off along the path. West leads toward the lynchets of Charlbury Hill (medieval field patterns), the great earthworks of Alfred's Castle and Uffington Castle, the mysterious long barrow of Wayland's Smithy, and the White Horse of Uffington (over-popular on summer weekends). To the east the path descends gradually past the enormous Devil's Punchbowl and more earthworks at Segsbury Camp, to the A338. An attractive loop walk includes the dozing villages of Letcombe Bassett and Letcombe Regis where King John once had his hunting box. In the height of summer you'll probably be walking with others, but in quieter seasons you'll have the hills to yourself. Far in the northern distance is the sweeping Vale of White Horse described so temptingly by Thomas Hughes in his *Tom Brown's Schooldays* as 'a land of large rich pastures, bounded by ox-fences, with here and there a nice little gorse or spinney and villages, queer, old-fashioned places . . .'.

But up here there are no villages and few fences. On quiet days the legends of these hills seem all too real. The White Horse, 365 ft long, the most ancient of all seventeen chalk-cut horses in England, possibly dates from the first century BC and has all the power of the dragon that many say it is. Nearby Dragon Hill is claimed to be the site of St George's victory over the monster and the eternally bare patch marks the sterile ground where the blood fell. Ancient folklore contrasts rather markedly with Kenneth Grahame's description of the creature in *The Reluctant Dragon* as 'the most modest and retiring dragon in the world who lolled in the turf, enjoyed sunsets, told antediluvian anecdotes to the Boy, and polished his old verses while meditating on fresh ones'.

The restored Wayland's Smithy is an eerie place, a 2,000-year-old long barrow in a copse of tall trees guarded by enormous stones. Walter Scott immortalised the legend in *Kenilworth* and described how travellers on the Ridge Way could leave their horses and a token coin by the barrow, whistle three times and retire while the mystical demigod, Wayland Smith, shod the creature 'in ten minutes and not a minute more'. Tales of magical blacksmiths are not unusual in southern counties. Their lives were intertwined with the 'potent charms' – fire, iron and horseshoes – and they were often known as 'servants of the sacred horse'. Up here on one of those scowling downland days, the legend seems totally believable.

Waylands Smithy

Spend time in these hills. Be part of the silence for a while and feel their soaring emptiness. Watch the long shadows in the tumbling combes, the fresh light on the slopes and the sheep, bright as daisies. See the plain, sponged out by a tall white storm of rain. Then roll down again in the valleys, with a visit to Ashdown House close by the earthworks of Alfred's Castle. This pert Dutch-style mansion, c.1665, is an unusually tall creation topped by an octagonal cupola, 'a doll's house writ too large, seeming to have been transported from a Dutch canal and stranded'. The two low pavilions on either side, framed by large chimneys, help relieve the verticality, and the restored formal garden provides a jewel-like setting against the chalk hills. This was the home of William, 1st Earl of Craven, devoted follower of the Stuarts and particularly of Charles I's sister, Elizabeth, Queen of Bohemia. When she returned to Britain in ill health during the Reformation he nursed her in his London house and in return she bequeathed her valuable paintings, some of which are on display at Ashdown.

Wandering eastwards, one passes through a series of snuggling valley and downland villages. Childrey sits close to the ancient Icknield Way, an Iron Age route following the base of the downs from Ashbury at the Wiltshire border to its fork at Wantage. Beyond the thatched cottages, the stern little Methodist chapel, and a Working Men's Club and Reading Room by the duck pond, is Childrey Church with a lead font and a notable array of brasses. The font, similar to the famous one at Dorchester to the north, is surrounded by standing figures, twelve mitred bishops with their croziers. The brasses memorialise the Finderne, Walround and Kyngeston families and, as was the fashion, picture the deceased adorned in their finest clothes or armour. The brass for William Fettiplace and his wife, founders of the sixteenth-century almshouses in the village, shows their shrouded figures rising from coffins into immortality.

While the Norman Church at Wantage also contains impressive brasses, the statue of King Alfred is the town's main attraction. The sculptor was Count Gleichen, a German appointed by Queen Victoria as a British admiral. Bankrupted in middle age, he took up sculpture as a serious occupation and was installed in St James's Palace to work on his commissions. This is considered to be one of his finest pieces and shows the resolute ninth-century monarch, battle-axe at the ready, defeater of Danes, designer of ships (rather inadequate vessels in storms), atrocious cook and revered scholar, still observing the antics of his minions with a combination of love and scorn.

East Hendred, a village of cob cottages, thatched timber-framed houses and raised causeways, is the home of Sir Thomas More's descendants.

Hendred Manor contains many mementoes of the unfortunate man, executed by Henry VIII for a resoluteness that would have impressed Alfred. A famous Holbein portrait shows the More family. An ecclesiastical staff was once the property of John Fisher, a colleague of More and similarly executed for his refusal to take the Oath of Supremacy to Henry. According to the legend, the King was particularly incensed when the Pope made Fisher a cardinal and declared with typical Henry vehemence: 'The Pope may send him a hat, but, Mother of God, he shall wear it on his shoulders, for I will leave him never a head to set it on.'

Quiet, pastoral East Hagbourne has long attracted artists with its leaning cottages and carefully shaped trees. I sat by the side of the lane and attempted my own rendition. It was a hot day and I was sweatily engrossed in my task when an elderly lady leaned over a garden gate and asked if I'd enjoy a cup of tea. She brought it to me on a round tray covered in a crochet cloth with a plate of hot scones and a pot of honey. 'I won't disturb you now,' she said quietly, 'but if you need to know anything about our little village, just knock.' I completed the sketch, drank the tea, ate all the scones and honey, and knocked. She was ready for me – walking shoes, stick and hat. 'I thought you'd come,' she beamed, and off we went marching through the village, peering in at windows, bidding good afternoon to everyone we met and ending up at the church. She showed me the Italianate paintings on the nave walls and the great arms of Charles II, the village's favourite monarch, who ordered a collection to rebuild the community after a disastrous fire in 1659. Then she led me to 'Henry', as she called him, a hideous head on the northern corbel of the chancel arch. 'He'd be a fine drawing,' she suggested. So, rather hastily. I made two sketches, one for her and one for the book. She was delighted. 'Sign it, sign it,' she insisted, and took me back for another plateful of fresh scones and more tales of downland villages.

It was thanks to her that I left the gentler Icknield Way country and climbed up again onto the high hills. Signs along narrow lanes pointed to 'Downs only'. I passed the perfect thatched pub, the Four Points, slumbering in the warm afternoon, lopsidedly intoxicated on its own ale.

At West Ilsley a spritely white goat guarded his territory by the village pond. A path meandered off across the cornfields to nearby Farnborough and the ponderous monument on the crest of the downs to Lord Wantage, founder of Reading University College. At East Ilsley, a lovely sprinkling of cottages and Georgian mansion around a hilltop church and duckpond, I found a few hand-drawn waterpumps in front gardens and rolled on into Aldworth, famous for its canopied well, one of the deepest in England at more than 370 ft. My elderly informant and scone-maker had referred to the

East Haqbourne

Capital. East Hagbourne church

village as 'Home of the Giants' and she was right. I passed the sharded remnants of a 1,000-year-old yew tree (held together with wire rings) and set in a round, possibly pagan, burial ground. At first it was difficult to see anything in the gloom of the church. Then I noticed the carved memorials, the nine enormous figures of the De la Beche family, filling the nave and lined along the side aisles under ornate canopies. The villagers refer to three of the figures as 'John Long, John Strong and John Never Afraid' (John Ever Afraid has vanished from his niche), and during the sixteenth century the figures had apparently become a focus of local superstitions. Even though the male line of the family ceased around the mid 1300s, a form of ancestor-worship is thought to have been practised here, encouraging the wrath of indignant officials during the Reformation and partial destruction of the monuments. Today their broken remnants lie quietly in this vault-like church. They possess a Henry Moore flavour, fragments of bodies, separate yet related. One of the best preserved is the effigy of Lord Nicholas, an important figure during the reign of Edward III, Constable of the Tower of

London and custodian of the Black Prince. He rests, hands in prayer and dressed for battle complete with pointed helmet. Under one of the canopies lies the huge Sir Philip, valet to Edward II, and attended by a dwarf to exaggerate his imposing stature. Elizabeth I was attracted here by the legends and Alfred Tennyson indicated his affection for this secluded village by adopting the title, Lord Tennyson of Freshford and Aldworth. Other lesser known visitors have left their initials all too plainly cut into the flanks of the slumbering giants and their wives.

Beyond the village, paths and lanes lead up once again on to the empty slopes of the downs. In the tinkling evening a racehorse canters over high meadows starred with sheep. Mostly, though, it's just the silence and strange foldings of ground along the Ridge Way – the ancient marks of those ancient men so admired by Rudyard Kipling:

> And see you, after rain, the trace
> of mound and ditch and wall?
> O that was a Legion's camping-place
> When Caesar sailed from Gaul.
>
> And see you marks that show and fade,
> Like shadows on the Downs?
> O they are the lines the Flint Men made,
> to guard their wondrous towns.

One of the Aldworth Giants

19. The Dorset Hills and Vales

'You've got a bit of ev'thing round these parts.' The farmer, reeking of earth and other more redolent odours, tumbled the remaining half-pint down his throat without spilling a drop. 'You'd think most of 'em comin' in had never heard of Dorset. They're through it in a flash off to t' West Country. S'daft really – 'specially when there's all this empty country doin' nothin'.' His purple-veined nose flashed. He was ready for a refill and the landlord asked me knowingly, 'Same again, sir?' I nodded and spread out my map on the table. After two pints we'd established that Dorset was an eminent candidate for hidden-corner exploration. Now it was just a matter of specifics and that looked like being a long, slow job.

Thomas Hardy loved the bold sweep of the Wessex landscape and populated real towns and stately homes with imaginary people always at loggerheads with themselves and the elements. From schoolday readings I remembered the sombre presence of Egdon Heath, the great wasteland of southern Dorset: 'grand in its simplicity . . . the great inviolate place of ancient permanence which the sea cannot claim . . . the sea changed, the rivers, the villages, and the people changed, yet Egdon remained'.

Immediately to the north rise the windswept chalk hills peppered with prehistoric earthworks, white horses, odd mounds of indistinct purpose and that magnificent penis-proud turf giant above Cerne Abbas. A swathe of forest, the remnant of Cranborne Chase, brings relief to the openness. Then abruptly comes the dropping away off the northern escarpment to the Vale of Blackmoor and the vaulted glories of Sherborne Abbey. Then on into little lost vales and fantasy-realms of dozing hamlets with such unlikely names as Fifehead Neville, Purse Caundle, Child Okeford, Beer Hackett, Toller Fratrum and Toller Porcorum, Compton Pauncefoot, a few Winterbornes named after winter-rising springs, and the impossible Ryme Intrinseca!

My extended enquiries at the pub were eventually fruitful and I began explorations in the Puddles of Piddle Valley under the much-propped sycamore tree at Tolpuddle. Here was the home of the famous 'Martyrs' and the site of a pathetic incident in 1834 which marked the beginning of Britain's trade union movement. George Loveless, a lay Methodist preacher, and five companions found decent life impossible on the 8s 6d weekly wage paid by local farmers, and after two years of abortive negotiations as the 'Friendly Society of Agricultural Labourers' were suddenly arrested under some obscure law. Their offence was 'administering illegal oaths concerning trade activities' and they were sentenced to seven years' penal servitude in Australia. A local flurry of protest brought an eventual free pardon, but not until the men had been transported, and their reputations made the stuff of legend. The Martyrs' Inn was renamed in their honour and a hundred years later the TUC built a row of six memorial cottages and instituted an annual July service to commemorate their courageous stand.

They were the kind of men who made the novice colonies so resentful of arrogant British rule. George Washington would have found them good grist for his revolutionary mill in America and, appropriately, the nearby St Laurence church at Affpuddle is the burial-place of his mother's family. A lady arranging flowers in the chancel told me proudly that the small carved coat-of-arms on Edward Lawrence's tablet, horizontal red stripes under a row of five-painted stars, was the inspiration for 'Old Glory', the stars and stripes of the US flag. She also asked me if I'd heard about the strange creatures said to haunt the heathland hollows above nearby Briantspuddle (Bryants Puddle). I went to look and found a number of 'swallet holes' possibly formed by collapsed water-passages in the underlying chalk. The largest, 'Culpeppers Dish' (thankfully not another 'Devil's Punchbowl') was a hundred yards across, thirty or so feet deep, very overgrown and not at all ominous. Maybe on a moonlit night these holes might assume a different character, although, strangely enough, Thomas Hardy never integrated them into his novels. Just about everywhere else in the area is mentioned. Dorchester, of course, was the prominent town of Casterbridge. Tolpuddle became Tolchurch, and Puddletown (a cosy streamside village of thatched cottages) was Weatherbury. Here Gabriel Oak finally married his rather well-used Bathsheba whose home has been identified as nearby Waterston Manor. The ceremonies took place at St Mary's church where Hardy's real-life grandfather played the cello in the choir loft above the creaky box pews. A mile west along the valley is Druce Farm, Squire Boldwood's home, and over at Higher Bockhampton is Hardy's birthplace where he wrote his first (but unpublished) novel, *The Poor Man and the Lady*.

As far as I could tell, though, from my reading, the almost over-perfect Milton Abbas, a model estate village a few miles to the north of the Piddle Valley built by Lord Milton in the late 1700's, never appeared in any discernible guise. And the once-vast heathlands, now much reclaimed and crisscrossed by army tank-tracks, would doubtless send the poor author into paroxysms of rage. Even T. E. Lawrence's chintzy-yellow Clouds Hill home, shrouded in a rhododendron wilderness here, rattles and shakes as armed vehicles career by on caterpillar tracks. Segments of heath remain, most notably around Winfrith Newburgh (although an atomic energy establishment has emerged here) and Black Down, but these are mere shards of the original – a sad reflection on the rate at which we consume our wild landscape.

Some of the better-known downland features, such as the Cerne Abbas giant, Maiden Castle near Dorchester, and the extensive Badbury Rings, tend to appear rather frequently on tourist-itineraries. I prefer the quieter places like the ruined flint church at Knowlton, a tiny robust structure built in the centre of a 4,000-year-old ditch-and-rampart wing. Yew trees huddle on the edge of the ring, doubtless a place of pagan ceremonies, and in the adjoining field a large, bush-covered barrow rises abruptly from the earth.

Locals claim it to be haunted by all manner of spirits, which seems quite probable in this lonely country. They also talk of flickering lights inside the 120 ft high Horton Tower, an eccentric eighteenth-century folly on the open hilltop above Horton village. Built by Humphrey Sturt after he acquired the manor in 1697, it never possessed interior floors and the lively squire is said to have bounded up by means of ladders to spot deers herds and satisfy his zeal for hunting.

Further to the west I explored lonely country around Hod Hill and Hambledon Hill, topped by yet one more prehistoric barrow. At Child Okeford, General Wolfe trained troops for his Quebec assault in 1759. Yew woods hug the upper slopes. These dark groves, thick with twisted trunks and broken branches, are strangely damp, as if the sun never reaches the ground, and a sharp contrast to the beechy mellowness of nearby Cranborne Chase.

This ancient deer forest once stretched along the southern slope of downs from Shaftesbury to Salisbury and was famed not only for the quality of its fallow deer but also for the smugglers and criminals who found sanctuary in its secluded combes. Few tracks crossed here except the Ackling Dyke, a fine Roman road leading from Badbury Rings to Old Sarum, and the Dorset Cursus, a Neolithic ceremonial route parallel with the A354 and almost lost now in the rich vegetation of the forest. Cranborne village itself, once a burgeoning community with a Chase Court and Benedictine abbey, has been owned by the Marquesses of Salisbury since the early seventeenth century. The manor house, a Jacobean creation, peers over the church and village green, and its grounds and garden centre are usually open to the public. Cranborne, however, is now a few miles from the wooded Chase hills. Sixpenny Handley is closer and was the headquarters of Isaac Gulliver, one of the fiercest of the Chase smugglers, whose operations centre was the local pub. His coterie of deer-poachers used to hide their catch in a grave by the north-west gate of the churchyard and their antics are memorialised by an inscription on the tombstone. Across the road the 1896 butcher's shop, adorned with ornate wood-carvings of rams' heads and cows' hindquarters, has now become a more official repository.

Tollard Royal nestles in the heart of the Chase surrounded by mature oak and beech woods. King John's House contains remnants of thirteenth-century construction and is thought to have been used by the monarch on his frequent sorties in the forest. The delightful Larmer Gardens with their temples, statues and open-air theatre, once contained the old wych elm where he often met his huntsman-compatriots.

And then abruptly the forest falls back and the downlands emerge again, broad sweeps of hills curling to the dome of Win Green. Crowned by a circle

Knowlton church

of trees, this is a superb vantage-point with unbroken views in all directions. Big bulbous clouds float by almost close enough to touch, and swirls of black rooks rise from the cornfields. Below is 'Zig-zag hill' a switchback descent to Cann Common and on to Shaftesbury. Clusters of farms and barns dot the tiny fields and streams flash under a brilliant sun. The mound to the east, accessible from Berwick St John, is the Winkelbury, yet one more ancient fortified settlement. Three thousand years ago, such prominent sites provided admirable vantage points for defence. Today's villages seem to have found more sheltered spots away from those sweeping winds. Even tiny Ashmore, with broad views to the south from its green, is Cotswold-cosy round a duck-laced pond.

The hill road south, with more vistas, passes along the edge of the downs to the primly Georgian town of Blandford Forum. Such architectural unity is rare in a region where the long histories of most towns are reflected in a jumble of building styles. Blandford Forum, however, lost most of its physical heritage in 'God's dreadful visitation by Fire' of 1731, commemorated by a plaque over the grandiose classical church. The two Bastard brothers, John

258

and William, aided by a public collection of funds, set about rebuilding the town with all the vigour and some of the sensitivity of Christopher Wren. The place is compact with a refined dignity unusual in Dorset, and visitors may wander the estate grounds of Bryanston School in an 1890 mansion on the outskirts, and visit the Royal Signallers' museum at Blandford Camp.

The A350 leads north along a soft valley with delicate church spires sheltered by woodlands. Then abruptly it bounds up a steep hill into the centre of Shaftesbury, an obviously ancient town and a favourite of King Alfred who founded the nunnery here in 880. The sinuous, cobbled Gold Street, tumbling down from behind the town hall past the museum of Shaftesbury-made buttons and knick-knacks, is one of the most evocative places in the county and an immediate subject for photographers and artists. But the ravages of supermarketed frontages and blacktop car parks have broken the continuity of other streets, leaving only the charming terrace-walk alongside the abbey ruins, a perfect example of an Olde English tea-room in King Alfred's Kitchen, and a rather worn fifteenth-century church whose crypt was once the beer cellar of an adjoining pub. Of course, the

Gold Street . Shaftesbury

town has its ghost, a grey legless monk who haunts the abbey grounds endlessly seeking the abbess to show her where he hid the abbey treasure during the Dissolution. Apparently the digging of a secret pit wearied him and after burying the valuables there, he promptly died of heart failure and no one ever found them again.

The market town of Sturminster Newton has managed to retain more character in its mixture of brick, cob, stone and timber-framed buildings, and is another splendid sketch-subject with its medieval bridge and water mill by the river Stour. Be careful how you cross the bridge. According to a plaque, anyone damaging it is likely to be transported to the far colonies. Immediately behind me as I sat on an earth mound (presumably placed there for like-minded admirers) was the bowed, thatched sprawl of the Bull Inn. Johnny Cox keeps the mill active 'now 'n then, when he feels like it', according to a local. 'He enjoys meetin' people passin' through', my informant added, which was a shame because I couldn't find him.

Blackmore Vale Forge

Beyond Sturminster Newton stretches the Vale of Blackmoor (Blackmore), a welcome pastoral relief after the blustery downs. I crossed here on one of the first frosty mornings of autumn. The sun snapped brightly on silky mists over the fields. Hoar-frost sheened the trees, leaving them sugar iced, and birds shivered song-less, on fence posts. The silver chill was a stiletto-sharp warning of the winter months to come. But for Mike Malleson it was work as usual in his coke-hot Blackmore Vale Forge at Bishop's Caundle. The heat had melted the ice on his windows and he hammered away making toasting forks, oblivious to the whitened world outside. He had been a teacher but gave it up at the age of twenty-seven for something he enjoyed. Sparks exploded from the red-hot metal as his hammer crashed down on the anvil. 'I don't do shoeing – that's for the fellows with the portable furnaces now. They drive up to your stables and do it on the spot. I prefer this.' He indicated an impressive array of intricate wrought-iron gates. 'There's more fun – you use your imagination a bit.' I watched as the fork handle began to emerge from a tangle of steel strips – heat, shape with the hammer, 'puddle' in the cold water bath, re-forge, jump it up to keep shape, puddle again. It seemed a long time before he was satisfied with the finished product and I sketched him as he worked. 'I could have been in the same old job most of my life,' he told me, 'but it wasn't right. Took a while to get going in this, a lot of beans and bread. But the days are all mine now. I work as long as I choose and there's only me to get in my way.' He showed me a piece he was making for Sherborne Abbey. 'Have you been there?' I told him I was on my way. 'People often miss it.' He chuckled and puddled his fork handle for the final time. 'People miss a hell of a lot!'

Wandering across the vale I passed the Elizabethan Manor House at Purse Caundle with its graceful oriel window and flavour of other-worldliness. A few miles west the tiny stone church of St Cuthbert's sits back from the road in a burial ground of broken tombstones. Originally built in the sixteenth century, much of it was later demolished leaving only the tiny chancel with three pews, a simple octagonal font and rough stone floor under a barrel roof. A charming nook.

Then came Sherborne, a compact, cosy market town of castles, churches, almshouses and that beautiful Benedictine abbey. Gerald Manley Hopkins's rich description of Oxford seemed appropriate to the view from the west:

. . . a Towery city and branchy between towers:
Cuckoo-echoing, bell-swarmed, lark-charmed,
Rook-racked, river-rounded.

St. Cuthberts near Sherborne

The bleached ruins of the Old Castle built in the early twelfth century by Roger de Caen, Bishop of Sarum and Abbot of Sherborne, peer over the clustered town from a moated site. To the north and east are flat, marshy river meadows. To the south a landscaped lake forms a link with the 'new' castle, once the home of Sir Walter Raleigh. Elizabeth I bestowed the lease of the property on her favourite explorer-courtier in 1592 and he allowed the old castle to deteriorate while involving himself in the design of his new residence.

The town is a tumble of narrow streets. Cheap Streets swirls downhill lined by shops full of Dorset knobs (crisp biscuits), fresh-baked scones, the creamy Blue Vinny cheeses at Mould and Edwards grocery, sticky hive-honeys, and succulent hams. Chintzy frontages of warm-tinted stone, lichen-dappled, parade a bevy of architectural influences – Ionic pillars, mullioned windows, aloof Georgian doors and nudge-nudge Victoriana frills. A hefty covered water-trough, the Conduit, was once the monks' washing and shaving place and a narrow ginnel leads between the Cross Keys Hotel and the Sherborne Conservative Club, past the museum, into the broad green of the abbey grounds.

From the outside even the broad Perpendicular windows, the elegant pinnacles above the gargoyles and the Decorated flying buttresses cannot disguise the abbey's essential heftiness below its stumpy tower, containing the heaviest peal of eight bells in the world. The interior however is a miraculous transformation. Light pours in through enormous clerestories and columns splay out into the most graceful of stone fan-vaulted ceilings, untouched for 500 years. The choir ceiling vaults burst like a bouquet into brightly-coloured foliated bosses, painted flowers and crested heraldic devices shimmering down the walls and columns to the choir stalls and quaintly-carved misericords. I stood transfixed, feeding coin after coin into the floodlighting meter. At the eastern end the colours reflected on the gently swirling figures of the white stone reredos above the altar.

Bishops and kings are buried here along with members of the Horsey family and the inimitable lifesize Digbys on their baroque tomb in the south transept still scorning, perhaps a touch too complacently, 'the Hurry of a publick Life'. Behind the main altar one discovers the sunken Lady Chapel, once the residence of the abbey-school's headmaster. The surviving bay of an original three-bay unit suggests a continuance of the choir's sumptuousness with Purbeck marble shafts and delicately painted vault. The east bay is a recent addition and encloses a meticulous engraved-glass reredos symbolising the glory and fruitfulness of St Mary the Virgin by Laurence Whistler (1968).

Sherborne Abbey repays slow and careful appreciation, as does its companion piece thirty miles to the east, the dark-red and white chequered Wimborne Minster. I arrived here after a day of down-rambling to find yet another comely market town surrounding yet another sturdy church set in a generous swathe of green. Early Gothic and blind Norman arching on the ecclectic exterior led, a little more predictably this time, into sturdy Norman nave lined with chevron-decorated arches. The central tower rests on four round Norman arches, the oldest part of the church built around 1120. Fourteen steps lead up through the choir to the Early English chancel. An ornate organ 'Orchestral Trumpet Stop' flares out at the side of the chancel like a line of heralds, and by the sanctuary is the only known memorial brass effigy of an English king, King Ethelred, who 'fell by the hand of the pagan Danes' in 873.

This most harmonious of early churches contains a wealth of notable features. Below the chancel is a simply-vaulted crypt, uncluttered and quiet. Equally unadorned is the late Norman font in brown Purbeck marble stripped of its elegant decorations in the Cromwellian era. Fortunately the Quarter Jack on the outside north wall of the tower was left unmolested, as

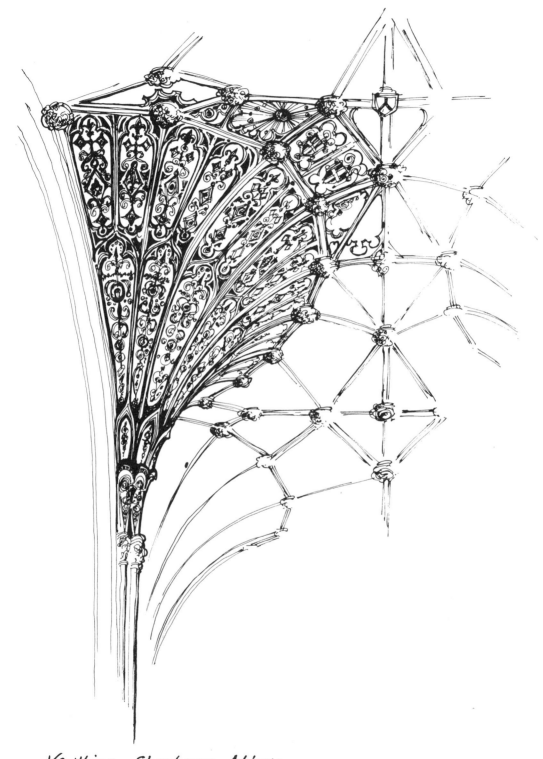

Vaulting. Sherborne Abbey

was the fourteenth-century astronomical clock on the south wall to which it is linked. Built by a Glastonbury monk in pre-Copernicus times, the clock portrays the sun revolving round the earth marking each hour of a twenty-four-hour day.

Particularly amusing are two of the tombs. The first is the Uvedale Monument erected by the wife of Sir Edmund Uvedale 'in dolefull duety'. It is the work of an Italian Renaissance sculptor and portrays the ornately-armoured knight resting nonchalantly on his elbow, eyes wide open, watching the world go by with a most benevolent expression. Anthony Ettricke, it seems had a rather different attitude toward his world and after suffering 'maliscious offence' from the people of Wimborne declined to be buried 'neither in their church, nor without it, neither in their ground, nor above it' and ended up being buried in the wall! He had the coffin placed there while he was still alive, inscribed with the year of his predicted death in 1693. His calculations went awry and he lived to 1703, hence the odd alterations to the date.

Up a spiral staircase above the vestry is a remarkable library founded in 1686 for the free use of residents and containing 240 leather-bound volumes redolent of age and ancient wisdom. Among the sombre tomes of Ignatius, St Thomas Aquinas, Plato and the Caroline Divines are such diversions as *The Gentleman's Companion* by A Person of Quality, Hughe's *Compleat Vineyard*, Evelyn's *French Gardiner*, and Burton's *Anatomy of Melancholy*. The oldest book is housed in a glass case, a 1343 vellum *Regimen Animarum* (The Direction of Souls).

In a region that seems to have avoided touristic panderings I was surprised, and delighted, to discover a complete model town of Wimborne Minster hidden at the rear of the Cornmarket. This Lilliputian one-tenth-scale creation shares the site with a small locomotive exhibition and funfair roundabout and is a totally magical place, with the miniature river Allen flowing round the backs of tiny flowering gardens. The model minster rises up, pinnacled and proud with its stained glass and 14,626 floor tiles, almost in the shadow of the real minster. Organ music plays softly and a tiny Quarter Jack strikes the quarter hour a respectful two minutes after its larger brother has performed his duties on the minster tower bells.

As my farmer-informant remarked at the outset of my journeys here, 'You've got a bit of ev'thing round these parts.'

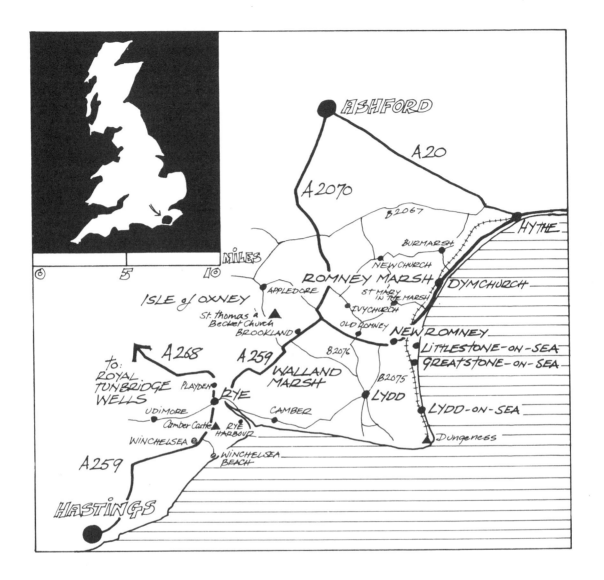

20. Romney Marsh and Dungeness

'Pebble-desert.' That's what the surf-fisherman called it as we slid across rounded rocks to the last ridge before the beach. 'Until the road came they used backsters to move around. There wasn't any other way.' I wondered what a 'backster' was. 'Proper name is "back-stay". It's like a small ski. You put it over your boots and sort of slid across the pebbles.'

He was right about the pebble desert. I turned and looked back from the ocean across miles of flat nothingness. Somewhere in the distance, he told me, was an army firing range and a complete dummy village of Hollywood-type fronts, but I saw no sign of that. There was little of anything except a faint haze of hills beyond Rye, scattered pockets of gorse, and gulls floating over the beige emptiness.

The fisherman was dressed for a long, blustery day in thick oilskins and high boots and moved off the shingle 'full' to the pebble beach. In the distance half a dozen other figures stood still as petrified trees silhouetted against the surf, waiting for whiting. Bass and cod, sometimes up to 10 lb, are also familiar catches. 'Had a shark once,' my fisherman-informant had bragged. 'Leastways, I think it was. I saw its fin, great grey thing, then the bugger broke the line.'

The illusion of desert is shattered by the awesome cubes and towers of the Dungeness atomic power station a mile away on the point of the shingle bank. During the summer tourists sing and chatter their way here on the miniature Romney, Hythe and Dymchurch Railway, visit the lighthouses, listen to the smuggling tales of old salts, and sunbathe on the sandy strand.

'They're a blasted nuisance,' an old fisherman told me in the Britannia, a sprawling pink shack of a pub near the power station. 'You don't really notice them. Compared to Hastings or Hythe it's as quiet as the grave here,' came a second opinion from a retired lifeboatmen living on 'the estate', a scattering of beach cottages south of Lydd-on-Sea. He wore a navy blue pullover with the RNLI insignia and was filleting whiting, hanging them to dry in the sun. His wife peered suspiciously through lace curtains as we chatted about life in this unusual community. 'Most of us round here are lifeboatmen. I was with them thirty-two year with a bit off for the war. I've still got my own boat and do some fishing when I feel like it.' He pointed across to a line of black tar-paper shacks cowering like beetles along the shingle. 'That's my place, the one with the flag.' By the side of the shack stood his high-stern beach-lugger boat hauled up the pebbles by winch and perched on top of the 'full'. 'We go for cod and plaice mainly. Some go after the whelks but they're not so many now. Haven't been out for a while. South-easters have been blowing and you don't launch when they're around unless you want to end back on the shingle fast.' It seemed a pleasantly relaxed pace of life. 'It's not so bad,' he agreed, 'but not half so cosy as those old Camber "keddlers" – lord, they had it easy enough, just stuck their keddle nets in the shallows and let the fish swim right in. Low tide they'd go down and pick 'em out. You don't see it now. They're all too busy making money off the tourists, all those Pontin campers.'

At the height of summer the beach at Camber village itself is a place to

Lifeboatman. Lydd-on-sea

avoid. But the magnificent Camber and Broomhill Sands stretch in a silver-gold sheen for miles, edged by grassy dunes, ideal for seclusion-seekers. Horse-riders race down the surfy fringes of the beach and sea-breeze-powered sand-yachts hiss by. Further down toward the Dungeness end the sands are lonely and deserted. I spent a day deep in the marram grass, with occasional strolls across the hot beach to the ocean, and saw a total of three people.

''Course, smugglin' were the best way to make a living.' The lifeboatman continued his reminiscenses while deftly filleting his whiting. 'Round Dymchurch was the best place for it. ''Marsh-Pilots'' they called them, 'least, that was one of the polite names. Most of them were just ordinary folk, fishermen and the like, bringing in a few boatloads of brandy and tobacco. Sometimes they'd carry tea because that was expensive stuff in those days. Most folk in the marshes couldn't afford it – they used herbs instead. My grandmother always did. She said Chinese tea would poison you anyway and stuck to her docks and dried flowers. It didn't taste bad at all if you ate something wi' it.'

Russell Thorndike's novels effectively portray this era of eighteenth-century Kent history. Dr Syn was the key character, the devious vicar of Dymchurch who led a double life as religious zealot and smuggling mastermind. His fictional antics are celebrated every year in Dymchurch's Dr Syn carnival culminating in a beach-battle between the smugglers and the excisemen. The town itself, like many others along the coast, has been transformed from a Kentish seaside village to an occasionally raucous resort inundated during the summer season. All that remains is the parish church of Saints Peter and Paul with its Norman west door (now a tower arch) and two of those rotund martello towers built in 1804 as part of a defence line against Napoleon's invasion that never came.

Littlestone has managed to retain a quieter charm. Crisp white hotels, stern as Victoria, peer out to sea across a neat beachfront park. The Diamond Jubilee fountain rises in rose granite splendour from the turf, and at the northern edge of the town the 1890 water tower is clad in buttresses, turrets and all the exotic trimmings of a true Victorian folly.

Other seaside towns have maintained their character for the simple reason that they are no longer at the seaside. The ocean has moved out, by up to two miles in places, leaving them high, dry and totally charming on old clifftops.

Winchelsea is my favourite and possesses a curious history. The original town was built on the flats, but after years of battling with the tides was finally submerged in the late thirteenth century by great waves that 'flowed twice without ebbing with a horrible roaring and a glint as of fire on the

Winchelsea · Strand Gate

waves'. With the enthusiastic backing of Edward I, a new town was established on adjoining higher ground and prospered in spite of frequent French raids. Together with Rye the town was made an associate member of the Cinque Ports, a defensive association of Sandwich, Dover, Romney, Hythe and Hastings created by Edward I. These towns guaranteed a supply of ships and seamen to the King in return for import monopolies and privileges of self-government. Then in the sixteenth century the fickle ocean receded and silted the port. There was talk of rebuilding further out, but Winchelsea Beach has become little more than a quiet backwater of summer cottages fringing a vast arc of pebble beach, and Winchelsea itself slumbers on a high island-like perch, surrounded by the rolling Kent–Sussex countryside.

Although most of the buildings here are less than a hundred years old, the ancient gates, the fourteenth-century church and Court Hall, and remnants of vaulted medieval cellars (as seen in the Manna Plat restaurant) are reminders of the town's earlier origins. I drove up the old cliffside, under the ponderous Strand Gate, and parked by the broad, open churchyard. A short

272

walking tour of the grid-patterned town took me along Hiham Green, North Street, Castle Street and Rectory Lane, past weatherboard cottages, brick and stone houses, tile-hung and stucco walls, timber-framed cottages, a town museum in the Court Hall and an eighteenth-century Doric-fronted mansion. The 1785 Methodist Church was where John Wesley ended his great open-air ministry on 7 October 1790. A lane on the left led out to the remnants of a 1760 post mill and long vistas across meadowed valleys to stately homes gleaming between trees. In the far distance on the marshes close to Rye I could see the bulbous sixteenth-century Camber Castle, a ring of semicircular towers around a central citadel outdated before it was completed and never used.

Winchelsea's church, resplendent in Decorated style, is merely the chancel and chapels of a far greater structure destroyed by the French on one of their seven invasions during the fourteenth and fifteenth centuries. The west door, framed by odd figures on either side of the arch, leads into the soaring space illuminated by rich stained-glass windows, six of which tell the story of Winchelsea and are the 1930 work of Douglas Strachan. Noble canopied tombs are set into the walls, three on the north side with carved figures and two even more elegant displays on the south wall containing the remains of Gervase Alard, Admiral of the Western Fleet under Edward I (Britain's first official admiral), and Stephen Alard, Admiral of the Cinque Ports and the Western Fleet. This was a favourite haunt of Ford Madox Brown and John Millais, and the pew by the Alard memorial is thought to be the setting for Millais' famous paintings of a little girl attending her 'First Sermon' (upright and reverent) and 'Second Sermon' (fast asleep).

Spend time here. A slow exploration of this unusual town repays itself with surprises before the descent to coastal marshes again.

Lydd was never made a member of the Cinque ports and is little more than an overgrown village circling its 'cathedral on the marsh', a noble and largely fifteenth-century parish church over 200 ft long with a 132 ft tower. Thomas Wolsey was once vicar here. Originally it was the site of a Saxon basilica built during the reign of King Otta and hazy remnants are evident in the north aisle. Even today's church was lucky to survive. Lydd was one of the few coastal towns to suffer damage during the Second World War. The chancel was totally destroyed and many of those ponderous, coffin-shaped tombstones in the surrounding graveyard show signs of shrapnel blast.

The Norman origins of New Romney's church are most evident in the four-ordered dog-tooth west door beneath a ponderous tower topped by pinnacles, and the massive octagonal pillars of the nave. The white interior is plain, with the traditional Romney Marsh three-aisle plan and open chancel.

Later fourteenth-century additions in the Decorated style create a pleasant sensation of increasing lightness as one moves along up the central nave from the west door. Stain marks on the pillars record the trauma of 1287 when gales and tidal waves buried most of the town beneath mud and shingle. The course of the river Rother was changed, leaving New Romney and Lydd high and dry and bringing instant good fortune to the village of Rye through which it has flowed ever since.

Across from the church at the rear of an antique shop I discovered the remnants of an ancient building with small Gothic windows and grotesque stone faces grimacing at passers by. I asked four local residents about its origins. Two admitted never having noticed it, another thought it was an old barn 'or something', and a fourth said he had no idea what it was and anyway the church was far better. I decided to visit the town hall and learn more about its origins, only to find that the town guidebook makes no mention of it, the receptionist didn't know what I was talking about and the gentleman in charge suggested I visit the antique shop itself because 'it's their property, so they must know something about it – I suppose'.

Fortunately, they did. A young woman explained its origins as a twelfth-century priory and invited me inside, apologising for its use as an antique furniture warehouse. She showed me the sturdy roof timbers and told me the building was linked by catacombs to the church. It had occasionally been a residence for lepers, although normally it was used by the priory monks. I peered out of the tiny window into an overgrown back garden. I could just discern the outlines of a pond and broken arches behind the scrub. 'They're still here, too.' I thought I'd mis-heard. 'The monks, they're still here. Even during the day we hear sounds in the old cloister.' She pointed through the windows. 'We thought it was cats at first, but I've stood and looked. The sounds come from the old pond, usually around midday. And I know it's not animals.' I wondered if she was joking. 'There's draughts, too. Even in summer you get a sudden blast of cold air from here. I've closed the door but it doesn't alter it. Goes right through the kitchen [the door from the old priory led into the rear room of the antique shop, once a kitchen with a vast ox-sized fireplace] then on into the showroom. Same time every day.' I must have looked sceptical. 'It's not just me,' she insisted earnestly. 'Customers have felt it too – it's like a lot of people rushing past you out of a cold room. It's scarey.'

Many times on my journeys I'd been regaled with such tales, but almost always from secondary or tertiary sources who usually shared my own cynicism. I include this anecdote only because the woman had actually experienced these occurrences herself and because (and here I become a little self-doubtful) I returned to the shop at midday and while examining the antique displays in the kitchen I felt that same chilling breeze waft out of the old priory, just as she had described it. She gave me a classic 'I-told-you-so' look and went on serving a customer. I left, rather perplexed.

The ghosts of Romney Marsh are less demonstrable, sleeping peacefully in the churches and mossy graveyards in this secluded corner of Kent. Here the crowds of the coastal resorts seem far away and one is left to wander at will along winding lanes through a Fen-like landscape below an enormous sky. Richard Barham, author of *The Ingoldsby Legends*, wrote: 'the world is divided into five parts, namely Europe, Asia, Africa, America and Romney Marsh', and on days when the mists creep in across Dungeness and marsh frogs croak in the dikes, this indeed feels like a land apart with its little villages silent under slow-moving clouds.

The marsh, which is actually an island separated from the wooded hills of the Weald by the 1804 Royal Military Canal (built, along with the martello towers, as a defence against Napoleon), was first drained by the Romans. They constructed enormous sea walls along the Dymchurch coastline and between Appledore and New Romney and slowly transformed these tidal 'saltings' into fertile land. The area to the west known as Walland Marsh was left until much later when Thomas à Becket and other church landowners sought to expose more of its 'marvellous rank ground'.

Romney Marsh became one of the most fertile corners of England, famous for its plump sheep and wheat which the often-critical William Cobbett described in his 1823 *Rural Rides* as the best he'd ever seen. It also gained other reputations for the secretiveness of its populace, the profusion of witches and warlocks and abundant under-the-bed wealth from smuggling activities. 'The marsh is dying now, though,' I was told by a retired shepherd, a 'looker'. We were standing by the church wall at St Mary in the Marsh. 'First you lose the shop, then the school. Now it's the buses that're going. The young 'uns have gone, most of 'em. We're even losing the trees.' He pointed beyond the churchyard. 'Six years ago there were a dozen elms by that wall, over 150 feet high, two of 'em. Now look at it.' One scraggy remnant peered over the church. 'And thats comin' down next week. It's ready for fallin' anyway.' The churches, a handful of Romney masterpieces, are feeling the pinch too. Signs plead for funds from diminishing congregations. Evidence of deterioration is everywhere. 'You want to see 'em quick before they start collapsing too,' said my droll shepherd. So I did and was entranced by their simplicity, their lightness (large windows but very little stained glass) and their brilliant whiteness.

I began at St Clement's, Old Romney, with its typical three-aisle plan, high pews, tile and stone floor and lopsided charm. Above the minstrels' gallery sturdy tie beams with oddly designed kingposts carry the nave roof to the Norman chancel arch. A fourteenth-century Purbeck marble font, square and plain, stands on a central pillar supported by four smaller shafts, one at each corner. Note the carved capitals – a dwarf, a monkey-like face, a green man of sorts, and a priest holding a chalice. The place is redolent of age and ancient traditions (thanks partially to a film company who financed its restoration and the removal of Victorian trimmings to create a suitable set for a Dr Syn movie). A ladder to the belfry is the precursor of all ladders – two halves of a tree trunk with solid wedge-shaped risers. The brass memorials date from the early sixteenth century.

At Ivychurch is a Decorated masterpiece built in the late fourteenth century. The sturdy, two-storey porch and parvise leads into a surprisingly spacious interior illuminated by large clear windows and free of pews. In the nave stands a hudd, a sentry-box-shaped hut used by the priest during burial ceremonies on wet days to keep his wig dry. Newchurch is equally light and All Saints at Burmarsh has a most unusual Norman doorway topped by a menacing (off-centre) head.

Brookland Church

Lead Font. Brookland

At St Mary in the Marsh the retired shepherd proudly showed me the grave of E. Nesbit, author of *The Railway Children*, and the ancient sedilias by the altar carved from Caen stone brought over by Norman stonemasons. 'Go see Brookland church,' he told me. 'You'll not find a tower like hers any-where.' And he was right. It stands by itself at the side of St Augustine's in Brookland, an octagonal belfry spire clad in weatherboarding said to date from the thirteenth century. So imposing is this structure that it distracts the eye from the mish-mash eclecticism of the church itself with a fourteenth-century wooden porch, Early English chancel, and tiny crenelated clock tower – all supported by a generous array of buttresses. Inside is a grandma's attic of delights. On the south wall are remnants of a wall painting of Becket's assassination and at the far western end a 'tithe pen' where the priest's 10 per cent of local produce was carefully weighed and measured. A large tomb with Bethersden marble top sits alone in the south chapel (a memorial to John Plomer, a sixteenth-century mayor of Romney) near the remains of a three-decker pulpit (the sounding board is now used as a table top at the west end of the nave). The pews are appropriately boxed and the supporting aisle pillars, even more appropriately in this rambling place, lean at a remarkable angle to the perpendicular and have done for centuries. From a distance the font resembles a gigantic circular pail resting unevenly on its base. Closer examination shows it to be an exquisitely detailed twelfth-century Norman lead font decorated with the Occupations of the Months motifs (see Chapter 13) and zodiac signs beneath cable and saw-tooth mouldings. I had seen nothing quite like it on my travels and so sat on the floor and sketched it as sun streamed in through the east windows.

Wandering northwards I paused at the St Thomas à Becket church at Fairfield, nestling in flat, moist fields, full of marshland flavour. The pulpit here is a real three-decker and well worth a visit. Then abruptly the long horizons ended at the Royal Military Canal. The road skimmed up a rise into the comfortable village of Appledore, home of Vikings, destroyed by the French in 1380, and a hotbed of agrarian reform during Wat Tyler's rising and Jack Cade's rebellion of 1450. The threat of a Hitler invasion brought a refurbishment of the canal and the construction of pill-boxes in the 1940s, but nothing happened and today the community snoozes with its weatherboard and brick cottages along a broad main street, at peace with the world and itself.

Which is more than can be said for Rye, another of these 'islanded' ports, one of the most charming places on the south coast, and unfortunately also one of the most hectic during the summer. In actual numbers the town can hardly match the commercial deluge of Hastings and Folkestone, but its clustered compactness can transform a few coachloads of visitors into an invasion. Steep pathways zig-zag up the old cliffs to winding alleys and prim Georgian streets. Silver knives and goblets sparkle on bright red tablecloths in cosy restaurants. Authentic blue-jerseyed fishermen, mingle with the weekend anglers and day-trippers and the smell of the ocean tumbles down cobbled ginnels.

I strolled past the half-timbered Mermaid Inn (one of Britain's most famous smuggling headquarters) and peered in the windows of Henry James's residence on the corner of West Street below the stalwart Rye Church with its 400-year-old clock. I explored the town museum in the Ypres Tower and then half-skidded down cobbles to the crouching black ware-houses by the waterfront and the old windmill. Lunchtime was aled away in beam-and-bottleglass locals, followed by a visit to Mrs Townsend's unusual collection of farming implements and domestic knick-knacks from the nineteenth century at her home, The Cherries, in nearby Playden. I ended up by Rye Harbour peering over the boat masts at the marshes beyond. It was early evening and there was no one about, just gulls above a hazy sea. Dinnertime was at least an hour away so I took Fred for a stroll until the birds made it abundantly clear that he was *persona non grata* in their territory. So we returned with dignity to the camper and began planning our final journey.

St. Thomas à Becket Church · Fairfield

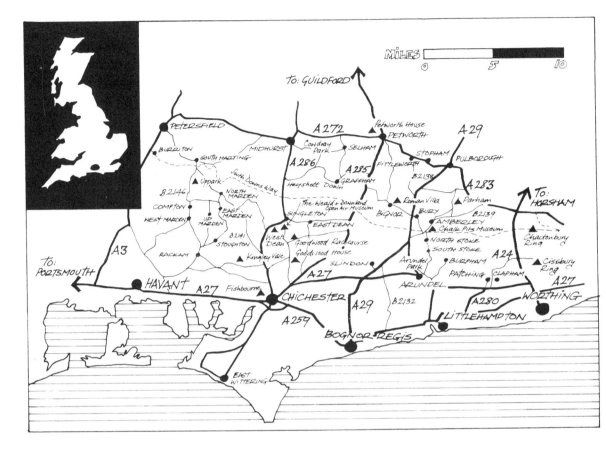

21. The South Downs

After the arcadian frimperies of London's southern suburbs and an all too crowded coastline, the South Downs offer fresh air, space and the broad curves of empty hills. Kipling's 'blunt, bow-headed whale-backed Downs' describes the landscape east of the river Arun where the break with the Weald is more distinct. Hilaire Belloc, whose book *The Four Men* contains one of the most evocative descriptions of Sussex, loved 'the line of the Downs, so noble and so bare'. West of Chanctonbury Ring, an ancient circular earthwork surmounted by a wind-shaped copse, the hills are heavily wooded. Beech forests sweep along curved flanks and paths meander into their depths from a tracery of backroads. Then abruptly the open hills emerge again, short-cropped ley pastures sprinkled with sheep. A tumble of combes

280

hide steep, nestling hamlets. Butterflies flicker over the springy turf and larks spiral under an immense skydome.

Crossing the whole bold sweep is the eighty-mile South Downs Way from Eastbourne to Petersfield, following prehistoric tracks littered with barrows and earthworks. The route is clearly marked with acorn waymarks and oak signposts, and walkers by the score do a John Hillaby from end to end, pausing at pubs and peering into tiny churches up tight valleys. Motorists are also attracted by woodland walks, the splendid mansions at Petworth, Goodwood, Uppark and Parham, the horse-racing at Goodwood racecourse and the unique attractions of the Weald and Downland Open Air Museum. The country towns on the fringe of the downs, Midhurst, Petworth, Arundel and Petersfield, suffer occasionally from summer-madness but many visitors never explore the real downland country. I wandered for miles at the height of the season on country lanes thick as thatch with silence. I discovered villages steeped in solitude, a nature reserve of 500-year-old yews, a chalkpit museum, remains of a Roman house, wineries, and miles of empty beech-wood paths. I was surprised so peaceful an area could still exist on the edge of the outer commuter-belt.

We begin a few miles north-west of Chichester. Here, hidden in a deep combe at the end of a mile-long track across cornfields, is the Kingley Vale Nature Reserve. According to local legend, this sinister grove of yew trees changes its shape at night and wanders the valley together with the ghosts of Vikings defeated here in 874 by the Saxons. The *Anglo-Saxon Chronicle* records that the local citizens 'put them to flight and killed many hundreds of them'. Even on a bright summer afternoon the place has an eerie quality. The upper slopes are dotted with clusters of bush-like yews spawned by their gnarled parents, huddled in deep gloom at the base of the hill. The Nature Conservancy pamphlet claims this to be one of Europe's finest yew forests. The ancient trees writhe silently under a canopy of exploding branches. Clematis or 'old man's beard' cascades in a grey curtain, shrouding the grove and cutting out the light. Streamers of creeping plants dangle like snakes in a tropical rain forest. Close up the grain bursts through thin bark, swirled and contorted as if every inch of growth was agony and death imminent. Branches lie broken and rotting on a brown carpet of needles. A single strand of sun pierces the darkness and falls on a patch of sponge-like moss. Drops of dew sparkle and the dampness of moist decay hangs thick in the grove. It's a magical place that stays in the mind.

Equally magic, but in a rather different way, is tiny Amberley south-east of Petworth. The rather dour reaction of the nineteenth-century writer E. V. Lucas, who referred to the village as 'a large stockyard smelling of straw and

Kingley Vale

cattle', contrasts with contemporary admirers claiming it variously as 'serenity epitomised' and 'the essence of bucolic rurality'. The smells have long gone and today one wanders through a fairytale setting of ivy-shrouded thatched cottages, tiny hedged gardens brimming with hollyhocks and flowering shrubs, the remnants of a fourteenth-century castle built for the Bishops of Chichester and the adjacent St Michael's Church at the end of a lane of doe-eyed houses. One should pause to admire the splendid twelfth-century chancel arch and remnants of wall paintings showing the resurrection of Christ and various scenes of Calvary. The yellow dividing strips between the paintings contain odd amphibious creatures. During renovations in 1967 a strange collection of objects was found embedded in the wall, including shards of medieval glass, walnut shells and the skull of a thrush. Their origins are obscure, as are those of John Wantele, the armoured gentleman commemorated in the large brass in the south aisle, which,

according to local records, was once enamelled in brilliant colours. Better known was the painter Edward Scott, who helped attract a colony of artists to the village in the early twentieth century (his memorial is the semi-circular stained glass window in the north doorway) and the gliding-pilot, E. C. Gordon England. He established an unofficial world record glide from Amberley Mount in 1909 in an odd canvas and bamboo structure known as 'The Albatross'. The flight lasted 58 seconds and he wrote afterwards in typical British understatement: 'The wind was just right and I found myself rising to about 40 feet above my starting point, and the machine – which was in charge of me, not I of it – headed out over the valley below, and proceeded to glide into a ploughed field adjacent to the Amberley–Storrington road, where it landed gently.' His record held until overtaken by the Wright brothers at Kittyhawk after the First World War.

More surprises await the explorer south of Amberley. At the back of the

283

The South Downs

hill by the railway station is the recently established Chalk Pits Museum with various exhibits of south-eastern industrial history in a scattering of chalk-works buildings. Quarrying began here around 1840. Most of the chalk was burned to make lime which was loaded onto barges in the specially created Canal Cut. The opening of the railway in 1863 led to a gradual abandonment of barge traffic and increased production from the site, although the mining methods remained rather crude. The chalk was dug out by hand and carried to the kilns in wheelbarrows or unusual three-wheeled horse carts backed directly to the top of the kiln. Records indicate that the occasional over-enthusiastic horse would misjudge the distance and vanish, cart and all, into the fiery furnace. Apparently the quality of the lime was not noticeably affected by such mishaps.

Nearby, on the fringes of Arundel Park, are the two villages of North and South Stoke nestled in the water meadows beside the Arun river. Only a footpath connects them and one can stroll southwards along the edge of the park into the fairytale town of Arundel itself with its enormous and much renovated castle of the Dukes of Norfolk towering over the steep streets, cream-tea shops and clustered inns. During the summer the place is hectic with tourists filling the castle grounds and the famous displays of armour and tapestries. Most, however, seem to miss the town's Catholic cathedral perched in proud French-Gothic fashion on a prominent site at the top of the hill. Built by the fifteenth Duke in 1868, it contains the remains of St Philip Howard, 13th Earl of Arundel and one of the 'forty martyrs' who died after incarceration in the Tower of London during the reign of Elizabeth I. There's a sense of soaring space and peace here. The architect, Joseph Aloysius Hansom, inventor of the hansom cab, proposed an even more dramatic edifice, but his enthusiasm had to be restrained when it was realised that foundations up to 70 ft deep would be required. The naturalist and taxider-mist, Walter Potter, was more fortunate in his ambitions and managed to leave to posterity a collection of over 2,000 stuffed animals and birds in his Museum of Curiosity crammed into a Victorian building in the High Street. Pertly-posed guinea pigs rollicking through a game of cricket may seem a little dated by today's aesthetic standards, but one must grant the man a remarkable imagination and an irrepressible sense of fun.

Only a few miles away from the coach-crowds one finds tranquility again in such tiny downland villages as Burpham, clustered at the end of a cul-de-sac on a broad ledge overlooking the Arun valley. The locals collect in the George and Dragon, smuggling centre and inn for more than 400 years and full of tales of illicit activities along the slow-moving river outside.

Further to the east are the villages of Patching and Clapham, only a stone's throw from the busy A280 and yet centuries removed from the coastal bustle. Patching possesses the Kinnard hurdle workshop, the last of many similar enterprises that flourished here in the days when the downs were littered with sheep and flexible inexpensive wattle fencing or 'flaking' was needed by the mile for sheep-folds. The simple finished product, a woven fence of split hazel rods, belies an involved process requiring years of experience to master the 'feel' of the rods, the twisting technique that avoids splitting, the exact cleaving of the rods to expose equal amounts of pith, and the even tautness of the completed hurdle.

Slindon to the west lies on the fringe of the vast 3,500-acre Slindon Park Estate (National Trust) with yet more shaded beech forests. Hilaire Belloc lived here for a while at Court Hill Farm with his wife Elodie, and on one of his later sea-journeys wrote of these woods:

> A deeper sympathy even than that of the senses came . . . and brought me the beeches and the yew trees also, although I was so far out to sea, for the loneliness of this great water recalled the loneliness of the woods and both these solitudes . . . mixed in my mind together as they might in the mind of a sleeping man.

Belloc's appreciation was shared by earlier men, most notably Thomas à Becket and other archbishops of Canterbury who summered here on lands transferred to the See of Canterbury by St Wilfrid in 686. A palace was built in the mid thirteenth century, almost entirely restructured in the mid sixteenth century and is now used as a boys' public school. Stephen Langton, one of the instigators of Magna Carta, is memorialised on a plaque in the church near the unusual and expressive wooden effigy of the 'Slindon Knight', thought to be a Sir Anthony St Leger who died in 1539. Outside, horses clip by and walkers seek out the elusive Roman road of Stone Street which passes through the woods to the remains of the Roman villa at Bignor.

I wandered over here through Bury, another tiny village embraced by sappy foliage and wrapped in its own mellowness, and found one of the finest Roman sites in Britain, an equal of the famous Chedworth villa in Gloucestershire. Discovered accidentally by a farmer in 1811, it extends over four and half acres and offers a glimpse of the leisured life of the Romans immediately prior to their departure in the fourth century AD. A complex of courtyards, servants' quarters, cattle sheds, outbuildings and granary form the supportive framework for the finely-mosaic'd chambers and ante-rooms of the prime family, all centrally heated and equipped with temperature-controlled bathrooms. A large room in the north wing contains a 'Venus and the Gladiators' full of flailing figures, some in combat, others writhing from wounds. An adjoining chamber is decorated with an elaborate pavement of interlocked geometric figures and colourful flowers and the whole creation is enclosed under a series of thatched roofs. There is evidence to suggest that the villa was taken over and possibly expanded by families of Romano-Britons, but eventually the secrets of a too-sophisticated culture were lost to the mental-murkiness of the Dark Ages.

Bignor's 'Old Shop' is an indication of the comparatively slow emergence of ordinary domestic architecture from daub and wattle huts and early cruck-frame structures to this half-timber creation with brick panels and upper floor projections on enormous oak joists. The result is totally charming but one cannot help wondering how different our communities might have looked if the Romans had stayed longer.

Once again, woods await the backroader beyond the village of Graffham, and, unlike Cowdray Park, a few miles to the north-west, these are quiet, often pathless places inviting languid rambles. Enthusiastic walkers can join one of the most scenic stretches of the South Downs Way here, leading from Bignor Hill through the forest out onto the vast spaces of Heyshott Down. Views splay out to the north over the pinewoods and heaths of the Weald and south across the Solent to the Isle of Wight flecked with tiny villages on a green-field chess board. The path continues over Cocking Down and Linch Down past the remains of an Iron Age camp on Beacon Hill, along Hastings Down and the northern edge of the Uppark estate to end at Sunwood Farm, near Burriton. These are the real downs – broad sweeps of empty landscape, furred with forests in the hollows, windshaped and bare. The silence here is the silence of the sky. The wind is unfunnelled and unbroken. The clean, curved lines of copses echo the shapes of the hills. Even during summer weekends one can find solitude and quiet combes for sun-snoozing.

Equally undiscovered are the lanes and villages between Chichester and Petersfield. An elderly farmer at Rackam ('Fifty-seven years in this place and never a day off in m' life') showed me his local church sparkling with the colourful canopied tombs of the Gunter family and pointed out the thatched cottage next door where the Gunters hid Charles II after the battle of Worcester. High on the hillside above his pastures sat an odd towered folly almost identical in design to Horton Tower (see Chapter 19) but in a state of imminent collapse. 'Some Greek's gone an' bought it now,' the farmer told me. 'Paid a fortune for it. Says he's going to make a house in it.' He shook his head sadly as if the world had finally lost its reason. 'They say it takes all kinds, but you can't help wondering sometimes what's going on.'

I wandered north along wriggling lanes through the flint and brick villages of West Marden and Compton, and rolled unexpectedly into the secluded picture-postcard scene of East Marden. Here a barn-like church peered down

Bignor's 'Old Shop'

across greens at a triangle of cottages and a water pump under a thatched awning. Scattered among the gravestones were half a dozen white beehives. The hedgerows were filled with summer perfumes and the only sign of life was a black kitten topsy-turvying in pursuit of butterflies.

The churches at North Marden and Up Marden are tiny affairs lost up lanes and hardly altered since the thirteenth century. In South Harting's broad main street one finds the stocks and whipping post still in workable condition by the church gate. Nearby Uppark Mansion is a 'rose-coloured altar among columned beech trees' perched on a steep hill with views across the downs to the Isle of Wight. The interior was lavishly decorated by Sir Mathew Fetherstonhaugh and his wife who in 1750 alone are said to have spent over £100,000 on fittings and furnishings. His son was a rather prodigal character who brought the fifteen-year-old Emma Hart, later Lord Nelson's Lady Hamilton, to the house. He fêted and pampered her for a year before sending her off, six months pregnant, for purportedly dancing all over the dining room table.

I travelled east through tunnelled lanes and hanging woods past the Chilsdown Winery (visitors welcome) to the gardens of West Dean College. Here, dominated by huge specimen trees of beech and cedar of Lebanon, is a thirty-acre complex of lawns, sunken gardens, a palm house, gazebo, pergola, water gardens and wild gardens surrounding a sprawling 1804 flint-faced mansion, now a college for adult crafts. The original manor house was built in 1622 and the garden was subsequently improved and expanded over three centuries. The massive walls of the estate erected by French prisoners during the Napoleonic wars partially hide a much-restored Saxon church and inside the college one comes eyeball to eyeball with a remarkable array of moose heads, lions, polar bears and buffalo in a baronial setting of enormous marble fireplaces and tapestries.

In a somewhat less dramatic vein, the nearby Weald and Downland Open Air Museum is an evocative repository of regional architecture scattered over a sloping site above the Lavant river. The most notable of the eighteen buildings assembled here include the Catherington Tread Wheel (boy-sized), a 1730 granary raised above the ground on 'staddle stones' (to ensure protection against damp and rodents) and a half-timbered seventeenth-century market hall from Titchfield. Exhibitions of traditional crafts and trades present a picture of rural life in the south-east from the sixteenth century to the nineteenth, and the organisers hope to double the number of structures here over the next few years.

As is the nearby village of Singleton, which became popular after the opening of the Goodwood racecourse in 1801 on the downs below Trundle Hill. Edward VII, when Prince of Wales, stabled his horses here and subsequent parish priests denounced the 'licentious antics of tipplers and touts' during the race season.

Tourists flock to admire the Van Dycks and Canalettos at Goodwood House and Petworth House's Turners and Reynolds. The town of Petworth, a quaintly congested knot of alleys and narrow streets, contrasts markedly with the open 2,000-acre estate beyond the high wall. Landscaped by Capability Brown, it was beloved by Turner who had a studio here in the early nineteenth century. Both are delightful day-long diversions outside the peak season.

Then once again we enter broad beechwoods, deep in shade and mellowed with autumnal golds, as we journey through Cowdray Park towards Midhurst. Gun-shots clatter in the distance, and at the side of the road tweedy gentlemen in plus-fours stand by a Range-Rover admiring their braces of pheasants, limp and bloody. Mud-splattered retrievers tail-wag excitedly nearby and along a woodland path trot two perfect Thelwell ponies

East Marden

topped by Thelwell girls, podgy and pink-cheeked under their velvet riding hats. A churned polo-pitch suggests the popular pastime of the upper-crust families in this region of long-lineages and centuries-old heritages.

Midhurst is an appropriate centre, slightly horsey and full of elegant shops, with all the robust flavour of an old market town. Georgian, timber-frame and Regency buildings mingle with comfortable old inns around small squares and narrow streets. At the Spread Eagle a fire glows in the bowed-beam lounge. The deep leather armchairs smell of polish and the pints pour out cream-topped and glowing amber. There's a Raj flavour in the menu of more than thirty curry dishes as well as traditional fare of chops, ducks and pheasant. I'd planned to move on, but the aromas from the kitchen persuaded me otherwise. Travelling, after all, should be a leisurely process with plenty of time allowed for the unexpected. And a rich Indian curry served on a silver salver in an ancient English inn was exactly the kind of unexpected I expected to enjoy.

Granary on 'staddle stones'

Index

Index